'In the work before us, we find the convergence of three researchers who, faithful to their Freudian roots, demonstrate what Freud himself once warned us: in psychoanalysis, research and treatment coincide. And if this encounter proves so fertile – this being neither the first, nor the second, nor the last time they write together – it is undoubtedly linked to their differences: differences in theoretical backgrounds, life paths, and generations. This book makes it clear that difference can be profoundly generative, provided that a good portion of the enthusiasm psychoanalysis stirs in us for life is also devoted to a rigorous theoretical-clinical journey – one that is not without good encounters, or rather, excellent ones.'

Ana Suy, *Psychoanalyst, PhD in Psychoanalysis from the State University of Rio de Janeiro (UERJ), and best-selling author*

'This book invites us to make a fundamental gesture: to recognise that the human cannot be contained within a single theoretical framework. When clinical listening yields too readily to the rigidity of systems, it risks betraying what is most essential to it: transference and its transformative potential in analysis. Honouring this movement requires a willingness to inhabit uncertainty, to move between different authors, to formulate new questions and, above all, to sustain the complexity that underpins our practice. By mapping, with both rigour and sensitivity, some of the theoretical and clinical contributions of Klein, Winnicott, and Bion, this work offers not final answers, but a partial cartography of a vast and ever-changing field. Like a compass, it offers orientation – never at the expense of a direct journey through these and other authors. A call to thought in motion: faithful, in that sense, to the Freudian spirit.'

Berta Hoffmann Azevedo, *Psychoanalyst, author, full member and training analyst of the Brazilian Society of Psychoanalysis of São Paulo (SBPSP), with a Mhgjhyyyaster's degree in Clinical Psychology (PUC-SP). Editor of the* Journal of Psychoanalysis (SBPSP) *from 2021 to 2024 and current editor of the* Brazilian Journal of Psychoanalysis (Febrapsi)

'My interest in psychoanalysis began when I was a teenager facing hard times, and met a psychoanalyst. That first session really moved me, somehow made me think something quite magical was about to happen – it gave me hope. It was only the first of many sessions full of life. To my surprise this is what this book is all about. Taking the challenges of contemporary clinic and allowing Winnicott, Klein, and Bion to exchange ideas, these three Brazilian authors with outstanding academic careers and creative clinical approaches reaffirm that it is the clinical practice that keeps moving theory – and, magically, the patient's being. This analyst, born back in 1979 in that first session, is thankful for this wonderful gift. It has been a pleasure to savour such potent pages.'

Vera Maria Guilherme, *Psychoanalyst, Master in Criminal Sciences from the Pontifical Catholic University of Rio Grande do Sul (PUC-RS), and researcher in the fields of psychoanalysis and gender*

'Analytic identity is shaped upon a terrain in constant rearrangement, composed of multiple inner voices: theories, supervisors, colleagues, texts, and patients. We are formed through a series of losses, but also through many encounters. Born out of the convergence of three theoretical and clinical journeys – those of Alexandre Patricio de Almeida, Alfredo Naffah Neto, and Filipe Pereira Vieira – this book emerges from the desire to think of psychoanalysis as a living field, one capable of engaging with the transformations of subjectivity and the challenges posed by contemporary clinical work. By bringing Freud, Klein, Bion, and Winnicott into dialogue – sometimes in harmony, often in tension – the authors affirm their belief in the creative potential of difference. It is this plurality that keeps psychoanalysis alive, able to respond to the wounds of our time without submitting to rigid models or static certainties. To chart these conceptual landscapes is to follow the traces and fragments each author has left behind – an undertaking that demands stamina, a willingness to welcome the unfamiliar within the familiar, and the courage to sustain contradiction. For an analyst to find their own voice – rather than simply echoing inherited discourses – psychoanalysis must be held "by heart", *etched on the string of the heart*, as the ancient Greeks would say. This gesture entails recognising, embracing, and transforming one's theoretical and clinical heritage, thereby making room for a living form of listening.'

Helena Cunha Di Ciero, *full member of the Brazilian Psychoanalytic Society of São Paulo (SBPSP), affiliated with the International Psychoanalytical Association*

Klein, Bion, and Winnicott

This book fills a gap in psychoanalytic literature by offering a rigorous analysis of the intersections and divergences between the three foundational figures in psychoanalysis: Melanie Klein, Wilfred Bion, and Donald Winnicott.

Klein, Bion, and Winnicott: Theoretical and Clinical Convergences and Divergences invites professionals and academics into a comparative dialogue across psychoanalytic traditions and equips them to understand how the ideas of these three authors interweave and unfold in distinct directions, impacting clinical practice and the comprehension of complex psychic processes. By exploring aspects such as Klein's theory of internal objects, positions, and envy; Bion's alpha function, reverie, and capacity for thinking; and Winnicott's notions of emotional development, transitional space, and therapeutic regression, this book provides a comprehensive view of the implications of each theory in the contemporary clinical context.

With copious clinical material and a deep understanding of all three subjects, this book is key reading for psychoanalysts, psychotherapists, and advanced trainees at all stages of their careers, as well as anyone wishing to broaden their understanding of the works of Klein, Bion, and Winnicott.

Alexandre Patricio de Almeida is a Psychoanalyst with a Master's and PhD in Clinical Psychology from the Pontifical Catholic University of São Paulo (PUC-SP). He has authored several scientific articles and books and is a Finalist for the Jabuti Literature Prize. He is also the creator of the podcast *Psicanálise de Boteco* and is currently undertaking a postdoctoral fellowship at PUC-SP.

Alfredo Naffah Neto is a Psychoanalyst with a Master's in Philosophy from the University of São Paulo (USP) and a PhD in Clinical Psychology from the Pontifical Catholic University of São Paulo (PUC-SP), where he is a full professor on the Postgraduate Programme in Clinical Psychology. He has also authored several books and scientific articles.

Filipe Pereira Vieira is a Psychoanalyst with a Master's degree and currently a doctoral researcher in Clinical Psychology at the Pontifical Catholic University of São Paulo (PUC-SP). He has authored several scientific articles and books and is the co-creator of the podcast *Psicanálise de Boteco*.

Klein, Bion, and Winnicott

Theoretical and Clinical Convergences and Divergences

Alexandre Patricio de Almeida, Alfredo Naffah Neto, and Filipe Pereira Vieira

Translators: Alexandre Patricio de Almeida and Filipe Pereira Vieira

Translation Reviewer: Vera Maria Guilherme

Routledge
Taylor & Francis Group

LONDON AND NEW YORK

Designed cover image: Getty Images

First published in English 2026
by Routledge
4 Park Square, Milton Park, Abingdon, Oxon OX14 4RN

and by Routledge
605 Third Avenue, New York, NY 10158

*Routledge is an imprint of the Taylor & Francis Group, an informa
business*

© 2026 Alexandre Patricio de Almeida, Alfredo Naffah Neto, and Filipe
Pereira Vieira

The right of Alexandre Patricio de Almeida, Alfredo Naffah Neto, and
Filipe Pereira Vieira to be identified as authors of this work has been
asserted in accordance with sections 77 and 78 of the Copyright,
Designs and Patents Act 1988.

For Product Safety Concerns and Information please contact our EU
representative GPSR@taylorandfrancis.com. Taylor & Francis Verlag
GmbH, Kaufingerstraße 24, 80331 München, Germany.

Trademark notice: Product or corporate names may be trademarks
or registered trademarks, and are used only for identification and
explanation without intent to infringe.

British Library Cataloguing-in-Publication Data
A catalogue record for this book is available from the British Library

ISBN: 9781041078463 (hbk)
ISBN: 9781041075875 (pbk)
ISBN: 9781003642503 (ebk)

DOI: 10.4324/9781003642503

Typeset in Optima
by KnowledgeWorks Global Ltd.

"For our patients, who teach us so much."

Contents

Acknowledgements

This book was born out of dialogue. A dialogue between generations, between styles, between distinct – yet committed – ways of thinking about psychoanalytic theory and clinical practice. With each page, we moved through doubts, revisited concepts, returned to authors, wrote, and rewrote – not without friction, but always with a genuine desire to listen. This work would not have been possible without the trust we placed in one another, and without the quiet, daily wager that theory can indeed emerge from encounter.

First and foremost, we thank our patients who, with courage and openness, allowed us to enter their stories – and, in doing so, transformed our listening. Each case discussed in this book is, above all, an expression of deep respect for the singularity of those who seek us out.

To our colleagues, students, and supervisors who, directly or indirectly, contributed with suggestions, questions, and sparkles that helped us refine our thinking – our dialogue with you has been an essential part of our clinical and academic journeys.

We are also grateful to the institutions we have been part of – especially PUC-SP, the space where our paths first intertwined, and where we learned that psychoanalysis is sustained not only by tradition, but by the possibility of reimagining it with care and rigour.

We would like to express our heartfelt thanks to Vera Maria Guilherme, our translation reviewer, for reading this book with such attentive and generous eyes. Her willingness to join us on this journey – at times arduous, always intense – was essential to bringing this work to its final form. Our exchanges, from early mornings to late nights, revealed not only Vera's technical precision, but also her sensitivity to the nuances of the text. To her, our most sincere gratitude.

And finally, to our partners in life, who stood by us through the long – and at times solitary – hours of writing. This book, now in the hands of readers, was woven by many hands, many voices, and many affections.

May it inspire, as it inspired in us, new encounters.

Foreword
Between Singularities: A Clinical Dialogue Composed of Distinct and Engaged Voices

Samantha Dubugras Sá[1]

Thinking together is an act of resistance against the isolation of knowledge that turns inward and closes upon itself. Any theory that remains alive does so because it is questioned; it is doubt that prevents it from hardening into dogma and returns it to its most fertile ground: the clinic. The clinical space does not demand certainty, but presence – that rare quality of listening which relinquishes prior knowledge in favour of the encounter that unfolds *in between*. And when such listening is sustained by affection, between colleagues who share the vocation of thinking human suffering, it gives rise to something even more precious: a friendship in which thought does not stagnate, but circulates, transforms, and is transformed. Between what is already known and what is yet to come, psychoanalysis continues: wandering, engaged, and alive.

There are books born of a solitary author's quiet reflection, and others that emerge in the warmth of friendship, through constant dialogue and mutual listening. This volume is one of those rare cases in which thought is shaped by many hands – in conversations that extend beyond academic research, reaching into bonds of genuine friendship and an ethical commitment to psychoanalysis.

Alexandre, Alfredo, and Filipe – my colleagues, friends, companions along the way, and generous interlocutors – offer here a work that is, at once, rigorous in its scholarship and deeply engaged with the living clinic: that space which calls on us, day after day, to rethink what we believed we already knew.

Klein, Bion, and Winnicott are not merely established references in the field of psychoanalysis; they are presences who illuminated the darker regions of psychic life, each guided by a singular mode of listening, attentive to the delicate nuances of human suffering. In this book – the fruit of many years of study and clinical experience – the authors' gesture is not one of idolisation, but of critical listening: a comparative approach to their propositions – their scope and their limits – in search of a more sensitive understanding of the analytic experience and its demands.

In my view, to compare within psychoanalysis is not to assume a neutral stance, nor to carry out a technical operation devoid of ethical and clinical consequences. It is not a matter of aligning theories like pieces in a logically coherent system, nor of establishing hierarchies to declare one author more legitimate or one school more authentic. When undertaken with rigour and genuine attentiveness – as it is in the pages that follow – comparison becomes a living method of approximation. It opens a space for what pulses between the lines: the impasses of clinical practice, the questions that unsettle us, and the historical and subjective contexts that have given shape to those very questions.

By examining the differences between authors and theoretical lineages, we open the possibility of recognising the extent to which each formulation responds to singular forms of psychic suffering. Far from fragmenting the field of psychoanalysis, such a comparative method enriches it: it expands the analyst's repertoire, sharpens their sensitivity to the diversity of cases, and demands a more flexible stance – less bound to certainties, more attuned to the complexity of each unique encounter. The true value of comparison lies precisely there: in what it displaces, in what it interrogates, in what it enables to be transformed. In this sense, it is always an unfinished task – reinvented with each reading, each clinical encounter, each surprise that emerges from the transferential field.

It is in this spirit that the authors remind us: the direction of a psychoanalytic treatment cannot – and must not – follow a single, rigid path. Every treatment implies a point of departure that is not pre-established; it is constructed through the interweaving of listening and transference, grounded in the singularity of each subject.

In this book, Alexandre, Alfredo, and Filipe invite us into a state of creative unease: how can we sustain a clinical mode of thinking that resists classificatory imperatives, without relinquishing conceptual rigour? By privileging theory as it is woven into the analysis of clinical cases, they offer us a reading of psychic suffering that avoids the comfort of universal parameters and instead draws closer to the nuances of lived experience – to that place where symptoms do not repeat themselves, and where forms of suffering defy any attempt at capture.

Our authors, therefore, reaffirm that people are always more complex than any classificatory system could ever encompass – and that it is precisely this complexity which psychoanalysis must never lose sight of.

More than a theoretical treatise, this work is also a passionate defence of psychoanalysis as a field in perpetual evolution – renewed by the very questions that unsettle it. In reading it, we rediscover not only Klein, Bion, and Winnicott, but also something of Freud – not as a figure frozen in the past, but as an inexhaustible source of unease and invention. In this way, the book quietly fulfils its promise: it reinscribes the Freudian gesture in the present, challenging us to think with the ethics of clinical commitment.

As a reader, as a colleague, and as a friend, I receive this work with admiration and joy. And I hope it reaches those who, as Bion proposed, do not seek ready-made truths, but rather offer themselves to emotional experience – even when it is confusing, undigested, still in its raw state. May they, in the spirit of his suggestion, be willing to relinquish preconceived knowledge and antici-pated expectations, and instead embrace that which has not yet taken form,

> […] discard your memory; discard the future tense of your desire; forget them both, both what you knew and what you want, to leave space for a new idea. A thought, an idea unclaimed, may be floating around the room searching for a home. Amongst these may be one of your own which seems to turn up from your insides, or one from outside yourself, namely, from the patient.
>
> (Bion, 1977–1978/2018, p. 4)

May Klein, Bion and Winnicott: Theoretical and Clinical Convergences and Divergences thus serve as a space of welcome – an ethical and sensitive con-tainer for thoughts still untamed, ideas yet to be born, and experiences waiting to be heard.

An invitation, ultimately, to that subtle metamorphosis that only authentic thinking can bring about.

Note

1 Psychoanalyst, PhD in Psychology from the Pontifical Catholic University of Rio Grande do Sul (PUC-RS) and postdoctoral researcher at the Pontifical Catholic University of São Paulo (PUC-SP).

Reference

Bion, W. R. (2018). *Bion in New York and São Paulo and Three Tavistock Seminars*. London: The Harris Meltzer Trust. (Original work presented in 1977–1978)

Introduction

Some Considerations on the Comparison of Psychoanalytic Lineages

Alexandre Patricio de Almeida, Alfredo Naffah Neto, and Filipe Pereira Vieira

We begin the Introduction of our book by quoting the following words by Clarice Lispector which, in our view, seem to encapsulate what we are proposing here:

> This book is like any other. But I would be glad if it were read only by people whose souls are already formed. Those who know that any kind of approach, whatever it may be, happens gradually and painfully – even passing through the opposite of that which one seeks to approach. Those people, and only they, will slowly understand that this book takes nothing away from anyone.
>
> (Lispector, 2020, n.p.)

In 2022, we – Alfredo and Alexandre – published *Near to Darkness: Depression in Six Psychoanalytic Perspectives* which, to our pleasant surprise, reached a significant readership and came to be cited as reference in various university programmes across Brazil.[1] In early 2025, *Psychoanalytic Interpretation: Revisiting Klein and Winnicott* was released. Authored by Filipe, the book stems from his current doctoral research, supervised by Alfredo, which investigates the origins and treatment of psychosis in the works of Bion and Winnicott.

Although each of these works addresses a distinct thematic focus, both had already begun – albeit tentatively – to outline a comparative movement between different psychoanalytic traditions. This movement now finds greater depth and consolidation.

It is with renewed satisfaction, therefore, that we continue along this path, now through the present work in English, published by Routledge.

We consider that this book emerges from the intertwining of three theoretical and clinical trajectories which, though distinct, share a common starting point: the understanding of psychoanalysis as a living field of research, attentive to the mutations of subjectivity and the demands of contemporary clinical work. Developed as part of a joint project – coordinated by Alfredo – within the Postgraduate Programme in Clinical Psychology at the Pontifical Catholic University of São Paulo (PUC-SP),[2] this volume is the result of close

DOI: 10.4324/9781003642503-1

(and critical) reading of the works of Melanie Klein, Wilfred Bion, and Donald W. Winnicott. Over years of academic collaboration, the three of us have turned ongoing dialogue into a kind of "method of conceptual elaboration", choosing the comparison between psychoanalytic lineages as a means for theoretical deepening and clinical refinement (Almeida and Naffah Neto, 2021; Almeida and Naffah Neto, 2022; Almeida and Naffah Neto, 2024; Almeida, Naffah Neto, and Vieira, 2024; Vieira, 2024; Almeida and Vieira, 2025; Almeida, 2025).

At a time when psychoanalysis is often caught between dogmatic stagnation and the hasty dilution of its concepts into generic discourses on "care", we believe it is urgent to recover the critical vitality of the psychoanalytic tradition. This urgency, in our view, corresponds to the growing complexity of psychic suffering, which in many cases can no longer be grasped by the frameworks of classical neurosis nor by the references established in the early decades of the psychoanalytic movement.

Far from reducing this phenomenon to mere nomenclature or hastily fitting it into ready-made diagnostic categories, we propose the opposite movement: to subject theory to the test of clinical practice, allowing experience – with all its zones of indeterminacy and real impasses – to function as both filter and provocation. This gesture aims to recirculate the interpretative possibilities of psychoanalysis, while also recognising its limitations – so that it may be reinscribed as a field of elaboration, always stretched between what is already known and what is yet to be thought.

With regard to this issue, we stated in a recent text:

> Thus, the real challenge is to preserve the essence of psychoanalysis even when its technique must be adapted. This demands solid training, a fundamental understanding of what is at stake, and, above all, constant vigilance to ensure we are not, inadvertently, emptying psychoanalysis of its transformative core. Because, in the end, if our practice is no longer guided by the principles Freud established – if we do not work with the unconscious, if we do not confront resistances, if we do not engage transference and interpret – then what are we actually doing?
> (Almeida, Naffah Neto, and Vieira, 2025, p. 26)

Let us recall, then, that Klein, Bion, and Winnicott were, each in their own way, authors who knew how to respond to the impasses imposed by clinical practice. Not by chance, their theoretical contributions emerged largely from a mode of listening that did not retreat in the face of "difficult cases": psychoses, borderline personalities, disorganised states, early environmental failures, or situations of helplessness. By rejecting the limitations of theory centred on neurosis and the Oedipus complex, these authors enacted a decisive shift: they reinscribed the Freudian legacy within a broader horizon, in which themes such as symbolisation, primary communication, and the constitution of the self become structuring axes. This does not represent, in any way, an abandonment of Freud. On the contrary, it implies his *continuity*: the common trunk remains, but the branches multiply, responding to new demands of psychic reality (Mezan, 2019).

In light of this, we believe it is precisely in the friction between concepts – the points of inflection among clinical proposals, and the tension between styles of thought – that the richness and relevance of these classical authors can be fully appreciated. Thus, the comparative approach we propose here is far from any form of hierarchical judgement. To be clear: what drives us is not the selection of a "superior theorist", as if we were engaging in an epistemological tournament, but the desire to map – with as much rigour as possible – the territories each author has occupied, the impasses they encountered, and the paths that have been opened – or closed – through their respective clinical practices.

It is worth highlighting a matter that is often overlooked when psychoanalytic training becomes rigidified by excessively doctrinaire institutional frameworks: comparative reading is neither quick nor comfortable. It requires stamina, a willingness to engage with contradictions, and, above all, the renunciation of certainties that tend to offer an illusory sense of theoretical security. Comparing is, first and foremost, estranging oneself from the familiar and accepting that different models may illuminate – or unsettle – clinical work in unexpected ways. Perhaps that is precisely why such an exercise is so rarely encouraged in certain training contexts, where one prefers to adopt a "pet author" and build around them a closed, coherent system conveniently immune to dissent.

Indeed, there are not few – one might even say surprisingly numerous – institutions that, in the name of a "supposed theoretical cohesion", choose to relegate Freud to the status of a mere footnote in their curricula. The justification, often adorned with respectable jargon, tends to revolve around the notion that "we have already moved beyond Freud" – or that "Freud gets in the way of understanding". Such a stance, which could be described as hasty revisionism or institutional amnesia, reveals, at best, a curious forgetfulness regarding the very origins of the psychoanalytic field – and at worst, a poorly resolved unease in the face of the grandeur of Freud's legacy. That one wishes to read Freud critically – excellent; that one seeks to erase him from the map is, at the very least… unsettling. Not to say symptomatic.

What strikes us most, however, is the realisation that the directors of such institutions have themselves travelled long paths of reading and discussion of Freud's works. This is not a matter of ignorance, but of strategy: a kind of programmed forgetting – or, to use a sharper image, a deliberate "short circuit", in which what is being erased is precisely what is well known.

By contrast, universities – when faithful to its public vocation – remain one of the few spaces where access to knowledge does not depend on institutional lineage, doctrinal allegiance, or the approval of peers invested with symbolic authority. Without intending to idealise it – since we are well aware that academia is not immune to bureaucracy, power struggles, or vanity – it is nonetheless within this setting that the possibility of coexisting psychoanalytic traditions is still preserved today, without one needing to annul the other in order to assert its legitimacy. It is also within the academic environment that psychoanalysis can benefit from contact with other fields of knowledge, renewing itself to the extent that it is challenged by questions that surpass it.[3]

That said, a cautionary note is in order: this project was not conceived as a technical manual, nor as a compendium of applicable solutions. We do not offer protocols. Our aim is something else – more modest, or perhaps more ambitious, depending on one's point of view. We seek to build a reflective tool to help refine the clinical ear, bearing in mind the most demanding dimension of psychoanalytic listening: the capacity to welcome what resists classification, what escapes ready-made categories, and what cannot be captured by any theory that attempts to reduce suffering to a formula.

Following this path, the first chapter opens our journey by examining the notion of interpretation in Klein and Winnicott. Starting from two distinct perspectives – interpretation as a tool for accessing unconscious phantasies in Klein, and the creation of a holding space (*management*) in Winnicott – we outline the clinical consequences of these positions and their effects on the construction of the analytic bond.

In the following chapter, we discuss the concept of phantasy. For Klein, it is an archaic activity, inseparable from instinctual life and from the formation of the internal world. For Winnicott, by contrast, it emerges from play and appears after the distinction between inner and outer reality, being rooted in relational experience and linked to creativity.

In the third chapter, the discussion moves to the so-called "depressive position", a key concept in Klein's thought which marks the capacity to recognise ambivalence and begin the work of reparation. Although reticent about the term, Winnicott formulates the "capacity for concern" as an index of emotional maturity and self-integration. This chapter shows how these ideas – though developed in distinct theoretical registers – converge in their attempt to reflect upon the foundations of an ethics of care within psychoanalysis.

Next, we delve into the process of thought formation by comparing the proposals of Bion and Winnicott. While Bion understands thought as a response to frustration – a product of the metabolisation of raw elements of experience through the alpha function – Winnicott privileges the transitional space and play, proposing a differentiation between mind (as the cognitive part) and psyche.

The fifth chapter focuses on the question of symbolisation, drawing on the contributions of Klein and Bion. For Klein, symbolising is transforming persecutory anxiety into representation, with an emphasis on the configuration of internal objects. For Bion, symbolisation is a continuous emotional process whose effectiveness depends on the presence of a psychic container. The comparative analysis highlights the importance of both models, particularly in the treatment of patients with impaired symbolic capacities.

Maternal function – and, by extension, the function of the analyst – is the theme of the sixth chapter, where the concepts of *reverie* in Bion and *holding* in Winnicott are contrasted. On one hand, the mother who thinks the baby;

on the other, the mother who physically and emotionally sustains the baby. These are distinct functions, yet equally essential to the constitution of the individual. The chapter demonstrates how these operations shape the analytic setting, particularly in the listening of patients in regressed states.

The following chapter addresses therapeutic regression, highlighting its understanding in Klein and Winnicott. While Klein describes regression as a return to primitive positions in which archaic anxieties and defences are reactivated, Winnicott conceives it as a legitimate need of the patient to relive, under favourable conditions, early experiences of dependence. By situating these particularities, we explore their implications for the clinical work with borderline states.

The discussion in the eighth chapter centres on the concept of the superego, whose early emergence and severity are emphasised by Klein, marked by the introjection of persecutory objects. In Winnicott, by contrast, the superego appears later, as an achievement of emotional maturation. The contrast between an intrapsychic model and a more relational one allows us to rethink forms of psychic suffering and possible modes of intervention.

The ninth chapter offers a dense reflection on the body in the works of Winnicott and Bion. Drawing on Merleau-Ponty, the authors examine how the body becomes a territory of psychic expression and inscription. In Winnicott, it is the cradle of the psyche-soma unity; in Bion, it appears as the seat of the unthinkable, requiring from the analyst an embodied form of listening – the so-called somatic *reverie*.

Finally, the last chapter investigates the origins of psychosis through the models proposed by Bion and Winnicott. Bion's framework emphasises the failure of the alpha function and the collapse of links as triggering factors. Winnicott's perspective, in turn, points to severe environmental failures in the early stages of life, which impair the constitution of the self. Although they stem from different axes – one more intrapsychic, the other more relational – both approaches attribute a decisive role to the presence (or absence) of a sufficiently sustaining environment in the organisation (or fragmentation) of the psyche.

By bringing together authors who are often read in isolated compartments, this book embraces the fecundity of contrasts and the vitality that emerges when we take up the challenge of thinking with – and, at times, against – the masters. If clinical work demands listening, and research requires precision, then perhaps the convergence of both can only be sustained when we cultivate doubt as a method. This is the invitation we extend to readers: to preserve wonder and curiosity as the pillars of psychoanalytic practice.

Notes

1 The book remained for several months on the list of "bestsellers" in the Psychoanalysis category on Amazon.
2 Alfredo Naffah Neto is responsible for the research project entitled *The Ferenczian-Winnicottian Psychoanalytic Lineage and Its Singularity in Relation to Other Traditions: Theoretical and Technical Convergences and Divergences*, developed within the Postgraduate Programme in Clinical Psychology at PUC-SP (Pontifical

Catholic University of São Paulo). The study aims to investigate, through a theoretical-clinical methodology, the specificities of the psychoanalytic tradition that unfolds from Ferenczi to Winnicott, contrasting it with other schools such as the Kleinian, Lacanian, and American ego psychology approaches. Among the key analytical axes is the place of therapeutic regression – central to the Ferenczian-Balintian-Winnicottian lineage – in contrast with the handling of transference in approaches designed for psychotic and borderline patients. The goal is to provide clearer criteria for the conceptual and technical delineation of psychoanalytic fields, thereby contributing to a clinical practice that is more consciously aware of its assumptions and effects.

3 Freud himself, in his text *On the Teaching of Psycho-analysis in Universities*, states that:

> In the investigation of mental processes and intellectual functions, psycho-analysis pursues a specific method of its own. The application of this method is by no means confined to the field of psychological disorders, but extends also to the solution of problems in art, philosophy, and religion. […] The fertilizing effects of psycho-analytic thought on these other disciplines would certainly contribute greatly towards forging a closer link, in the sense of a *universitas literarum*, between medical science and the branches of learning which lie within the sphere of philosophy and the arts.
>
> (Freud, 1919/1981, p. 173)

References

Almeida, A. P., and Naffah Neto, A. (2021). Sándor Ferenczi e Melanie Klein: a análise do analista como alicerce da formação [Sándor Ferenczi and Melanie Klein: The Analyst's Analysis as the Foundation of Training]. *Trivium – Estudos Interdisciplinares*, *13*(2): 92–102. https://doi.org/10.18379/2176-4891.2021v2p.92

Almeida, A. P., and Naffah Neto, A. (2022). Psicanálise e educação escolar: contribuições de Freud e Winnicott à compreensão do fenômeno da violência escolar [Psychoanalysis and School Education: Contributions of Freud and Winnicott to the Understanding of the Phenomenon of School Violence]. *Dialogia*, *40*: 1–16. https://doi.org/10.5585/40.2022.20478

Almeida, A. P., and Naffah Neto, A. (Orgs.). (2022). *Perto das trevas: a depressão em seis perspectivas psicanalíticas* [*Near to Darkness: Depression in Six Psychoanalytic Perspectives*]. São Paulo: Blucher.

Almeida, A. P., and Naffah Neto, A. (2024). Um estudo comparativo entre as teorias de Klein e Winnicott: analisando o conceito de fantasia [A Comparative Study of the Theories of Klein and Winnicott: Analysing the Concept of Phantasy]. *Revista Latinoamericana De Psicopatologia Fundamental*, *27*: 1–23. https://doi.org/10.1590/1415-4714.e230636

Almeida, A. P., Naffah Neto, A., and Vieira, F. P. (2024). A construção do pensar: um estudo comparativo entre Bion e Winnicott [The Construction of Thinking: A Comparative Study between Bion and Winnicott]. *Natureza Humana*, *26*(1): 40–59. https://doi.org/10.59539/2175-2834-v26n1-692

Almeida, A. P. (2025). Reflexões psicanalíticas sobre a separação amorosa: contribuições de Melanie Klein e Winnicott [Psychoanalytic Reflections on Romantic Separation: Contributions from Melanie Klein and Winnicott]. *Psicanálise & Barroco Em Revista*, *22*(1): 14–32. https://doi.org/10.9789/pb.v22i1.14-32

Almeida, A. P., and Vieira, F. P. (2025). A regressão na clínica psicanalítica: um estudo comparativo entre Klein e Winnicott [Regression in Psychoanalytic Practice: A Comparative Study between Klein and Winnicott]. *Analytica: Revista De Psicanálise*, *13*(26): 1–23. https://doi.org/10.69751/arp.v13i26.5465

Almeida, A. P., Naffah Neto, A., and Vieira, F. P. (2025). *A clínica winnicottiana: os casos difíceis* [*The Winnicottian Clinic: Difficult Cases*]. São Paulo: Blucher.

Freud, S. (1981). On the Teaching of Psycho-analysis in Universities. In S. Freud, *The Standard Edition of the Complete Psychological Works of Sigmund Freud (Vol. 17)*. London: The Hogarth Press. (Original work published in 1919)

Lispector, C. (2020). *A paixão segundo G.H.* [*The Passion According to G.H.*]. Rio de Janeiro: Rocco. E-book.

Mezan, R. (2019). *O tronco e os ramos* [*The Trunk and the Branches*]. São Paulo: Blucher.

Vieira, F. P. (2024). A depressão em adolescentes na atualidade: um estudo comparativo a partir da psicanálise de Freud e Winnicott [Depression in Contemporary Adolescents: A Comparative Study Based on the Psychoanalysis of Freud and Winnicott]. *Revista Da Faculdade Paulo Picanço*, 4(3): 1–17. https://doi.org/10.59483/rfpp.v4n3121

Vieira, F. P. (2025). *A interpretação psicanalítica: revisitando Klein e Winnicott* [*The Psychoanalytic Interpretation: Revisiting Klein and Winnicott*]. São Paulo: Blucher.

1 Psychoanalytic Interpretation in Klein and Winnicott

A Comparative Study

Filipe Pereira Vieira, Alfredo Naffah Neto, and Alexandre Patricio de Almeida

The Freudian Origins of Psychoanalytic Interpretation

Freud – throughout much of his work – emphasised the use of psychoanalytic interpretation as the only means of transforming the roots of unconscious conflict. In one of his earliest books, *Studies on Hysteria* (1893–1895), co-authored with Josef Breuer, the fundamental thesis of Freudian theory regarding psychoanalytic interpretation is already clearly formulated, particularly in Chapter 4, entitled "The Psychotherapy of Hysteria". Let us consider:

> Experiences like this made me think that it would in fact be possible for the pathogenic groups of ideas, that were after all certainly present, to be brought to light by mere insistence; and since this insistence involved effort on my part and so suggested the idea that I had to overcome a resistance, the situation led me at once to the theory that *by means of my psychical work I had to overcome a psychical force in the patients which was opposed to the pathogenic ideas becoming conscious (being remembered)*.
>
> (Freud, 1893–1895/1981, p. 268, original emphasis)

Later, in the text "Freud's Psycho-Analytic Procedure" (1904), written as part of an encyclopaedia entry, Freud states that repressed content can only find representation once certain resistances have been overcome – a process made possible through the use of interpretations:

> Freud has developed on this basis an *art of interpretation* which takes on the task of, as it were, extracting the pure metal of the repressed thoughts from the ore of the unintentional ideas. This work of interpretation is applied not only to the patient's ideas but also to his dreams, which open up the most direct approach to a knowledge of the unconscious, to his unintentional as well as to his purposeless actions (symptomatic acts) and to the blunders he makes in everyday life (slips of the tongue, bungled actions, and so on).
>
> (Freud, 1904/1981, p. 252, emphasis added)

DOI: 10.4324/9781003642503-2

At this early stage in the history of our discipline, the main task of the psychoanalyst was to listen, to understand, and to interpret the resistances in order to allow the repressed content to reach consciousness – just as Freud explained, "Interpreting means finding a hidden sense in something" (Freud, 1916/1981, p. 87, emphasis added).

Moving forward to 1937, the year in which Freud wrote the essay "Constructions in Analysis", the author opens with the following words:

> It has always seemed to me to be greatly to the credit of a certain well-known man of science that he treated psychoanalysis fairly at a time when most other people felt themselves under no such obligation. On one occasion, nevertheless, he gave expression to an opinion upon analytic technique which was at once derogatory and unjust. He said that in giving interpretations to a patient we treat him upon the famous principle of "Heads I win, tails you lose". *That is to say, if the patient agrees with us, then the interpretation is right; but if he contradicts us, that is only a sign of his resistance, which again shows that we are right.* In this way we are always in the right against the poor helpless wretch whom we are analysing, no matter how he may respond to what we put forward.
>
> (Freud, 1937/1981, p. 257, emphasis added)

As we can observe, concerned with the development of psychoanalysis, Freud draws our attention to misguided practices within psychoanalytic technique – that is, he offers a critique of the analyst's authoritarian stance, in which one essentially "commands" (the analyst) and the other "obeys" (the patient). Still in this 1937 essay, he revisits fundamental principles of our clinical practice:

> What sort of material does he put at our disposal which we can make use of to put him on the way to recovering the lost memories? All kinds of things. He gives us fragments of these memories in his dreams, invaluable in themselves but seriously distorted as a rule by all the factors concerned in the formation of dreams. Again, he produces ideas, if he gives himself up to 'free association', in which we can discover allusions to the repressed experiences and derivatives of the suppressed affective impulses as well as of the reactions against them. And, finally, there are hints of repetitions of the affects belonging to the repressed material to be found in actions performed by the patient, some fairly important, some trivial, both inside and outside the analytic situation. Our experience has shown that the *relation of transference*, which becomes established towards the analyst, is particularly calculated to favour the return of these emotional connections. It is out of such raw material – if we may so describe it – that we have to put together what we are in search of.
>
> (Freud, 1937/1981, p. 258, emphasis added)

In other words, when the analyst adopts an excessively authoritarian and assertive stance, interpreting the patient's disagreements merely as forms of resistance, the transference tends to become weakened. In such a configuration, the analyst comes to occupy the place of a kind of unquestionable "law", which may, even if unconsciously, inhibit the process of *free association*[1] – one of the fundamental rules of our discipline.

Faced with this, we may ask ourselves: is interpretation the only possible path within the analytic practice, or might there be other ways of conducting it?

In this very article, Freud (1937) proposes a model of treatment more guided by the exchanges between analyst and patient than solely by the interpretation of unconscious content into consciousness. Indeed, interpretations come to be used not merely in an assertive manner, but as possible forms of communication established through *intersubjective* interaction – after all, in analytic practice, two unconscious minds are in communication, and therefore the dynamic does not follow a vertical logic.

In summary, as we move through Freud's work, we find essays that highlight an analytic treatment more closely guided by the *interpretative* method of unconscious (intra-psychic) content – as is especially the case in the records of his early clinical cases, such as Dora, Little Hans, the Rat Man, among others. On the other hand, in his later writings, we come across a stronger emphasis on "constructions in analysis" – which reveals a more intersubjective perspective of clinical practice.

We quote Freud:

> The analyst finishes a piece of construction and communicates it to the subject of the analysis so that it may work upon him; he then constructs a further piece out of the fresh material pouring in upon him, deals with is in the same way and proceeds in this alternating fashion until the end. If, in accounts of analytic technique, so little is said about "constructions", that is because 'interpretations' and their effects are spoken of instead. *But I think that "construction" is by far the more appropriate description.*
>
> (Freud, 1937/1981, pp. 260–261, emphasis added)

Although Freud did not explicitly use the term, we can nonetheless discern, embedded within the notion of construction, what has come to be referred to in our field as "object relations" (Gurfinkel, 2017; Greenberg and Mitchell, 1983) – that is, a phenomenon which encompasses the exchange and dynamics of instinctual movement, functioning as a kind of equation between patient and analyst.

From this perspective, Karl Abraham (1924) played a fundamental role in broadening the psychoanalytic understanding of so-called object relations, directly influencing authors such as Melanie Klein and Ronald

Fairbairn in the development of their theories. According to Thomas Ogden:

> Working within the framework of Freud's theory of sexual instincts, Abraham (1924) attributed greater importance than Freud to the role of the object in the development of the libido and placed greater emphasis on the role of unconscious fantasy in psychological life.
>
> (2017, p. 143)

After this brief introduction, we shall turn our attention to the Kleinian clinic, grounded in the concept of *phantasy*[2] and in the role of interpretations within psychoanalytic practice.

The Function of Interpretation in Kleinian Theory

Inspired by Abraham, Klein was one of the most prominent authors to extend and disseminate the concept of object relations, devoting herself to the study of unconscious phantasies and the significant impact they have on both child and adult development. Her theoretical framework was largely shaped by this very premise. According to the *New Dictionary of Kleinian Thought* (2011):

> In Kleinian theory unconscious phantasies underlie every mental process and accompany all mental activity. They are the mental representation of those somatic events in the body that comprise the instincts, and are physical sensations interpreted as relationships with objects that cause those sensations. Phantasy is the mental expression of both libidinal and aggressive impulses and also of defence mechanisms against those impulses. [...] Klein adopted his idea of unconscious phantasy but broadened it considerably because her work with children gave her extensive experience of the wide-ranging content of children's phantasies. She and her successors have emphasised that phantasies interact reciprocally with experience to form the developing intellectual and emotional characteristics of the individual; phantasies are considered to be a basic capacity underlying and shaping thought, dreams, symptoms and patterns of defence.
>
> (Spillius et al., 2011, p. 3, emphasis added)

"Since she did not require the quasi-physical speculation that obscured Freud's work, Klein was able to delineate the territory he had opened up without concern for the scientific status of her own work" (Caper, 1990, p. 141). Klein penetrated, with intense sensitivity and precision, "the heart of the child", as Jones remarked (Steiner, 1985). Her theoretical-clinical path expanded our understanding of the origins of the most primitive mental states. Here, we turn to the author's own words:

> Paranoid disturbances in adults are, in my view, based on the persecutory anxiety experienced in the first few months of life. In the paranoid patient the essence of his fears of persecution is the feeling that there is a hostile agency which is bent on inflicting on him suffering, damage and ultimately annihilation. This persecutory agency may be represented by one or many people or even by the forces of nature. There are innumerable and in every case specific forms which the dreaded attack may take; but the root of persecutory fear in the paranoid individual is, I believe, the fear of annihilation of the ego – ultimately by the death instinct.
>
> (Klein, 1948/2011, n.p.)

However, the Kleinian stance is regarded by many analysts as excessively authoritarian and direct. However, would that really be true?

According to Hinshelwood, Klein's work "was so dismissed by certain colleagues from the mid1920s onwards" (2018, p. 136). We would venture to say that this still occurs today. Like all great researchers, Melanie Klein had a thesis to prove and, for that reason, she paid close attention to the *finer details* – the micro-processes – of clinical material. This aspect "has remained a prominent dimension of Kleinian writing to the present day" (Hinshelwood, 2018, p. 136).

Indeed, it does not take much effort to understand the origins of the "disregard" shown by much of the psychoanalytic community towards Kleinian ideas. At this point, it is necessary to consider the misogyny, prejudice, and resistance – all so present in our field – and how these factors directly affect the reception of a woman's work. Let us recall that Klein was a *divorced* woman with *no formal academic qualifications* – unlike most analysts of her time, who were typically trained in medicine (Almeida, 2023).

In this light, it is quite likely that her rigid stance may have been constructed precisely as a defence mechanism in response to that position (or would it be more accurate to say, "absence of position"?). In other words, had Klein not been so assertive in her claims, her theories might well have been forgotten over time.

Through her careful observation of children's play, Klein realised that the stories enacted by the child contained important elements of their internal conflicts. These symbolic narratives, often repeated in play, revealed profound aspects of the psychic pain experienced by the young patients. For this reason, she began to regard the level of anxiety expressed during play as a kind of "thermometer" of emotional suffering. When an interpretation led to a reduction in that anxiety, Klein understood that a significant change had occurred in the process, indicating that the treatment was progressing satisfactorily.

Conversely, although the use of interpretation is the cornerstone that consolidates analytic work within the Kleinian tradition, we must not mistake this stance for a lack of sensitivity. As Hinshelwood reminds us, "When she conducted therapeutic analyses, she became interested in what actual impact interpretations had. It was very important to her that an interpretation felt right *to the patient*, rather than merely feeling right to the analyst" (Hinshelwood, 2018, p. 136, original emphasis).

According to the author, Klein's primary aim was for the interpretation to make sense *to the patient*; that is, for the patient to be able to recognise it as true based on their own emotional experience. She herself emphasised that, depending on the psychic defences at play, some patients might struggle to grasp the meaning of the interpretations offered. This was because certain aspects of the personality could be "split off":

> Patients with schizoid features may say: 'I hear what you are saying. You may be right, but it has no meaning for me.' Or again they say they feel they are not there. The expression 'no meaning' in such cases does not imply an active rejection of the interpretation but suggests that parts of the personality and of the emotions are split off. These patients can, therefore, not deal with the interpretation; they can neither accept it nor reject it.
>
> (Klein, 1946/2011, n.p.)

It is true that Klein drew upon the psychic material that emerged in the "here and now" to construct her interpretations. However, this does not mean that her technique was rigid or unchanging – on the contrary, she recognised the importance of adapting it whenever the patient required a more attentive listening or a differentiated clinical approach. Not by chance, the author herself stated:

> As a rule the analyst would base his first interpretation on fresh material coming up in that session; but if anxiety is so acute that the patient cannot express it, an interpretation referring to the material of the previous session (or sessions) is required.
>
> (Klein, 1961/2011, n.p.).

In other words, although she prioritised the "here and now" of the analytic encounter, she also emphasised the importance of the patient's historical continuity (temporal logic) – especially when difficulties in the process of symbolisation arose.

In this sense, interpretation was not limited to naming content; on the contrary, it required the analyst to "construct words" that would touch the patient with precision – words capable of operating within the psyche, unsettling omnipotent certainties and opening space for new possibilities of elaboration (Vieira, 2025).

To summarise: the Kleinian technique may be understood as a process of "translation" of the clinical material into a symbolic dimension which, once introjected, results in the relief of anxiety (Almeida, 2020).

Klein also observed that, in some cases, the child's ego developed precociously as an attempt to deal with intense anxieties from a very early stage (Vieira, 2025). This led the child to display a kind of "exaggerated empathy" with the suffering of their internal objects, a phenomenon linked to the excessive use of projective identifications. In such situations, the subject would end up repressing their aggressive impulses for fear of harming these objects, already perceived as fragile (Almeida, 2020).

Analytic work, by reducing anxiety and offering appropriate interpretations, allowed such patients to gradually come into contact with their more violent feelings – *sadism proper* – in a "less threatening" way. Over time, this integration made it possible to expand their interest in other objects, fostering richer and less inhibited relationships.

The focus of Kleinian work thus developed as a constant attempt to reduce anxiety – driven by both intrapsychic and intersubjective conflicts. Within this psychoanalytic tradition, interpretation is regarded as the *primary tool* that enables access to the patient's internal world. Depending on the establishment of transference, it is as if the patient offers their hand to the analyst, allowing them to enter their psyche and, together, "search through" the objects that provoke terror and anxiety.

In a footnote from *The Psycho-Analysis of Children* (1932/2011), Klein points out "[...] interpretation has the effect of changing the character of the child's play and enabling the representation of its material to become clearer" (Klein, 1932/2011, n.p.).

Let us consider:

After the termination of its analysis the child cannot alter the circumstances of its life as the adult often can. But analysis will have helped it very greatly if it has enabled it to develop more freely and to feel better in its actual environment. Furthermore, the removal of the child's neurosis often has the effect of minimizing the difficulties of its milieu.

(Klein, 1932/2011, n.p.)

Although the author's writings may evoke a certain discomfort in readers – particularly when we critically examine her more visceral use of interpretation – she consistently made her epistemological assumptions explicit, drawing upon numerous descriptions of clinical cases. Klein's writing thus presents itself as living material, pulsing within us and raising several concerns.

In what follows, we offer some reflections on Winnicott's interpretative technique, highlighting the role of *management*, which he defended as an essential resource in clinical practice.

From Interpretation to Management: The Winnicottian Clinic

Winnicott, following in the footsteps of Sándor Ferenczi (Almeida, 2019[3]), was one of the great pioneering authors to rethink the dynamics of psycho-analytic technique. He introduced the notion of *clinical management*, understood as the construction of a setting that should be modified (adapted) according to the needs of each individual patient. We quote the author:

> In the work I am describing the setting becomes more important than the interpretation. The emphasis is changed from the one to the other. The behaviour of the analyst, represented by what I have called the setting, by being good enough in the matter of adaptation to need, is gradually perceived by the patient as something that raises a hope that the true self may at last be able to take the risks involved in its *starting to experience living*.
>
> (Winnicott, 1955/2017, p. 63, emphasis added)

Unlike Kleinian theories, the Winnicottian tradition prioritises, first and foremost, an environment (*setting*) that is sufficiently good in terms of predictability and reliability. It is from this sense of safety that the patient is able to relax, creating (and inhabiting) their "potential space" – where play becomes possible and creativity can expand into a wide range of elaborations.

To Winnicott:

> The thing about playing is always the precariousness of the interplay of personal psychic reality and the experience of control of actual objects. This is the precariousness of magic itself, magic that arises in intimacy, in a relationship that is being found to be reliable.
>
> (Winnicott, 1968/2017, p. 308)

However, it is only in states of relaxation – made possible by the environmental care the infant receives – that a sense of trust can emerge, allowing the child to move within an overlap between their subjective (personal) reality and objective (shared) reality. Winnicott named this phenomenon the *transitional area* (or third area).

> This third area has been contrasted with inner or personal psychic reality and with the actual world in which the individual lives, which can be objectively perceived. I have located this important area *of experience* in the potential space between the individual and the environment, that which initially both joins and separates the baby and the mother when the mother's love, displayed or made manifest as human reliability, does in fact give the baby a sense of trust or of confidence in the environmental factor.
>
> (Winnicott, 1967c/2017, p. 436, original emphasis)

To Winnicott, analytic work takes place fundamentally within this third area, where the capacity for *creativity* is enhanced. Winnicott emphasises that, "From the beginning, the baby has the most intense experiences in the potential space between the subjective object and the objectively perceived object, between the extensions of the self and the not-self" (Winnicott, 1971a/2019, p. 162). Therefore:

> It is only here, in this unintegrated state of the personality, that that which we describe as creative can appear. [...] We experience life in the area of transitional phenomena, in the exciting interweave of subjectivity and objective observation, and in an area that is intermediate between the inner reality of the individual and the shared reality of the world that is external to individuals.
>
> (Winnicott, 1971/2017, p. 179)

Nevertheless, it is also crucial to emphasise that, within the psychoanalytic field, Winnicott was the first theorist to formulate a theory of emotional (or maturational) development, in which – among other aspects – he emphasised the importance of the baby having their needs adequately and reliably met.

According to his ideas, it is only through the creation of that which is there to be found – that is, the subjectively perceived object, created and discovered by the infant within their illusion of omnipotence – that the individual will come to feel they can trust their new environment. This is one of the necessary conditions for healthy – and creative – maturation. In the author's words:

> In the early development of the human being the environment that behaves well enough (that makes good-enough active adaptation) *enables personal growth to take place*. The self processes then may continue active, in an unbroken line of living growth. If the environment behaves not well enough, then the individual is engaged in reactions to impingement, and the self processes are interrupted. If this state of affairs reaches a quantitative limit the core of the self begins to get protected.
>
> (Winnicott, 1955/2017 p. 214, original emphasis)

To Winnicott, if we are forced to protect ourselves from the experience of living due to an unsatisfactory environment (marked by failures or intrusions), the core of the self – that is, the true self – will not mature, remaining frozen in anticipation of a favourable environment that might allow it to "come into being". As a result, in situations where environmental failures are frequent, the defences of the self become more rigid, and false self develops in order to protect the true self from further intrusions. According to Winnicott:

> This false self is no doubt an aspect of the true self. It hides and protects it, and it reacts to the adaptation failures and develops a pattern

corresponding to the pattern of environmental failure. In this way the true self is not involved in the reacting, and so preserves a continuity of being. However, this hidden true self *suffers an impoverishment that derives from lack of experience.*

(Winnicott, 1956/2017, p. 62, emphasis added)

It is not uncommon for us to receive, in the clinical setting, individuals who appear well *adapted* to treatment. However, as they begin to relax in the presence of the analyst's attentive care, they may *regress* to primitive stages of development which, due to some failure in the early environment, could not be properly *experienced* by the self or integrated through the *imaginative elaboration of body functioning* (see Chapter 9 of this book). Broadly speaking, if the environment is excessively failing, the infant will attempt to protect itself by reacting to the intrusion.

Well, if we are speaking of experiences that remained *frozen*, there is not sufficient psychic material available to be interpreted in more regressed patients – that is, those who endured traumatic experiences in the earliest phases of life. As radical as this statement may sound, it is important to stress that, within the Winnicottian tradition, an individual who has not undergone a process of integration – *built from the inside out* – does not possess an ego capable of repressing unconscious content. This is, therefore, a weakened psychic structure – one that had to react in order to survive.

Throughout his work, Winnicott sought to describe how the human being progresses from their initial state – in which immaturity prevails, marked by total dependence on the environment and, therefore, a state of *non-integration* – to the various forms of integration that occur throughout life (reaching differentiation between the external and internal worlds, achieving a sense of individual unity, and distinguishing the self from the not-self). To him, the earliest stage of life is an extremely delicate period, as the infant will require all of the mother's care in order to *come into being* (Almeida and Naffah Neto, 2021). Let us follow Winnicott:

I wish to postulate a state of being which is a fact in the ordinary baby before birth as well as afterwards. This state of being belongs to the infant and not to the observer. *Continuity of being is health.* If one takes the analogy of a bubble, one can say that if the pressure outside is adapted to the pressure inside, then the bubble has a continuity of existence and if it were a human baby this would be called 'being'. If on the other hand the pressure outside the bubble is greater or less than the pressure inside, then the bubble is engaged in a reaction to impingement. It changes in reaction to the environmental change, not from personal impulsive experience. *In terms of the human animal this means that there is an interruption of being, and the place of being is taken by reaction to impingement.*

(Winnicott, 1988/2017, p. 144, emphasis added)

In less favourable contexts, the relational pattern is configured as a response by the baby to the environment, rather than as an expression of their spontaneity. It is a matter of intrusion, as the environment imposes itself traumatically, disconnected from the child's spontaneous gesture. Depending on how often this experience is repeated, a different relational model is established – with outcomes that differ significantly from those that result from an *active* and *devoted* adaptation by the caregiving environment.

In situations where the early environment failed to provide predictability, the psychoanalyst must, above all, wait for the gradual reduction of the defences that keep the patient protected by a split and pathological false self. It is the analyst's task to sustain (*holding*) and manage (*management*) the analytic setting, supporting the *imaginative elaboration of body functioning* and enabling the revival of the experience of being within a sufficiently adapted therapeutic environment. This new beginning depends on sensitive management, carefully attuned to the patient's state of integration throughout the process of regression.

In these terms, the analyst must, as needed, take on the role of either the "environment mother" or the "object mother". We quote Winnicott:

> It is helpful to postulate the existence for the immature child of two mothers – shall I call them the object-mother and the environment-mother? I have no wish to invent names that become stuck and eventually develop a rigidity and an obstructive quality, but it seems possible to use these words 'object-mother' and 'environment-mother' in this context to describe the vast difference that there is for the infant between two aspects of infant-care, the mother as object, or owner of the part-object *that may satisfy the infant's urgent needs, and the mother as the person who wards off the unpredictable and who actively provides care in handling and in general management.*
> (Winnicott, 1963/2017, p. 353, emphasis added)

In summary, "[...] the environment-mother who receives all that can be called affection and sensuous coexistence; it is the object-mother who becomes the target for excited experience backed by crude instinct-tension" (Winnicott, 1963/2017, p. 353). Winnicott explains that it is precisely at the stage of *using the object* that the infant brings together the figure of the environment-mother and the object-mother. For this complex task to be successfully accomplished, the survival of the mother becomes essential. Later, in the stage of concern, a *benign cycle* is established, enabling the development of the capacity for reparation – in other words, the emergence of *genuine* guilt, which is indispensable for the gradual construction of concern for the other as a fellow being (see Chapter 8 of this book).

Winnicott specifies these two forms of maternal care, linking them to the calm and excited states that the infant constantly presents as vital indicators. Before reaching the "stage of the use of the object", the baby is not yet able to integrate these maternal functions and modes of existence within their still immature psyche. Similarly, this is an important aspect to consider when working with disintegrated patients, or with those who, for some reason, have not reached the stage of object use and, consequently, the stage of concern. In such cases, the analyst's survival is fundamental: "When confidence in this benign cycle and in the expectation of opportunity is established, the sense of guilt in relation to the id-drives becomes further modified, and we then need a more positive term, such as 'concern'" (Winnicott, 1963/2017, p. 355).

In light of these scenarios, it would make little sense to regard interpretation as the sole form of psychoanalytic intervention. Survival within the setting implies holding and presence, so that the benign cycle may unfold in the continuous and secure company of the analyst. Thus, frequently cancelling sessions, arriving late, or even offering overly assertive interpretations are all examples of behaviours that may negatively affect the progress of a case with such characteristics. After all, an "abandoned child" who turns to an analyst and regresses to the most primitive stages of development begins to experience – perhaps for the very first time – a state of total dependence on environmental care. If all goes well, the analyst will come to occupy the place of the "good enough mother" herself, and will know how to step back at the moment the individual reaches emotional maturity.

However, aside from situations of spontaneous regression, when the patient is in a state of *transference neurosis*,[4] Winnicott resorts to interpretation, like any classical psychoanalyst. Nevertheless, even under such conditions, his style is characterised by being less emphatic and less frequent than that of Kleinian interpretations. This is because, to him, the function of interpretation is not to reduce the patient's anxiety – such anxiety should be alleviated through the growing development of trust in the psychoanalytic process, fostered by the setting and by the analyst's own attitude.

In such cases, the function of interpretation is to translate into symbolic elements contents that are already within the patient's preconscious sphere, so that they may finally acquire conscious *meaning*. Even so, in one of his final writings, Winnicott (1967a/2017) tells us that, early in his professional career, he interpreted everything he discovered in the patient – until he realised the futility of doing so. In that same text, he states that the premature interpretation of a dream often deprives the patient of the opportunity to work through it on their own, preventing them from bringing it back repeatedly in sessions and, thus, from reaching a deeper understanding of themselves through their own elaboration. Let us consider:

> I've been through the long process of interpreting everything I could possibly see that could be interpreted, you know, feeling awful if I couldn't find anything, and pouncing on something because I found I could put it into words. I've been through all that and realised that in certain cases *it was no good at all*, along with other people who I know

had done the same things. [...] Since realising this I've had to deal with a lot of silent phases in analysis that lasted a long time, and it's very difficult to know when it's wasted time and when it's extremely productive, but nevertheless all this is now something I love to study. Today, this afternoon, a patient brought me a dream – a patient who's getting near the end of analysis – and suddenly I saw ahead to a solution of where he was getting to, so I let him have my idea of where he was, and he was so dissatisfied [...]. He was absolutely angry with me and absolutely hopeless and he said, 'When will you ever learn?' If I was right, *I'd taken away his opportunity to be creative*, to bring it next time and the time after; and if I was wrong *I'd interrupted his reaching an important bit of understanding through this dream*.

(Winnicott, 1967a/2017, pp. 46–47, emphasis added)

Convergences and Divergences

Winnicott's work shows us, in broad terms, the importance of *management* throughout life – not only within the therapeutic setting. Let us recall that it is through this essential form of care that the infant, when adequately held (*holding*) and handled (*handling*), will be able to achieve *ego integration* (in time and space), *personalisation* (the progressive allocation of the psyche within the body, forming a psychosomatic unity), and finally, *realisation* (the experience of feeling real).

In clinical practice, a sequence of events unfolds:

1   The provision of a setting that gives confidence.
2   Regression of the patient to dependence, with due sense of the risk involved.
3   The patient feeling a new sense of self, and the self hitherto hidden becoming surrendered to the total ego. A new progression of the individual processes which had stopped.
4   An unfreezing of an environmental failure situation.
5   From the new position of ego strength, anger related to the early environmental failure, felt in the present and expressed.
6   Return from regression to dependence, in orderly progress towards independence.
7   Instinctual needs and wishes becoming realizable with genuine vitality and vigour.

(Winnicott, 1955/2017, pp. 209–210)

Here lies one of the main differences between the Winnicottian and Kleinian clinics: the idea of *regression to stages of dependence*[5] – mentioned earlier, although briefly. To Klein, regression to primitive stages is not considered a valid therapeutic tool, as in such cases the patient would be returning to the *paranoid-schizoid position*, which to her represents an even more acute stage of psychic suffering.

From a Kleinian perspective, the path to health does not depend on regression, but rather on a kind of *balance* between the depressive position and the paranoid-schizoid position – the result of a dynamic movement back and forth, without permanent fixation in either position. Regression to the paranoid-schizoid position occurs because something from the depressive position has been lost, thus requiring a return in order for it to be recovered. In other words, regression should be spontaneous and never used as a therapeutic tool. Moreover, it is a return to a *psychic state* – not to stages of dependence – since Klein did not propose a theory of maturation involving stages to be passed through and overcome.

It is worth remarking that one of the greatest achievements of Kleinian treatment is "attainment and working through of the depressive position" (Almeida, 2024), which enables the individual to take responsibility for their actions, becoming capable of dealing with ambivalence – without this implying an inability to return to the schizoid-paranoid position whenever necessary, as a way of maintaining balance between the two positions or of reclaiming lost achievements.

To Winnicott, this is equally important. However, as we have seen, there are a number of developmental achievements that must be *experienced* by the infant before they are able to feel *concern* for the damage they may inevitably cause to the object. In this sense, premature experiences – before certain ego capacities have been integrated – may be perceived by the individual as profoundly damaging to their psychic constitution.

Not by chance, Winnicott highlights:

> Psychotic illness is related to environmental failure at an early stage of the emotional development of the individual. The sense of futility and unreality belongs to the development of a false self which develops in protection of the true self.
>
> The setting of analysis reproduces the early and earliest mothering techniques. It invites regression by reason of its reliability.
>
> The regression of a patient is an organized return to early dependence or double dependence. The patient and the setting merge into the original success situation of primary narcissism.
>
> Progress from primary narcissism starts anew with the true self able to meet environmental failure situations without organization of the defences that involve a false self protecting the true self.
>
> To this extent psychotic illness can only be relieved by specialized environmental provision interlocked with the patient's regression.
>
> Progress from the new position, with the true self surrendered to the total ego, can now be studied in terms of the complex processes of individual growth.
>
> (Winnicott, 1955/2017, p. 209)

This quotation summarises the aims of analytic work to Winnicott – depending on the degree of ego-integration – and also highlights the importance of regression in the treatment of severely traumatised patients. Here we find another feature that distinguishes the technique of these two psychoanalysts, as Klein did not work with the notion of *trauma*. She emphasised the role of instinctual drive in the aetiology of psychic disturbances; above all, the death instinct. We quote her:

> The strength of the ego – reflecting the state of fusion between the two instincts – is, I believe, constitutionally determined. If in the fusion the life instinct predominates, which implies an ascendancy of the capacity for love, the ego is relatively strong, and is more able to bear the anxiety arising from the death instinct and to counteract it. To what extent the strength of the ego can be maintained and increased is in part affected by external factors, in particular the mother's attitude towards the infant. However, even when the life instinct and the capacity for love predominate, destructive impulses are still deflected outwards and contribute to the creation of persecutory and dangerous objects which are reintrojected. Furthermore, the primal processes of introjection and projection lead to constant changes in the ego's relation to its objects, with fluctuations between internal and external, good and bad ones, according to the infant's phantasies and emotions as well as under the impact of his actual experiences.
>
> (Klein, 1958/2011, n.p.)

From this excerpt, we can draw several important considerations which, for the sake of clarity, we have chosen to list: 1) Winnicott did not work with the concept of the death instinct, nor did he believe in the existence of an archaic ego capable of projection and introjection from birth. This alone significantly alters his understanding of psychopathology and, consequently, his clinical interventions. 2) Although Klein worked with the duality of instinctual drives, she by no means disregarded the role of the environment. However, her understanding of primitive phantasies profoundly shaped her analytic stance. In short, the aim of Kleinian analysis is to enable the introjection of the good object, which, in turn, will mitigate the intensity of the destructive instinct – all of this, of course, relying on the interpretation of unconscious fantasies.

By contrast, Winnicott is unequivocal in asserting that:

> *Psychotherapy is not making clever and apt interpretations;* by and large it is a long-term giving the patient back what the patient brings. It is a complex derivative of the face that reflects what is there to be seen. I like to think of my work this way, and to think that if I do this well enough the patient will find his or her own self, and will be able to exist and to feel real. Feeling real is more than existing; it is finding a way to exist as

oneself, and to relate to objects as oneself, and to have a self into which to retreat for relaxation.

(Winnicott, 1967b/2017, p. 217, emphasis added)

This statement clearly summarises Winnicott's position regarding interpretation when working strictly within the classical technique – that is, as we noted earlier, with neurotic patients (or even with more severe patients, once they have emerged from regressive states), based on the clinical phenomenon of transference neurosis.

Thus, interpretation is always of material that is already in a preconscious state and therefore emerging into consciousness – very close to what the patient brings, or, as Winnicott puts it, "[...] a complex derivative of the face that reflects what is there to be seen" (1967b/2017, p. 217).

This does not mean that Winnicottian clinical practice, in employing the classical technique, operates in a superficial manner or neglects the becoming-conscious of unconscious processes (Almeida, Naffah Neto, and Vieira, 2025). The difference lies in how this transition occurs: not through interpretation, as in the Kleinian technique, but through the gradual dismantling of defences, made possible by the growing trust in the analytic setting. Interpretation merely concludes this process, granting it a symbolic dimension.

A Few Final Words

In certain corners of contemporary psychoanalysis, a curious phenomenon can be observed: the exaltation of one author at the expense of the belittlement of another – as if theory could be reduced to a podium. On one side, altars are erected; on the other, verdicts of oblivion are pronounced. It is almost as though each school of thought had its own cheerleading squad, complete with battle cries and an aversion to dissent.

We do not subscribe to this rigged game. The clinic does not bend to the theoretical preferences of analysts, no matter how much they try to mould it to their bedside manuals. It demands, above all, listening and presence – and, more importantly, the humility to recognise that every intervention carries with it a theoretical choice, even when disguised as neutrality.

In proposing this comparative study on the notion and use of interpretation, our aim was not to crown one author and depose another, but rather to trace the fertile – and at times irreconcilable – tensions that shape their legacies. Idealisation, after all, is the graveyard of any serious enquiry. When academic debate becomes merely a pretext for confirming one's own beliefs, we are left with a domesticated form of knowledge, useful only for decorating lecterns or feeding famished egos.

Something more is needed. More openness, more honest confrontation, less fear of difference. For, paradoxically, it is difference – not forced assimilation – that sustains the richness of any dialogue.

To conclude, without the pretension of resolving the irresolvable, we borrow the words of Guimarães Rosa, who perhaps, with his crooked and luminous wisdom, expresses better than we can what we seek to convey. "I say: the real is not in the departure or in the arrival: it reveals itself to us in the midst of the crossing" (Rosa, 1994, p. 86).

Notes

1 "Free association" can generally be understood through the well-known instruction Freud (1900) used to give to his patients at the beginning of psychoanalytic treatment: "Speak whatever comes into your mind, without censorship or restriction".
2 The difference between the spellings *fantasy* and *phantasy* will be discussed in more detail in Chapter 2 of this book.
3 As argued by Almeida (2019), Winnicott may be regarded as a direct heir to the thought of Sándor Ferenczi, not only for his appreciation of emotional experience within the setting, but above all for his clinical boldness in working with non-neurotic patients, his emphasis on the role of the environment in psychic development, and his openness to the use of regression as a therapeutic pathway. Both shared an ethical commitment to listening to suffering in its singularity, even when it did not conform to the dominant theoretical framework.
4 For Winnicott's notions of "transference neurosis" and "transference psychosis", we recommend reading Chapter 10 of this book.
5 For further clarification on this topic, see Chapter 7 of this book.

References

Abraham, K. (1970). Breve estudo do desenvolvimento da libido, visto à luz das perturbações mentais [A Short Study of the Development of the Libido, Viewed in the Light of Mental Disorders]. In K. Abraham, *Teoria psicanalítica da libido* [*Selected Papers on Psychoanalysis*], pp. 81–160. Rio de Janeiro: Imago. (Original work published in 1924)

Abram, J., and Hinshelwood, R. D. (2018). *The Clinical Paradigms of Melanie Klein and Donald Winnicott: Comparisons and Dialogues*. London: Routledge.

Almeida, A. P. (2019). Para além da interpretação: Repensando os enquadres e a escuta na psicanálise com crianças [Beyond Interpretation: Rethinking Settings and Listening in Psychoanalysis with Children]. *Estilos da Clínica*, 24: 121–133. https://doi.org/10.11606/issn.1981-1624.v24i1p121-133

Almeida, A. P. (2020). Melanie Klein e o processo de formação dos símbolos: revisitando o caso Dick [Melanie Klein and the Process of Symbol Formation: Revisiting the Case of Dick]. *Estilos da Clínica*, 25(3): 552–567. https://doi.org/10.11606/issn.1981-1624.v25i3p552-567

Almeida, A. P. (2023). A sombra do machismo e a formação psicanalítica: revisitando Melanie Klein [The Shadow of Machismo and Psychoanalytic Training: Revisiting Melanie Klein], pp. 55–94. In A. P. Almeida (Org.), *Muito além da formação: diálogos sobre a transmissão e a democratização da psicanálise* [*Beyond Training: Dialogues on the Transmission and Democratization of Psychoanalysis*]. São Paulo: Blucher.

Almeida, A. P. (2024). A depressão para Melanie Klein: um estudo teórico-clínico [Depression according to Melanie Klein: a theoretical-clinical study]. *Revista da Faculdade Paulo Picanço*, 4(1): 1–13. https://doi.org/10.59483/rfpp.v4n1.105

Almeida, A. P., Naffah Neto, A., and Vieira, F. P. (2025). *A clínica winnicottiana: os casos difíceis* [*The Winnicottian Clinic: Difficult Cases*]. São Paulo: Blucher.

Caper, R. (1990). *Fatos imateriais: a descoberta de Freud da realidade psíquica e o desenvolvimento kleiniano do trabalho de Freud* [*Immaterial Facts: Freud's Discovery of Psychic Reality and the Kleinian Development of Freud's Work*]. Rio de Janeiro: Imago.

Couto, M. (2016). *Poemas escolhidos* [*Selected Poems*]. São Paulo: Companhia das Letras.

Freud, S. (1981). Constructions in Analysis. In S. Freud. *The Standard Edition of the Complete Psychological Works of Sigmund Freud (Vol. 23)*, pp. 255–269. London: Hogarth Press. (Original work published in 1937)

Freud, S. (1981). Difficulties and First Approaches. In S. Freud. *The Standard Edition of the Complete Psychological Works of Sigmund Freud (Vol. 15)*, pp. 83–99. London: Hogarth Press. (Original work published in 1916)

Freud, S. (1981). Freud's Psycho-Analytic Procedure. In S. Freud. *The Standard Edition of the Complete Psychological Works of Sigmund Freud (Vol. 7)*, pp. 249–254. London: Hogarth Press. (Original work published in 1904)

Freud, S. (1981). The Psychotherapy of Hysteria [Freud]. In S. Freud. *The Standard Edition of the Complete Psychological Works of Sigmund Freud (Vol. 2)*, pp. 254–312. London: Hogarth Press. (Original work published 1893–1895)

Freud, S. (1971). The Interpretation of Dreams. In S. Freud. *The Standard Edition of the Complete Psychological Works of Sigmund Freud (Vol. 4)*. London: Hogarth Press. (Original work published in 1900)

Fulgencio, L. (2022). *Winnicott & companhia: Winnicott, Klein e Ferenczi (vol. 2)* [*Winnicott & Company: Winnicott, Klein and Ferenczi (vol. 2)*]. São Paulo: Blucher.

Greenberg, J. R. and Mitchell, S. (1983). *Relações objetais na teoria psicanalítica* [*Object Relations in Psychoanalytic Theory*]. Porto Alegre: Artes Médicas.

Gurfinkel, D. (2017). *Relações de objeto* [*Object Relations*]. São Paulo: Blucher.

Jaques, E. (2011). Prologue. In M. Klein, *Narrative of a Child Analysis*. London: Vintage Books. E-book. (Original work published in 1961)

Klein, M. (2011). *Narrative of a Child Analysis*. London: Vintage Books. E-book. (Original work published in 1961)

Klein, M. (2011). Notes on Some Schizoid Mechanisms. In M. Klein, *Envy and Gratitude and Other Works (1946–1963)*. London: Vintage Books. E-book. (Original work published in 1946)

Klein, M. (2011). On the Development of Mental Functioning. In M. Klein. *Envy and Gratitude and Other Works (1946–1963)*. London: Vintage Books. E-book. (Original work published in 1958)

Klein, M. (2011). On the Theory of Anxiety and Guilt. In M. Klein, *Envy and Gratitude and Other Works (1946–1963)*. London: Vintage Books. E-book. (Original work published in 1948)

Klein, M. (2011). *The Psycho-Analysis of Children*. London: Vintage Books. E-book. (Original work published in 1932)

Ogden, T. (2017). *A Matriz da mente: relações objetais e o diálogo psicanalítico* [*The Matrix of the Mind: Object Relations and the Psychoanalytic Dialogue*]. São Paulo: Blucher.

Rosa, J. G. (2019). *Grande sertão: veredas* [*The Devil to Pay in the Backlands*]. São Paulo: Companhia das Letras. E-book.

Spillius, E. B. et al. (2011). *The New Dictionary of Kleinian Thought*. London: Routledge.

Steiner, R. (1985). Some Thoughts About Tradition and Change Arising from an Examination of the British Psycho-analytical Society's "Controversial Discussions" (1943–44). *International Review of Psychoanalysis*, 12: 27–71.

Vieira, F. P. (2025). *A interpretação psicanalítica: revisitando Klein e Winnicott* [*The Psychoanalytic Interpretation: Revisiting Klein and Winnicott*]. São Paulo: Blucher.

Winnicott, D. W. (2017). Clinical Varieties of Transference. In D. W. Winnicott, *The Collected Works of D. W. Winnicott (Vol. 5)*, pp. 61–66. Oxford: Oxford University Press. (Original work published in 1956)

Winnicott, D. W. (2017). D. W. W. on D. W. W. In D. W. Winnicott, *The Collected Works of D. W. Winnicott (Vol. 8)*, pp. 35–48. Oxford: Oxford University Press. (Original work published in 1967a)

Winnicott, D. W. (2017). Human Nature. In D. W. Winnicott, *The Collected Works of D. W. Winnicott (Vol. 11)*, pp. 25–183. Oxford: Oxford University Press. (Original work published in 1988)

Winnicott, D. W. (2017). Metapsychological and Clinical Aspects of Regression Within the Psycho-Analytical Set-Up. In D. W. Winnicott, *The Collected Works of D. W. Winnicott (Vol. 4)*, pp. 201–218. Oxford: Oxford University Press. (Original work published in 1955)

Winnicott, D. W. (2017). Playing: Creative Activity and the Search for the Self. In D. W. Winnicott, *The Collected Works of D. W. Winnicott (Vol. 8)*, pp. 169–180. Oxford: Oxford University Press. (Original work published in 1971)

Winnicott, D. W. (2017). Mirror-Role of Mother and Family in Child Development. In D. W. Winnicott, *The Collected Works of D. W. Winnicott (Vol. 8)*, pp. 211–218. Oxford: Oxford University Press. (Original work published in 1967b)

Winnicott, D. W. (2017). Playing: A Theoretical Statement. In D. W. Winnicott, *The Collected Works of D. W. Winnicott (Vol. 8)*, pp. 299–312. Oxford: Oxford University Press. (Original work published in 1968)

Winnicott, D. W. (2017). The Development of the Capacity for Concern. In D. W. Winnicott, *The Collected Works of D. W. Winnicott (Vol. 6)*, pp. 351–356. Oxford: Oxford University Press. (Original work published in 1963)

Winnicott, D. W. (2017). The Location of Cultural Experience. In D. W. Winnicott, *The Collected Works of D. W. Winnicott (Vol. 7)*, pp. 429–436. Oxford: Oxford University Press. (Original work published in 1967c)

2 The Notion of Fantasy in Klein and Winnicott

Alexandre Patricio de Almeida
and Alfredo Naffah Neto

The Kleinian Concept of Phantasy

Melanie Klein was the great pioneer of child psychoanalysis – but not only that. She was also responsible, among other contributions, for introducing the term *phantasy* into the history of the psychoanalytic movement. "The initial *PH* serves to emphasise how the Kleinians understand *phantasy* or *phantasm*, these are *always unconscious*, having nothing in common with daydreaming or conscious fantasy" (Prado, 2021, p. 200, emphasis added).

> Susan Isaacs (1948, p. 80) suggests the use of the "ph" spelling for un- conscious phantasy and the "f" spelling for conscious phantasy. Some analysts have adopted Isaacs' suggestion, but most British analysts now use the "ph" spelling for both unconscious and conscious phantasies, at least in part because it is often difficult to be sure whether a pa- tient's phantasy is unconscious, tacitly conscious, or fully conscious. Laplanche and Pontalis (1968) criticise Isaacs' usage because, in their view, it disagrees with the profound kinship that Freud wished to em- phasise between the conscious phantasy of perverts, the delusional fears of paranoid patients, and the unconscious phantasy of hysterics. The spelling situation is further complicated by the fact that most Ameri- can analysts use the "f" spelling for both conscious and unconscious phantasies.
>
> (Spillius et al., 2011, p. 5)

However, in this text, we will use the term *fantasy*, spelled with an "f", fol- lowing the convention widely adopted in Brazilian psychoanalytic literature. Although the distinction between *phantasy* and *fantasy* was originally pro- posed to differentiate unconscious from conscious aspects of psychic activity, the Portuguese translation tradition has consolidated the use of a single term – *fantasia* – to refer to both instances.

Our aim, therefore, is not to disregard the conceptual nuances discussed by Isaacs or the critiques raised by Laplanche and Pontalis, but rather to main- tain terminological consistency that supports textual fluidity and accessibility

DOI: 10.4324/9781003642503-3

for an academic readership across different countries. We thus consider that the meaning of the word should be drawn from the context in which it appears, preserving theoretical rigour without compromising the clarity of the argument.

Before we proceed, it is essential to recognise that the definition of this concept has broadened the horizons of clinical practice, allowing for a deeper understanding of the internal world and, consequently, of new forms of psychic suffering – such as psychoses and borderline disorders. Therefore, in the present introductory section, we will explore the notion of *fantasy* within Kleinian theory.

For Klein, *object relations* occur from a very early stage – initially between the infant's premature ego and the maternal breast. Based on this premise, she assumes the existence of a potential triangularity at the beginnings of life – the "Early Stages of the Oedipal Conflict" (Klein, 1928). However, it is important to note that, at this initial stage, these object relations take place with *part-objects*, since, for Klein, the first defence mechanism employed by the infant's psyche is *splitting*. In other words: facing anxieties generated by the intense activity of the death instinct – which, in Kleinian theory, is considered constitutive in nature – the infant's fragile ego (still primitive and endowed with limited resources) becomes fragmented, projecting the bad parts *outward*. This phenomenon ends up "colouring" the environment, which comes to be assimilated by the newborn as something bad.

As the child receives maternal care marked by love and gratification, they experience the environment – or the breast, as Klein originally termed it – as something good, introjecting these benevolent aspects into their internal world. Thus, at the origin of life, the mother (whether understood as the environment and/or caregiving figure) is experienced by the infant as two entirely dissociated and uncommunicative objects: a *good mother* and a *bad mother*. This is the well-known Kleinian metaphor of the *good breast* and the *bad breast* which, unfortunately, remains poorly understood in parts of the psychoanalytic field.

All of these phenomena occur predominantly within the *intrapsychic* sphere – although they do involve interaction with the external world. They originate within the child's psyche, as the result of projection and introjection. For this reason, Klein maintains that external reality will always be "stained" by the influence of such processes – which in no way diminishes the significance of the environment for the constitution of human subjectivity (a topic we shall explore in more depth later on).

This, then, constitutes the backbone of the concept of *fantasy*. For Klein, *everything is fantasy* – including the activity of the defence mechanisms. In Kleinian theory, unconscious fantasies *underlie* all mental processes; they are psychic representations of somatic events and, from the very beginning, involve physical sensations arising from object relations – that is, from the ongoing interaction between the ego and the external world.

In his classic *Dictionary of Kleinian Thought*, Robert Hinshelwood (1992) notes that unconscious fantasies are transformed in two main ways: 1) through the development of the sense organs, leading to subjective perception – in other words, from the bodily to the psychic; and (2) through the emergence of the symbolic world of culture, rooted in the body itself – that is, the significance of the soma in cultural production (*intersubjectivity*).[1] Thus, fantasies may be elaborated as a means of relieving internal mental states, either through bodily manipulation and sensory experience, or through direct fantasising. Put differently, fantasy is both the mental expression of the instincts and the form taken by the defence mechanisms erected to counter the intensity of these instinctual forces.

This is one of the fundamental features that mark the uniqueness of Klein's thinking when compared to the Freudian framework. In Freud's work, fantasy appears explicitly in 1905, in the case study of Dora, and more precisely in the 1908 essay "Hysterical Fantasies and Their Relation to Bisexuality", in which the author argues that fantasies are unconscious at all times, although most of them initially exist as *daydreams* – that is, as *conscious fantasies* that are repressed (*Verdrängung*), passing into the unconscious by way of representation.

We must remark that, for Freud (1924a), the Oedipus complex emerges around the age of four, when the boy "falls in love" with the mother and turns against the father; or, conversely, when the girl "falls for" the father and begins to rival the mother. These affective conflicts are resolved by means of a *prohibition* or a signifier capable of preventing the fulfilment of incestuous desire – representing symbolic castration: the institution of the law, which will later result in the formation of the superego.

However, it is worth recalling that in 1923, with the development of the "Second Topography" presented in the text "The Ego and the Id", Freud reaffirmed the phylogenetic foundations of the superego: "Owing to the way in which the ego ideal is formed, it has the most abundant links with the *phylogenetic acquisition* of each individual – his archaic heritage" (Freud, 1923/1986, p. 36). As we know, the "ego ideal" forms the foundation of the Freudian superego, establishing morality at the end of the Oedipus complex.

In a similar vein, through her observations of very young children, Klein noted that, contrary to Freud's assumptions, the "Oedipal conflict" can be identified from the earliest stages of infant life.[2] For the author, this phenomenon occurs in a rather confused and disorganised manner, as the origins of the psyche are marked by what she termed the "paranoid-schizoid position". Therefore, even though there is triangulation at this early stage, it involves *partial objects* within a highly persecutory internal landscape. It is only later, when the child reaches the "depressive position" and begins to realise that the caring object is the same one that frustrates, that a sense of reality starts to prevail, and relationships with *whole objects* can emerge – thus, what was previously *split* into a good breast and a bad breast comes to be seen as one and the same breast possessing both characteristics simultaneously. This discovery demands a certain level of maturity from the individual, particularly the ability to cope with ambivalence and to face the guilt of having (in fantasy) *harmed* the loved object.

Based on her meticulous clinical observation, Klein perceived that the baby already had a fully active superego long before the age of four or five – thereby diverging from Freud's findings. To reach this conclusion, she gradually became aware that something was tormenting the child even in the earliest stages of development: feelings of guilt (depressive position) and persecution (paranoid-schizoid position) were extensively studied by the author. Let us consider:

> The effects of this infantile super-ego upon the child are analogous to those of the super-ego upon the adult, but *they weigh far more heavily upon the weaker, infantile ego*. As the analysis of children teaches us, we strengthen that ego when the analytic procedure *curbs the excessive demands of the super-ego*. [...] But, when we have freed the little child's ego from neurosis, it proves perfectly equal to such demands of reality as it encounters – demands as yet less serious than those made upon adults.
>
> (Klein, 1926/2011, n.p. emphasis added)

These aspects of primary development, which were not adequately explored by Freud, are essential for us to consider the dynamics of unconscious fantasy functioning. Indeed, in order to understand the nature and function of fantasy in mental life, a detailed study of the early stages of human existence is required, particularly through the lens of Klein.

Susan Isaacs (1885–1948), a prominent Kleinian psychoanalyst, articulated the concept of unconscious fantasy with great clarity and coherence. In a lengthy essay, presented in 1943 and published in an expanded version in 1952, entitled *The Nature and Function of Phantasy*, she argued that one of psychoanalysis's major errors lies in drawing a contrast between fantasy and reality. Such a gesture, according to Isaacs, underestimates the *dynamic* importance of fantasy, which appears not only in neurotic structures but also in psychotic ones. The distinction between normal and pathological thus lies in how unconscious fantasies are dealt with, and in the psychic processes through which they are worked through and transformed.

In this sense, fantasies are the mental representatives of instincts. "There is no impulse, urge, or instinctive reaction *which is not experienced as an unconscious 'phantasy'*" (Isaacs, 1952/1969, p. 96, emphasis added). Throughout the course of a child's development, *phantasy* also becomes a means of defence against anxieties, a way of inhibiting or controlling instinctual impulses, as well as a legitimate expression of reparative wishes. Below, we share a quotation from Isaacs that succinctly encapsulates the meaning of this Kleinian concept:

> Primary phantasies, the representatives of the earliest impulses of desire and aggression, are expressed and processed through mental operations far removed from words and conscious relational thought, and are governed by the logic of emotion. At a later stage, under certain conditions (sometimes through children's spontaneous play, at other times only in analysis), they may become capable of being expressed in words. There is abundant evidence to show that phantasies are active in the mind long before the development of language, and that even in the adult, they continue to operate alongside and independently of words.
> (Isaacs, 1952/1969, pp. 102–103)

Thus, in both childhood and adult life, we live and feel, fantasise and act far beyond our verbal meanings. We know that artistic expression – such as painting, drawing, sculpture, dance, and so on – can convey a vast array of implicit meanings. In social life as well, facial expressions, tone of voice, and numerous wordless gestures represent phenomena that are perceived, imagined, and felt – these form the foundation of experience. "Words are a means of referring to experience, real or phantasied, but they are not identical with it, nor do they replace it" (Isaacs, 1952/1969, p. 103).

In the interest of making our explanation more accessible, we share, in a summarised form, a case narrated by Susan Isaacs in this same 1952 article. It concerns a one-year and eight-month-old girl, whose speech was still poorly developed, who saw one of her mother's shoes with the sole coming loose and hanging off. The child was startled by the sight and screamed in terror. For a week, she would shrink back and try to run away, crying out, whenever she saw her mother wearing any shoes. Over time, she seemed to forget the episode and allowed her mother to wear shoes again. However, at the age of two, she suddenly asked her mother: "Where are those broken shoes?" The mother, fearing another bout of anxiety, quickly replied that she had thrown them away. The child then remarked: "They could have eaten me all up!" (Isaacs, 1952/1969, p. 104).

From a Kleinian perspective, it is possible that the shoe with the detached sole was perceived by the child as a threatening mouth, which explains her intense terror, even though the phantasy could not yet be translated into words until a year later. "Here we have, then, the most striking possible evidence that a phantasy can be felt – and felt as real – long before it can be expressed in words" (Isaacs, 1952/1969, p. 105).

It is worth noting that Klein places great emphasis on the infant's constitutional instincts, just as Freud had already proposed in his *Three Essays on the Theory of Sexuality* (1905) and in several other works – particularly those in which he addresses the theme of "culture and society" (Freud, 1915, 1921, 1927, 1930 (among others)). However, it is in the article *Beyond the Pleasure*

Principle (1920) – where the duality between life instinct and death instinct is introduced – that Freud explicitly reaffirms the significance of constitutional factors, a theme further developed in the classic "The Economic Problem of Masochism" (Freud, 1924b).

> Like Freud, Klein assumes that the activity of phantasising is innate, as are particular phantasies themselves. She goes further, for she thinks that not only are phantasising and phantasies inherited but so also is the ability to make certain sorts of realistic perception.
>
> (Spillius et al., 2011, p. 8)

In this sense, early phantasies are the result of physical impulses and are closely linked to bodily sensations. To clarify: initial bodily experiences give rise to the earliest memories, and external reality is gradually woven into the fabric of these archaic phantasies. It does not take long for the child's phantasies to be supported both by visual images and by sensations, which are gradually elaborated in accordance with perceptions shaped by the environment. However, for Klein, phantasies "do not *originate* from knowledge in relation to the external world; their source is internal, within the instinctual impulses" (Isaacs, 1952/1969, p. 107, original emphasis). This particular aspect diverges from the Winnicottian conception, as we shall see below.

Emotional Development According to Winnicott

First and foremost, it is essential to highlight that the English paediatrician and psychoanalyst Donald Winnicott did not work with the concept of the *death instinct*. In his view, this was the greatest theoretical error made by both Freud and Klein. In a letter addressed to Roger Money-Kyrle in November 1952, Winnicott writes: "It is a pity that Melanie has made such a big effort to bring her view round to a friendship with the life and death instincts, which are perhaps Freud's one blunder" (Winnicott, 1952/2017, p. 66). He also did not believe in the existence of an archaic ego, nor in the infant's capacity to project and introject in the earliest stages of life.

For Winnicott, at the origin, Id is external to the self and must be *experienced* and *appropriated* by the individual through a process called the "imaginative elaboration of body functioning". This is a phenomenon that is initially quite rudimentary, carried out by the infant's primitive psyche, but it depends on environmental care to maintain a minimum degree of consistency across time and space – bearing in mind that the infant initially exists in a *non-integrated* state, living in dispersed moments and assuming borrowed and provisional identities (such as the breast or the mother's arms, for example).

In short, the Winnicottian baby is born into a condition of extreme vulnerability, establishing an absolute dependence on the caregiving environment (Almeida and Naffah Neto, 2021). In this context, Winnicott develops a theory of emotional (or maturational) development in which he describes a series of stages that must be achieved by the individual in constant interaction with the environment. Let us examine them:

> I want to say that in these early, most significant weeks of the baby's life the initial stages of the maturational processes have their first opportunity to become experiences of the baby. Where there is good enough quality in the facilitating environment, which has to be a human one and a personal one, the inherited tendencies of the baby to grow have their first important achievements. One can give names to these things. The main thing is covered by the word *integration*. All the bits and pieces of activity and sensation which go to form what we come to know as this particular baby begin to come together at times so that there are moments of integration in which the baby is a unit although of course a highly dependent one.
>
> (Winnicott, 1966/2017, p. 336)

Winnicott focused his efforts on describing how a human being progresses from their initial state – in which they are immature, entirely dependent on the environment, and unintegrated – towards the various integrations that occur throughout life, culminating in the differentiation between external and internal worlds, the achievement of an individual unity, and the distinction between self and not-self. Furthermore, he was one of the psychoanalysts most devoted to understanding the impact of the environment on psychic development, and among those who most strongly emphasised the role of the environment as an essential factor in human growth. For Winnicott, the earliest stage of life is an extremely delicate period in which the infant will require every possible form of care provided by the maternal figure[3] in order to *come into being*.

It is the "mother" who becomes responsible for introducing the world to the baby in small doses, sustaining the infant's initial sense of omnipotence, within which there is a temporary experience of illusion – as if everything were created by the only existing thing: *the baby*. Everything external is perceived as stemming from this creation or from the baby's own spontaneous creative gestures (Fulgencio, 2016). From the observer's perspective, it is the environment that meets the child's needs; but from the baby's point of view there is no environment – there is only the self, and objects appear and disappear precisely in accordance with the baby's needs, as though they were elements of their own creation.

Schematically, we have: 1) the baby feels hunger; 2) the mother offers the breast; and 3) from baby's perspective the breast was created by him (a feeling of omnipotence). *Broadly speaking*, "it is up to the environment not to disappoint the child, not to force them, prematurely, to recognise external reality as such; not to impose upon them a unity for which they are not yet mature enough to assume" (Fulgencio, 2016, p. 30).

However, in the earliest stages of life, the environment must merely provide *holding* – sustaining the infant and ensuring that *becoming* is a personal achievement, arising from the child's spontaneous gesture. Within this logic, anything imposed from the outside inwards is experienced by the child as an *intrusion*, as it is not of their own making and does not belong to their area of omnipotence (as a perceived extension of themselves).

For example, if the baby is crying from hunger and the adult puts them to sleep instead, the adult ends up replacing the infant's *spontaneous gesture* with their own. On other occasions, when a child is left crying for hours on end in their crib, they may come to experience their instinctual impulses[4] as something intrusive and threatening to their very existential condition, leading them to erect defences against these sensations of helplessness. Such defences gather strength and, at a certain point, become dissociated from the healthy part of the individual's personality, thus creating what Winnicott termed a *split and pathological false self*, which prevents the true self from engaging with experiences acquired in the real world. In this way, life becomes devoid of meaning and the creative potential collapses (Almeida and Checchia, 2020). In the words of the English psychoanalyst:

> In one way I am simply saying that each person has a polite or socialized self, and also a personal private self that is not available except in intimacy. This is what is commonly found, and we could call it normal. If you look around, you can see that in health this splitting of the self is an achievement of personal growth; *in illness* the split is a matter of a schism in the mind that can go to any depth; at its deepest it is labelled schizophrenia.
>
> (Winnicott, 1964/2017, p. 28, original emphasis)

In other words: we all need to construct a false self in order to live in society. The problem, however, arises when this becomes a fixed, rigid structure, split off from the healthy part of the personality (the *true self*). In our view, this is one of the major complexities within Winnicott's theory which, when studied superficially, ends up generating misunderstandings or broad generalisations such as: "That person has a false self". But, as we have just seen in the quotation above, we all do. What differs, however, is the degree of dissociation or splitting that this defensive mechanism assumes throughout the developmental process.

It is worth emphasising that, towards the end of his work, Winnicott began to distinguish between the concept of *dissociation* and that of *splitting* (*scission*), using the former to describe communication failures between parts of the personality in an otherwise integrated individual, and the latter to describe both the initial state of the newborn (in which such early splittings gradually disappear through the process of integration made possible by environmental care) and the core defence mechanism in schizophrenia (Winnicott, 1988/2017).

Indeed, it is coherent to think of the modalities of the false self along a continuous gradation, ranging from varying degrees of dissociation to varying degrees of splitting – from the healthier to the more pathological forms.

To complement our explanation and synthesise our ideas, we quote an excerpt from an article by Naffah Neto (2019):

> However, it is also true that, in the earliest stages, the baby can only become the subject of their own destiny through an illusion. This is because, throughout the entire process of dependence, their matu-ration can only unfold through the presence of a sufficiently good environment – that is, one capable of sustaining them both physically and psychically. Only in this way can the small infant imaginatively elaborate their *body functions* and gradually create a psyche anchored in them, eventually forming a psycho-somatic[5] unity. [...] [With matura-tion] the first person remains at the forefront of their own story, but now aware of the limitations imposed by society and culture. At this stage, the child has already formed a healthy *false self* – that is, they are now able to pay their dues to the demands of social life without losing con-tact with their inner world, their spontaneity and creativity.
>
> (Naffah Neto, 2019, pp. 214–215, original emphasis, our brackets)

Winnicott's Conception of Unconscious Fantasy[6]

Following this brief and summarised explanation of Winnicott's theory of maturation, we believe it is now possible to enter the specific territory of the theme of fantasy.

Well then, if, according to the English author, the infant's ego is not mature enough to project and introject from birth, how does he conceive the notion of fantasy?

Let us begin by considering that, for Winnicott, fantasy must always be understood in a functional counterpoint to reality. In his classic 1945 text "Primitive Emotional Development", the author highlights:

> The point is that in fantasy things work by magic: there are no brakes on fantasy, and love and hate cause alarming effects. External reality has brakes on it, and can be studied and known, and, in fact, *fantasy is only tolerable at full blast when objective reality is appreciated well*.
>
> (Winnicott, 1945/2017, p. 365, emphasis added)

In other words, we can interpret this statement as suggesting that, until the distinction between fantasy and reality is established, everything functions "without brakes" in the infant's psyche. However, the text might also give us the false impression that fantasy exists in the infant's mind from the very earli-est stages – which, in fact, is not the case.

The fundamental essay for understanding the concept of fantasy in its proper sense appears in 1968, in the article "The Use of an Object and Relating Through Identifications", first published in the *International Journal of Psycho-Analysis* in 1969. A more complete and updated version of this text was later included in the book *Playing and Reality* (1971/2005).

For the British psychoanalyst, the infant's psychic plane is defined as a void pregnant with possibilities for becoming – a condition he refers to as *primary creativity*. In this sense, there is no inherited content or *proto-fantasies* transmitted phylogenetically, as posited by Freud (1923), nor are there unconscious fantasies in the Kleinian sense. Unconscious fantasy only emerges later, after the phase of "using an object", and as the counterpart to the real object – when the external world is created/discovered. In Winnicott's words:

> For instance, the object, if it is to be used, must necessarily be real in the sense of being part of shared reality, not a bundle of projections. It is this, I think, that makes for the world of difference that there is between relating and usage.
>
> (Winnicott, 1968 [1971]/2017, p. 357)

In order to use an object, the person must have *developed the capacity to use objects*. This is a fundamental aspect of the introduction of the reality principle. From a Winnicottian perspective, this capacity cannot be considered innate, nor can its development in any given individual be taken for granted. This achievement depends heavily on the presence of a facilitating environment. As Winnicott states:

> In the sequence one can say that first there is object-relating, then in the end there is object-use; in between, however, is the most difficult thing, perhaps, in human development; or the most irksome of all the early failures that come for mending. This thing that there is in between relating and use is the subject's placing of the object outside the area of the subject's omnipotent control; that is, the subject's perception of the object as an external phenomenon, not as a projective entity, in fact recognition of it as an entity in its own right. This change (from relating to usage) means that the subject destroys the object. [...] In other words [...] after 'subject relates to object' comes 'subject destroys object' (as it becomes external); and then may come 'object survives destruction by the subject'.
>
> (Winnicott, 1968 [1971]/2017, pp. 358–359)

However, the survival of the external environment may not occur. Through Winnicott's lens, we arrive at a new characteristic of object relations: "The subject says to the object: 'I destroyed you', and the object is there to receive the communication. From now on the subject says 'Hullo object!' 'I destroyed you'. 'I love you'" (Winnicott, 1968 [1971]/2017, p. 359). The object, then, begins to acquire value through its survival.

Although the individual loves the object, they continually destroy it in fantasy. It is at this point that fantasy begins to exist when the baby is able to *use* the object that has survived. "In these ways the object develops its own autonomy and life, and (if it survives) contributes in to the subject, according to its own properties" (Winnicott, 1968 [1971]/2017, p. 359). Thus:

> [...] because of the survival of the object, the subject may now have started to live a life in the world of objects, and so the subject stands to gain immeasurably; but the price has to be paid in acceptance of the ongoing destruction in unconscious fantasy relative to object-relating.
> (Winnicott, 1968 [1971]/2017, p. 359)

In summary: *fantasy* only comes into being as the counterpart to the *surviving object* – the object that remains immune to the infant's destruction and thus comes to represent the *real object*. Conversely, the object that continues to be destroyed at the infant's whim (through a ruthless/instinctual form of love) comes to represent *fantasy*.

But why does the infant continue to destroy the fantasied object?

This ongoing movement is necessary to maintain the distinction between fantasy and reality, given that this differentiation is not yet fully established.

Framing all of this within a more precise Winnicottian conceptualisation, we may say that, through the *imaginative elaboration of the survival of the "breast object"*, destroyed by the infant's sadistic attacks (at the height of their oral sadism), "[the] infant will gradually be able to discriminate a real, objective object – one that exists independently of their area of omnipotence – from a subjective object, which continues to be destroyed in fantasy" (Naffah Neto, 2023, pp. 147–148). This process occurs roughly between eight months and one year of age (which also marks a further divergence from Klein's thinking). Accordingly, "this stage marks the emergence of fantasies as *constituents of the internal world* – that is, within a domain that is now distinct from external reality" (Naffah Neto, 2023, p. 148, emphasis added).

Gradually, the infant reaches a more sophisticated form of imaginative elaboration, expanded through the use of fantasies. Little by little, the capacity to *repress* these fantasies develops, displacing them from consciousness – which gives rise to the *repressed unconscious*, as defined by Freud (Naffah Neto, 2023).

It is only through this arduous psychic process that the individual becomes able to make use of real objects and, whenever necessary, *can retreat* into their internal world, like someone who withdraws into their own shelter for rest (Naffah Neto, 2023). This interaction with external reality allows the individual to feel life is worth living, as it is not reduced to a purely mechanical adaptation. In this sense, *fantasy* plays the role of a *mediator* with the external world.

Regarding the question of projective and introjective mechanisms – which, for Klein, operate from the very beginning of life – for Winnicott, they are also shaped by the maturational process and develop over time.

In his final, unfinished book, *Human Nature* (1988/2017), published post-humously, Winnicott distinguishes between *incorporation* and *introjection*. Incorporating good objects in the form of care, in this distinction, is a spontaneous process that occurs from the start of life, as a natural manifestation of growth, without any defensive connotation. Introjecting good objects, by contrast, involves a magical idealisation of the internalised objects – functioning as a defence mechanism against anxiety when the environment becomes threatening. The same reasoning applies to *evacuation* and *projection*: we evacuate the remnants of what we have incorporated and which no longer serve us psychically. But we *project* persecutory internal objects – those that cause unbearable psychic pain – in an attempt to rid ourselves of them through magical means (Naffah Neto, 2019). Hence, we can clearly observe the intertwining of psyche and soma that runs throughout Winnicott's entire body of work.

However, *fantasy*, in the Winnicottian sense, also holds a psychopathological dimension. In his article "Dreaming, Fantasying and Living: A Case-Study of a Primary Dissociation", published in the book *Playing and Reality* (1971), Winnicott specifically explores this theme, offering a series of important arguments in which he seeks to show that the inability to access fantasy may be linked to *dissociation* – rather than repression.

To illustrate this, the author describes the case of a patient who, while participating in play with others, was at the same time entirely engaged in a fantasy. "She really lived in this fantasying on the basis of a dissociated mental activity" (Winnicott, 1971/2005, p. 291). He goes on to explain in detail:

> This part of her which became thoroughly dissociated was never the whole of her, and over long periods her defence was to live here in this fantasying activity, and to watch herself playing the other children's games as if watching someone else in the nursery group.
>
> (Winnicott, 1971/2005, p. 291)

As this patient grew older, she became capable of constructing a life in which nothing concrete that happened in her daily reality was truly meaningful to her. Over time, she became one of those many individuals who feel as though they are not fully human. Unconsciously, it was as if another life were taking place within the part of herself that was dissociated. Conversely, this meant that her experiences (which occurred in the part that played with the other children) were "separated" from her main self – the part that lived within an organised sequence of fantasies, running in parallel and functioning as if it were the central "me" – while the part that played appeared to her as a dissociated double: an *other*.

Through this clinical account, we observe that in certain pathological cases *fantasy* takes on a defensive role that the subject comes to inhabit predominantly, as an attempt to retreat from the external world – a kind of inversion in which fantasy, rather than enriching reality, becomes dissociated from it and begins to replace it. In such cases, there is no active interaction between fantasies and the real world; that is, we are faced with two domains that do not communicate and, consequently, do not enrich one another. This is a life lived at the margins, as this dissociated dimension of fantasy may come to constitute a schizoid-type psychic refuge, used as a defence mechanism against the real world.

For Winnicott, *fantasy* only occupies a healthy place when it forms part of what he called the "third area" or "potential space", which emerges precisely during the period of transitional phenomena. At this stage, the mother's presence begins to be replaced, for the infant, by various objects: a piece of cloth, a teddy bear, and so on. These *transitional objects*, in addition to facilitating the transition from the subjective world to the creation/discovery of the objective world – as a first "not-me possession" – also constitute a primitive form of access to the symbolic universe: an object that stands in for the other in their absence, for a limited time.

In this sense, what characterises the transitional object is its double inscription: the cloth remains a cloth, or at least a non-mother object (reality beginning to enter the subjective world, at the edges), while at the same time representing – by a kind of proxy – the mother in her absence.

With the advent of the phase of object use and the later development of the distinction between reality and fantasy, this intermediate region between the internal and external worlds becomes constituted by the overlap between *fantasy* and *reality*, forming the *third area* or *potential space* – the realm responsible for the infant's entry into the world of culture and symbols. It is only within this dimension – that is, a mode of functioning superimposed upon reality – that fantasy can occupy a healthy place in life, according to Winnicott. *Fantasy* thus becomes, at once, a form of late imaginative elaboration – an indispensable tool for the integration of the human psychosomatic unit – and a method of re-creating and/or reinventing reality (operating in conjunction with it).

In this way, Winnicott aligns with Manoel de Barros, when the latter declares: "Everything I do not invent is false" (Barros, 2005, p. 5).

A Few Closing Thoughts

Recently, our research in psychoanalysis has turned towards this theme involving the comparison of theoretical lineages. Certainly, this is a Herculean task, requiring an immeasurable amount of reading and in-depth study. Our aim is not to exalt the discoveries of one particular author while devaluing those of another. On the contrary – we simply wish to demonstrate how psychoanalysis is a broad discipline, open to infinite possibilities, provided it is approached with rigour and ethical responsibility.

To confine oneself to a single school of thought[7] reflects a kind of dogmatism that denies the very essence of our discipline, which has always been open to the unknown and to new avenues of investigation – even though some analysts defend the opposite, turning psychoanalysis into a kind of "indoctrination" which, incidentally, was one of Freud's greatest fears.

Klein was brilliant in formulating her theory of *unconscious phantasy*, opening up pathways that had previously been blocked to the extension of psychoanalytic clinical work with psychotic and borderline patients. However, before we proceed further, it is worth returning to the beginning of our article.

We affirm it is essential to understand that all these phenomena occur within the *intrapsychic* sphere. That is, they take place *within* the child's psyche, as the result of their projections and introjections. Thus, a more in-depth reading of Klein's theory allows us to glimpse a richer understanding of the notion of fantasy – one in which unconscious fantasy not only represents instinctual drives but also forms the symbolic matrix through which the subject experiences the world, the body, and the mind itself. In this framework, fantasies serve as true *organisers of experience*, shaping psychic form both for internal processes and for perceptions of the external environment.

It is a matter of recognising that every lived experience – whether physical or emotional – acquires subjective meaning through the ceaseless activity of fantasising. From the earliest moments of life, the psyche strives to endow bodily sensations, emotional experiences, and object relations with representational form, generating primitive sketches that will later evolve into symbols, narratives, and meaning.

According to Ogden:

> Phantasy for Klein (1952a) is the psychic representation of instinct. Instinct itself is a biological entity, and so phantasy is the psychic representation of one's biology. Instinct must undergo some type of transformation in order to generate "mental corollaries" (Isaacs, 1952) – i.e., phantasies. [...] The newborn infant's world at the outset is a bodily world, and phantasy represents the infant's attempt to transform somatic events into a mental form. Even into adulthood, phantasy never loses its connection with the body. Phantasy content is always ultimately traceable to thoughts and feelings about the workings and contents of one's own body in relation to the workings and contents of the body of the other.
>
> (Ogden, 2018, n.p.)

We may also presume that the Kleinian concept of phantasy *circulates* between the dimensions of *soma* and *psyche*, expressing the imaginative power of the body. As the individual projects aspects of their psyche onto external reality, that very reality is altered and subsequently introjected through those projections. There is, therefore, a process of communication – or rather, of *relation*. In this way, we move beyond the exclusively intrapsychic sphere and enter the intersubjective realm (Almeida and Vieira, 2025).

If we return to Susan Isaacs's classic 1952 work, *The Nature and Function of Phantasy*, we see how eating disorders, phobias, hysterical symptoms, somatic pains – in short, all bodily disturbances – have a psychic determination grounded in unconscious phantasy. Unconscious fantasies function as a vital link between the inner and outer worlds, articulating psychic reality with the experiences the subject undergoes in the social realm. They operate as a kind of *symbolic bridge*, enabling the individual to affectively translate what comes from the outside and to give internal expression to what dwells within. Although this definition was not literally recognised by Klein, it is we – today – who are able to understand this phenomenon through our own readings and implications. That, it must be said, is what constitutes research (Vieira, 2025).

It is worth noting that *The New Dictionary of Kleinian Thought* (Spillius et al., 2011) offers, among the core definitions of the term *phantasy*, the following proposition, which aligns perfectly with the preceding hypotheses:

> In her early work with children Klein found that their phantasies were especially concerned with their own bodies and with their beliefs about the bodies of their parents and the relationship between them. The way phantasies may be used by a child to explain bodily experiences has been well described by Robert Hinshelwood, who notes that an unconscious phantasy involves belief in the activity of concretely felt internal objects.
>
> (Spillius et al., 2011, p. 9)

Years later, in Winnicott, we come across the notions of *imaginative elaboration of the body* and *primary creativity* which, based on this premise, could be regarded as conceptual heirs to Klein's notion of phantasy – although Winnicott explicitly points to the interaction between psyche and environment in a far more direct way, starting from the notion of *experience* and situating the emergence of fantasy within the human maturational process over time.

Alongside this, we can observe – without much difficulty – that the notion of *imaginative elaboration of body functioning*, as proposed by Winnicott, refers to forms of psychic functioning that are far more *rudimentary* and *primitive* than fantasy as defined by Klein. It reflects a recognition of the infant's immaturity – a dimension largely absent in the Kleinian conception. We might say that, initially, imaginative elaboration is so primitive that it merely confers a general sense of *sufficiency* or *insufficiency* upon bodily experiences. In other words, a sensation of satiety or non-satiety during feeding; a sense of safety or insecurity in the mother's arms, and so on. It is only much later – once the infant has developed the maturity to create/discover the existence of the objective world – that fantasy can emerge as something distinct from perception, and only then does it begin to resemble more closely Klein's concept.

It is nonetheless accurate to affirm that the idea of a constant unconscious fantasising of lived experience is such a generative thesis that it functioned as an "embryo" – one capable of giving rise, in all subsequent authors, to an invitation to further develop and mature existing ideas.

That said, the influence of Melanie Klein on Winnicott's thinking is clear. At the same time, it is equally evident how the two diverge in several respects: 1) in Klein's emphasis on the *constitutional* nature of phantasy, as a direct manifestation of the instincts; and 2) in the central place phantasy occupies within the Kleinian lexicon – as the primary tool mediating everything from the very beginning – whereas, for Winnicott, fantasy only begins to exist from the phase of *object use* onwards, and only later does a superposition between fantasy and reality form the *third area*, whose function is to mediate between inner and outer worlds; and 3) in Klein's strong emphasis on the role of fantasy and projection/introjection as the founding activities of the psyche which are, in Winnicott's vocabulary, largely replaced by the importance attributed to the *environment* as the supporting structure for the maturational process and the formation of the *psyche-soma* (Almeida and Naffah Neto, 2024).

The dynamic of exchange and interaction observed when we specifically analyse the concept of *fantasy* can, in fact, be applied more broadly to the dialogue between these two authors. This is precisely what keeps their ideas alive, allowing for the enrichment of our clinical being and doing.

Finally, it is important to emphasise that we do not subscribe to the notion of *theoretical supplementarity* – that is, Klein and Winnicott do not supplement one another, but rather converge and diverge in various ways. We believe they begin from different starting points, giving rise to distinct theories and clinical practices (we prefer to think in terms of singular *epistemological lineages*). In our view, each psychoanalytic lineage opens up its own unique universe of inquiry, with theoretical and clinical tools that are irreducible to those of other traditions. We are referring here to fields of investigation that unfold independently – even though all of it remains psychoanalysis.

These are, indeed, threads that may cross in fruitful ways – provided we are mature enough to face the impasses without reducing them to mere childish argumentation.

After all, are these not the greatest riches of a psychoanalysis that is always in construction?

Notes

1 Like a craftsman who shapes a vase or a sculpture based on bodily perceptions, every human creation bears somatic traces – albeit fundamentally unconscious ones.

2 It is important to emphasise that Klein does not disagree with Freud regarding the onset of the Oedipus complex in the terms delineated by him. She merely argues that *Oedipal conflicts* begin far earlier than the timeframe proposed by Freud; however, their *peak*, as an ambivalent phenomenon crucial to genital sexuality, occurs at the same stage identified by Freud (around the ages of four or five). The early Oedipal complex relates to the original symbolic equivalence between the "breast" and the "penis", giving rise, from a very early stage, to a form of triangulation involving the mother and the father as partial objects, amidst the infant's jealousy and rivalry.

3 We have chosen to use this term instead of the word *mother*. It is important to remember that an author's work must always be considered within the social, cultural, and historical context in which it was produced. In Winnicott's time, it was common for mothers to carry out these primary caregiving functions. However, today, family structures have changed significantly, and this role is now often fulfilled not only by the mother, but also by other caregivers.

4 As previously mentioned, for Winnicott, at the beginning of life, the Id (instinctual impulses) is external to the infant's Self and must be experienced by the infant through a process the author called the *imaginative elaboration of body functioning*. However, this function can only take place if it is supported by maternal care (*holding*) and the necessary *handling* involved in the infant's early care: feeding, bathing, massage during moments of pain or discomfort, and so on.

5 We retain the Portuguese term with a hyphen, as in the English original, because we understand that, for Winnicott, *psyche* and *soma* are not reducible to one another; they have distinct identities, although they achieve a functional unity in healthy cases.

6 Unlike the Kleinian tradition, which adopts the spelling *phantasy* to refer to unconscious fantasies of primitive origin, Winnicott – like Freud – uses the term *fantasy*, without resorting to this orthographic distinction. This choice will be revisited and further developed throughout the text.

7 In the past, people referred to "schools of psychoanalysis" – for example, the English school and the French school. Today, however, this expression has fallen out of use, and we prefer to speak of *psychoanalytic traditions* or *lineages*. On this subject, see the book *O tronco e os ramos: estudos e história da psicanálise* by Renato Mezan (2014).

References

Almeida, A. P., and Checchia, A. K. A. (2020). O conceito de falso self no campo educacional: Sobre as dificuldades de encontrar a "si mesmo" no processo educativo [The concept of the false self in the educational field: On the difficulties of finding the "self" in the educational process]. *Natureza Humana, 22*(2): 204–218.

Almeida, A. P., and Naffah Neto, A. (2021). A teoria do desenvolvimento maturacional de Winnicott: Novas perspectivas para a educação [Winnicott's theory of maturational development: New perspectives for education]. *Revista Latinoamericana de Psicopatologia Fundamental, 24*(3): 517–536. https://doi.org/10.1590/1415-4714.2021v24n3p517-3

Almeida, A. P., and Naffah Neto, A. (2024). Um estudo comparativo entre as teorias de Klein e Winnicott: analisando o conceito de fantasia [A Comparative Study of the Theories of Klein and Winnicott: Analysing the Concept of Fantasy]. *Revista Latinoamericana De Psicopatologia Fundamental, 27*: 1–23. https://doi.org/10.1590/1415-4714.e230636

Almeida, A. P., and Vieira, F. P. (2025). A regressão na clínica psicanalítica: um estudo comparativo entre Klein e Winnicott [Regression in psychoanalytic clinical practice: A comparative study of Klein and Winnicott]. *Analytica: Revista De Psicanálise, 13*(26): 1–23. https://doi.org/10.69751/arp.v13i26.5465

Barros, M. (2005). *Memórias inventadas para crianças* [*Invented Memories for Chil-dren*]. São Paulo: Planeta Jovem.

Freud, S. (1981). *Three Essays on the Theory of Sexuality*. In S. Freud. *The Standard Edi-tion of the Complete Psychological Works of Sigmund Freud (Vol. 7)*, pp. 123–245. London: Hogarth Press. (Original work published in 1905)

Freud, S. (1981). Hysterical Fantasies and Their Relation to Bisexuality. In S. Freud, *The Standard Edition of the Complete Psychological Works of Sigmund Freud (Vol. 9)*, pp. 155–166. London: Hogarth Press. (Original work published in 1908)

Freud, S. (1981). Thoughts for the Times on War and Death. In S. Freud, *The Stand-ard Edition of the Complete Psychological Works of Sigmund Freud (Vol. 14)*, pp. 275–301. London: Hogarth Press. (Original work published in 1915)

Freud, S. (1981). Beyond the Pleasure Principle. In S. Freud. *The Standard Edition of the Complete Psychological Works of Sigmund Freud (Vol. 18)*, pp. 3–64. London: Hogarth Press. (Original work published in 1920)

Freud, S. (1981). Group Psychology and the Analysis of the Ego. In S. Freud, *The Standard Edition of the Complete Psychological Works of Sigmund Freud (Vol. 18)*, pp. 69–143. London: Hogarth Press. (Original work published in 1921)

Freud, S. (1981). The Ego and the Id. In S. Freud, *The Standard Edition of the Complete Psychological Works of Sigmund Freud (Vol. 19)*, pp. 3–66. London: Hogarth Press. (Original work published in 1923)

Freud, S. (1981). The Dissolution of the Oedipus Complex. In S. Freud, *The Stand-ard Edition of the Complete Psychological Works of Sigmund Freud (Vol. 19)*, pp. 171–179. London: Hogarth Press. (Original work published in 1924a)

Freud, S. (1981). The Economic Problem of Masochism. In S. Freud, *The Standard Edi-tion of the Complete Psychological Works of Sigmund Freud (Vol. 19)*, pp. 155–170. London: Hogarth Press. (Original work published in 1924b)

Freud, S. (1981). The Future of an Illusion. In S. Freud, *The Standard Edition of the Complete Psychological Works of Sigmund Freud (Vol. 21)*, pp. 5–56. London: Hogarth Press. (Original work published in 1927)

Freud, S. (1981). Civilization and its Discontents. In S. Freud, *The Standard Edition of the Complete Psychological Works of Sigmund Freud (Vol. 21)*, pp. 64–145. London: Hogarth Press. (Original work published in 1930)

Fulgencio, L. (2016). *Por que Winnicott?* [*Why Winnicott?*]. São Paulo: Zagodoni.

Hinshelwood, R. D. (1992). *Dicionário do pensamento kleiniano* [*A Dictionary of Kleinian Thought*]. Porto Alegre: Artes Médicas.

Isaacs, S. (1969). A natureza e a função da fantasia [The Nature and Function of Phan-tasy]. In M. Klein, P. Heimann, S. Isaacs and J. Riviere, *Os progressos da psicanálise* [*Developments in Psychoanalysis*]. Rio de Janeiro: Zahar Editores. (Original work published in 1952)

Klein, M. (2011). The Psychological Principles of Early Analysis. In M. Klein, *Love, Guilt and Reparation and Other Works (1921–1945)*. London: Vintage Books. E-book. (Original work published in 1926)

Klein, M. (2011). Early Stages of the Oedipal Conflict. In M. Klein, *Love, Guilt and Reparation and Other Works (1921–1945)*. London: Vintage Books. E-book. (Origi-nal work published in 1928)

Klein, M. (2011). A Contribution to the Psychogenesis of Manic-Depressive States. In M. Klein, *Love, Guilt and Reparation and Other Works (1921–1945)*. London: Vintage Books. E-book. (Original work published in 1935)

Klein, M. (2011). Notes on Some Schizoid Mechanisms. In M. Klein, *Envy and Grat-itude and Other Works (1946–1963)*. London: Vintage Books. E-book. (Original work published in 1946)

Klein, M. (2011). Our Adult World and Its Roots in Infancy. In M. Klein, *Envy and Gratitude and Other Works (1946–1963)*. London: Vintage Books. E-book. (Origi-nal work published in 1959)

Lispector, C. (2020). *Água viva* [*The Stream of Life*]. Rio de Janeiro: Rocco.

Mezan, R. (2014). *O tronco e os ramos: estudos de história da psicanálise* [*The Trunk and the Branches: Studies in the History of Psychoanalysis*]. São Paulo: Companhia das Letras.

Naffah Neto, A. (2019). Em primeira pessoa [In the First Person]. *Natureza Humana*, *21*(2): 211–219.

Naffah Neto, A. (2023). *Veredas psicanalíticas à sombra de Winnicott* [*Psychoanalytic Paths in the Shadow of Winnicott*]. São Paulo: Blucher.

Ogden, T. (2018). *The Matrix of the Mind: Object Relations and the Psychoanalytic Dialogue*. London: Routledge. E-book.

Prado, L. E. (2021). Impasse e solução: controvérsias entre Anna Freud e Melanie Klein, origens do Middle Group [Impasse and Solution: Controversies Between Anna Freud and Melanie Klein, Origins of the Middle Group]. *Revista Brasileira de Psicanálise*, *55*(3): 191–205.

Spillius, E. et al. (2011). *The New Dictionary of Kleinian Thought*. London: Routledge.

Vieira, F. P. (2025). Breves considerações sobre a clínica de Melanie Klein: o sentido das interpretações [Brief Considerations on Melanie Klein's Clinical Practice: The Meaning of Interpretations]. In F. P. Vieira, *A interpretação psicanalítica: revisitando Klein e Winnicott* [*The Psychoanalytic Interpretation: Revisiting Klein and Winnicott*], pp. 73–134. São Paulo: Blucher.

Winnicott, D. W. (2005). *Playing and Reality*. London: Taylor & Francis. (Original work published in 1971)

Winnicott, D. W. (2017) Dreaming, Fantasying, and Living: A Case-History Describing a Primary Dissociation. In D. W. Winnicott, *The Collected Works of D. W. Winnicott (Vol. 9)*. Oxford: Oxford University Press. (Original work published in 1971)

Winnicott, D. W. (2017). Human Nature. In D. W. Winnicott, *The Collected Works of D. W. Winnicott (Vol. 11)*. Oxford: Oxford University Press. (Original work published in 1988)

Winnicott, D. W. (2017). Letter to Roger Money-Kirle. In D. W. Winnicott, *The Collected Works of D. W. Winnicott (Vol. 4)*. Oxford: Oxford University Press. (Original work published in 1952)

Winnicott, D. W. (2017). Primitive Emotional Development. In D. W. Winnicott, *The Collected Works of D. W. Winnicott (Vol. 2)*. Oxford: Oxford University Press. (Original work published in 1945)

Winnicott, D. W. (2017). The Concept of the False Self. In D. W. Winnicott, *The Collected Works of D. W. Winnicott (Vol. 7)*. Oxford: Oxford University Press. (Original work published in 1964)

Winnicott, D. W. (2017). The Ordinary Devoted Mother. In In D. W. Winnicott, *The Collected Works of D. W. Winnicott (Vol. 7)*. Oxford: Oxford University Press. (Original work published in 1966)

Winnicott, D. W. (2017). The Use of an Object and Relating Through Identifications. In D. W. Winnicott, *The Collected Works of D. W. Winnicott (Vol. 8)*. Oxford: Oxford University Press. (Original work published in 1968 [1971])

3 The Depressive Position According to Klein and Winnicott

*Alexandre Patricio de Almeida
and Alfredo Naffah Neto*

As an Introduction

In the text "The Depressive Position in Normal Emotional Development" – presented to the Medical Section of the British Psychological Society in February 1954 and published in 1955 in the *British Journal of Medical Psychology* (Vol. 28) – Winnicott sets out his formulations on the classical concept of the "depressive position", developed by Melanie Klein (1935/2011, 1940/2011), emphasising its emergence as an achievement within emotional maturation.

Right from the opening pages, Winnicott reveals the original marks of his thinking: "The term 'depressive position' is a bad name for a normal process, but no one has been able to find a better. My own suggestion was that it should be called 'the Stage of Concern'" (Winnicott, 1955/2017, p. 187). The author's concern was that the word "depressive" might suggest a psychopathological condition, which would be entirely at odds with both his own ideas and those of Klein herself, it must be noted. In this regard, we cite a brief excerpt from Klein's text:

> [...] in my view, the infantile depressive position is the central position in the child's development. The normal development of the child and its capacity for love would seem to rest largely on how the ego works through this nodal position. This again depends on the modification undergone by the earliest mechanisms (which remain at work in normal persons) in accordance with the changes in the ego's relations to its objects, and especially on a successful interplay between the depressive, the manic and the obsessional positions and mechanisms.
>
> (Klein, 1935/2011, n.p.)

It is therefore evident that both authors shared the view that the depressive position is a vital milestone in psychic development, rather than a sign of pathology. However, Winnicott emphasises a distinct aspect by proposing the term *stage of concern*, highlighting that this process involves the infant's capacity to recognise the existence of the other as a separate being, with their

DOI: 10.4324/9781003642503-4

own desires and needs. This shift in perspective moves the focus away from depressive anxiety towards the emergence of genuine concern – that is, a fundamental step in the constitution of subjectivity according to Winnicottian theory.

For Klein, the depressive position emerges from the perception of ambivalence in the relationship with the object, leading the infant to experience guilt and to wish to repair what they imagine they have destroyed in fantasy. For Winnicott, however, this developmental phase is not limited to the struggle between love and aggression – that is, it does not concern the clash between life and death instincts – but rather represents an expansion of the individual's capacity to tolerate the complexity of interpersonal relationships, allowing acceptance of the idea of loving the very same object that (in fantasy) one destroys.

The stage of concern implies an emotional maturation that makes possible the emergence of empathy and affective responsibility. Moreover, Winnicott emphasises that this psychic achievement can only take place within a sufficiently good environment, through the support provided by parental figures – especially the mother. When this holding fails, development is compromised, hindering later achievements such as the "capacity to be alone" (Winnicott, 1958c/2017) and the appropriation of destructive aggressive impulses. This, in turn, undermines the healthy formation of the self and may lead to the emergence of a wide range of depressive pathologies.[1]

By reformulating Klein's concept, Winnicott does not reject it but rather expands upon it, shifting the focus from internal conflict to the quality of the environment and its influence on the individual's psychic health. This perspective, in turn, highlights the importance of the relationship with the other in the constitution of the self, anticipating some of his central formulations regarding dependence and the continuity of being (*going on being*). By contextualising this concept within the framework of Kleinian theory, we seek to highlight its role in psychic development and its implications for psychoanalytic practice.

Brief Notes on the Personal Life of Melanie Klein

Before we delve into the formulation of the concept of the depressive position, it is essential to gaze at Melanie Klein's own personal trajectory. Her life – marked by losses, displacements, and intensely ambivalent relationships – runs through and gives shape to her theory, making it impossible to dissociate her work from her personal experience. Understanding the context that shaped her thinking allows us to grasp more deeply how her theory of human emotional development was conceived – not only in books and consulting rooms, but also in the imprints left by her living experience.

Thus, we will undertake a brief journey through her life story, as we believe that a concept can only be truly understood when one is familiar with the web of experiences from which it originated.

In September 1926, Klein arrived in England, having given a number of lectures in London the previous year. The following year, she was elected a full member of the British Psychoanalytical Society. In 1932, she published *The Psycho-Analysis of Children*, her first major work, which would become a landmark in child psychoanalysis and remains an essential reference to this day.

By that point, her trajectory had undergone a significant transformation. Through her personal analysis – first with Sándor Ferenczi (between 1914 and 1920) and later with Karl Abraham (between 1924 and 1925) – she was able to overcome depressive and melancholic states that had accompanied her for years (Almeida and Naffah Neto, 2021). At the same time, she was consolidating her theoretical output, grounded in careful clinical observation, and freeing herself from a relationship that had kept her in a state of dissatisfaction. Furthermore, her name was gaining increasing recognition within the psychoanalytic field, establishing her as one of the leading thinkers of her generation.

However, as the popular saying goes, "life is not a bed of roses". In April 1934, Klein would face one of her greatest losses: the death of her beloved son Hans. As Grosskurth (1992) describes in her biography, this tragedy left a profound mark on Klein's life and influenced her thinking, adding new layers of complexity to her understanding of the human psyche. Let us take a closer look:

> [...] Hans was working at a paper factory founded by his grandfather, not far from Ruzomberok. He loved hiking in the Tatra Mountains, which had formed the backdrop of his childhood; but during one walk, the path suddenly gave way beneath his feet, causing him to plunge down the side of a cliff. The funeral was held in Budapest, where Erich was visiting his aunt Jolan. Arthur Klein came from Berlin, but Melanie was so shaken that she was unable to leave London. Eric Clyne states that Hans's death remained a source of sorrow for her for the rest of her life.
> (Grosskurth, 1992, p. 230)

Regarding this tragedy, the immediate reaction of Melitta, Klein's eldest daughter, was to claim that Hans's death had been a suicide – a rumour that quickly spread among psychoanalysts. However, due to the lack of concrete evidence, the details of this episode remain obscure and without a definitive explanation. Klein, on the other hand, always committed to her involvement in scientific events, only reappeared in public on 6 June. The impact of this loss, however, would accompany her for the rest of her life, drawing her attention even more closely to themes such as mourning and solitude – experiences that permeated her personal history and inevitably left their mark on her theoretical work.

Hans's death was the culmination of all her losses – for, as Tolkien (1954/2019b, n.p.) writes: "no parent should have to bury their child".

Yet paradoxically, as Nietzsche (1886/2017) points out, suffering is an essential part of existence and, often, a catalyst to profound transformation. Instead of succumbing to pain, Klein was able to channel this experience into the construction of a creative theory that would become one of the pillars of contemporary psychoanalysis. Between 1935 and 1937, she published three foundational papers: "A Contribution to the Psychogenesis of Manic-Depressive States" (1935), "Weaning" (1936), and "Love, Guilt and Reparation" (1937). In 1940, she released her most emblematic work on the subject, "Mourning and Its Relation to Manic-Depressive States" – a study that introduced the concept of the depressive position, marking a turning point in her theoretical framework (Almeida, 2022).

In this 1940 essay, Klein interprets the dreams of a patient identified as "Mrs A." – who, in fact, was herself. Through this dense and painful narrative, we follow her internal effort to work through the absence of her lost son and parents, gradually reconstructing them within her psychic world until she could feel life beginning to flow once again.

Grosskurth (1992, p. 233) states: "Just as Freud's greatest work, *The Interpretation of Dreams*, was the result of his self-analysis, *The Psychogenesis of Manic-Depressive States* is an investigation into Klein's own psyche". For her, mental health depends on the internalisation of a good object, whose preservation ensures the integration of the ego. When this process fails, a psychic vulnerability is established, which may lead to later psychotic anxieties.

Klein's (1952/2011) view of the mind represents one of the most significant contributions to psychoanalysis. In her writings, we find the notion of a psyche that is alive, dynamic, and at the same time intensely anguished – far from the idea of a linear and predictable development. We do not go from schizoid-paranoid position towards the depressive position in a definite way, as if they were overcome stages, but rather oscillate between them throughout life.

Indeed, if Kleinian psychoanalysis teaches us anything essential, it is that our inner world is marked by cycles and returns, and it is precisely this interplay that gives depth to subjectivity and shapes our experience of existence. In this sense, we are in full agreement with Ogden, when he emphasises that:

> The Kleinian notion (1935) of *positions* is fundamentally different from the concepts of developmental stages and developmental phases. [...] The positions neither follow nor precede one another; rather, each coexists with the others in a dialectical relationship. Just as the concept of the conscious mind only makes sense in relation to the concept of the unconscious mind, each of the Kleinian positions only makes sense in relation to the other. The Kleinian subject does not exist in a specific position or in a hierarchical level of positions, but within a *dialectical tension* created between positions.
>
> (Ogden, 1996, p. 30, original emphasis)

With that in mind, we will now explain the functioning of the depressive position from the Kleinian perspective, analysing its main psychic mechanisms and clinical implications.

The Depressive Position According to Melanie Klein

For Klein, working through the depressive position is a fundamental step for the child to begin stitching together the loose threads of their emotions, integrating love and hate within the same psychic fabric. It is within this movement – marked by the pain of loss and the desire for reparation – that the path to symbolisation is opened, along with the possibility of naming what was previously experienced in a "raw state". Language then ceases to be an external noise and becomes a territory of one's own; that is, a device through which affections may be processed, narrated, and reinvented. The author states that, "Feelings of guilt, which occasionally arise in all of us, have very deep roots in infancy, and the tendency to make reparation plays an important role in our sublimations and object relations" (Klein, 1959/2011, n.p.). In a successful attempt to synthesise this Kleinian concept, Robert Hinshelwood affirms:

> The depressive position is a state of mind that can allow the reality of things to take precedence; the self becomes tinged with bad, and the environment with good. The meticulous spitting out and taking in has to be reined in. In addition, the infant ego performs its functions imperfectly: sometimes good objects will be spat out, and sometimes bad objects will be taken in. And this creates not just confusion but alarm.
> (Hinshelwood, 2018, p. 73)

According to Klein's thinking, during the second quarter of the infant's first year of life, certain changes can be observed in terms of emotional development. Such changes are the result of the ego's integration process: the child begins to take responsibility for their destructive impulses.[2] But how does this occur?

At this stage of life, a subjective perception emerges that the hated object is also the loved object. "There is thus a confluence of different sources of libido and aggression, which colours the infant's emotional life and brings into prominence various new anxiety-situations" (Klein, 1952/2011, n.p.). As a result, the range of fantasies expands, becoming more mature and elaborated within this position.

Indeed, the relationship with the mother as a whole person begins to take shape, allowing a strong identification with her. "The processes of synthesis operate over the whole field of external and internal object-relations" (Klein, 1952/2011, n.p.). All these movements of integration and synthesis open up a world of new experiences and bring forth, with full force, the conflict between love and hate – that is, the very feeling of ambivalence.

Depressive anxiety and guilt do not merely increase or decrease in intensity; they are transformed in their very essence. Although the strength of the destructive impulses – rooted in the death instinct – seems to subside, they continue to hover as a silent threat, now directed at an object perceived as whole and loved. The infant, while wishing to preserve this object, feels consumed by an insatiable voracity – a hunger not merely for nourishment, but for the complete possession of the other. Behind the scenes of psychic development, this voracity continues to act, feared as a force capable of devastating both external and internal objects.

It is through this delicate balance between desire and guilt that the ego begins to repress previously unrestrained impulses, seeking ways to contain its own intensity. The fear of destroying what is loved may lead the infant to withdraw from pleasure, avoiding full contact with satisfaction – something reflected, for instance, in difficulties accepting and enjoying food, as Klein observed in the case of Dick (1930/2011). Thus, the relationship with food becomes more than a biological matter; it expresses, at its core, an emotional conflict between the impulse to devour and the need to preserve, between the desire for fusion and the fear of annihilation.

In the transition from relationships with fragmented objects to connections with whole objects, as well as from the splitting of personal experiences to a continuous sense of self-perception, the infant gradually comes to constitute themselves as a human being capable of empathy (Almeida, 2021). These advances include a clearer distinction between self and object, the maturation of symbolic capacity, the development of more refined emotional regulation skills, the ability to discern reality, and the emergence of memory.

Still within the depressive position, the child becomes aware of their dependence on the mother. This perception, coupled with ambivalence, leads the infant to experience an intense fear of loss, as well as feelings of sadness, pain, and guilt in relation to their object – both external and internal. In an attempt to deny depressive anxieties, the ego tends to resort to "manic defences". Thus, in the face of overwhelming anxiety, the ego inclines towards denial and, when the anxiety becomes excessively strong, may even deny its love for the object. The result of such an experience may be an intense suppression of love and a rejection of the integrated good object. This situation may lead to an increase in persecutory anxiety – in other words, a regression to the paranoid-schizoid position – activating mechanisms such as splitting, idealisation, and projective identification, among others.

Let us imagine a small being, immersed in the discovery of the world, who suddenly realises that their safe haven – the maternal figure – might leave them at any moment. When faced with this duality, the ego, still in the process of formation, tries to protect itself. Manic defences arise as a kind of armour against the sharp darts of reality. Yet this armour may prove too heavy, suppressing the very desire for connection and belonging. When the ego rejects the affection offered by the other, it creates an empty space – a distance that longs to be bridged.

Here, the paranoid-schizoid position comes into play. In attempting to shield itself from the pain of loss, the individual also deprives themselves of the warmth of love – a paradox that is, to say the least, difficult to reconcile. The splitting of the ego and the object, for instance, serves to keep feelings of love and hate apart, but in doing so, it blocks the possibility of experiencing the full spectrum of human emotion. After all, to paraphrase Caetano Veloso's (1976) song, "nothing is more precious than the pain and delight of being what one is", is it not?

The ongoing experience of confronting one's psychic reality – essential to the working-through of the depressive position – broadens the infant's capacity to perceive and understand the external world: "when the infant introjects a more reassuring external reality, his internal world improves; and this by projection in turn benefits his picture of the external world" (Klein, 1952/2011, n.p.).

The baby, until then sailing smoothly in calm waters, discovers that there are unpredictable tides. The mother – this secure continent who once seemed an extension of the self – can come and go, be present or absent. With this revelation, a new storm begins to gather. The little sailor, once certain of their course, realises that they depend on winds they cannot control, on currents that may carry them away or bring them closer to their primordial island. This awakening is the depressive position: it marks the recognition that the other is a separate being, who may be present or not, who may love or frustrate, comfort or withdraw.

As discovery strikes, the still-fragile ego struggles. Like a frightened sailor, it tries to devise strategies to avoid shipwreck. Manic defences act like sails hoisted against anguish. If the pain of loss is unbearable, the baby denies their dependence; if the fear of harming the object is overwhelming, they reject their own love. Yet such denial comes at a cost: the boat may indeed move forward, but without direction, adrift – lacking the anchorage of emotional truth.

And when denial fails – when fear seeps through the cracks of that emotional fortress – the paranoid-schizoid position resurfaces. Like a damaged compass, the subject splits the world in two: on one side, a stormy and threatening sea; on the other, an illusory refuge. Splitting offers protection, yet it also isolates. In fragmenting the object, one also fragments oneself, preventing the full experience of love and loss, of desire and mourning.

As the infant introjects a more reliable and comforting reality, their internal world also reorganises, projecting this renewed sense of security outward. The ocean, once perceived only as threat (or promise), reveals itself as a fluid, changeable space – and, above all, a navigable one. Perhaps this is the great lesson of the depressive position: learning to bear uncertainty without fleeing from it; to feel the pain of absence without destroying the love that preceded it. Crossing this emotional ocean is an essential part of growing up – not only for the infant, but for each of us, who continue, throughout life, to relearn how to navigate among our affects.

It is worth noting that, for Klein, the tendency to make reparation derives from the life instinct and forms part of all sublimations which, from this stage onwards, will be maintained as a means of warding off depression in its pathological sense (Almeida, 2022). According to Garvey:

> The infant in the depressive position must recognize that he neither possesses nor controls his mother; she is not his, she is not always there with him. At times she is somewhere else with someone else; she has other relationships. It is not easy for any of us to face that we are not the only or the most important person; it is not easy to bear the horrible feelings of being left out of an important relationship and to feel jealous, small and unwanted. Working through the depressive position involves working through the Oedipus complex and vice versa.
>
> (Garvey, 2023, p. 57)

The importance of experiencing sadness and engaging in reparative processes lies, therefore, in enabling the individual to fully integrate these ambivalent feelings. Sadness, though painful, is a profoundly human emotion that connects us to the reality of our vulnerability (and imperfections). By allowing oneself to feel this pain while simultaneously working to repair the perceived damage, the individual learns to take responsibility for their destructive impulses and to develop a more mature capacity to deal with conflict and object relations.

We can observe this emotional dynamic in many narratives from our popular culture – such as films, television series, artworks, and literature. A particularly fitting example, in our view, is the journey of Simba, the protagonist of the classic film *The Lion King* (Disney, 1994).

As a young cub, Simba believes himself to be the centre of the world. His father, Mufasa, is always present to protect and guide him, reinforcing the illusion of childhood omnipotence. However, Mufasa's death shatters that sense of security and casts the young lion into a dense depressive anguish. Unable to face his guilt and grief, Simba resorts to manic defences, escaping into a carefree life in the jungle with Timon and Pumbaa, where he attempts to deny his pain and responsibility.

Simba's flight is a typical representation of the manic defences described by Klein (1940/2011): rather than confronting his sadness and his role in the loss, the young lion represses his guilt and takes refuge in denial. However, reality calls him back. His reunion with Nala and the vision of Mufasa in the sky mark the moments in which he begins to work through the depressive position, realising that he cannot simply erase the past or hide from his own origins. In order to become king – and, symbolically, a more integrated subject – Simba must face his pain, acknowledge his mistakes, and repair what has been destroyed.

In confronting Scar and reclaiming his place in the kingdom, Simba not only restores a devastated land, but also re-establishes his own internal balance.

The final battle goes beyond a mere physical conflict; it symbolises a psychic confrontation between denial and acceptance, destruction and the possibility of reparation – that is, reconciliation with the past.

Just as Simba must pass through mourning to reclaim his identity, we too go through similar cycles. Indeed, the depressive position is not a stage that is definitively overcome. Rather, it is an ongoing task of embracing our contradictions. When we are able to face pain without surrendering to it, and to make reparation without denying the destructiveness that dwells within us, we take a fundamental step towards the strengthening of intersubjective relationships.

On the other hand, manic defences arise as a kind of shield against the pain inherent in the depressive position. Instead of confronting and integrating sadness and guilt, the ego protects itself through denial, projection, or the pursuit of immediate and excessive pleasures. In adults, substances such as drugs and alcohol are often used as means of dulling this anguish, offering temporary relief from suffering. However, such behaviours are merely palliative and frequently serve to amplify the underlying problem. In Klein's words:

> The *sense of omnipotence*, in my opinion, is what first and foremost characterizes mania and, further (as Helene Deutsch, 1933, has stated) mania is based on the mechanism of denial. I differ, however, from Helene Deutsch in the following point. She holds that this 'denial' is connected with the phallic phase and the castration complex (in girls it is a denial of the lack of the penis); while my observations have led me to conclude that this mechanism of denial originates in that very early phase in which the undeveloped ego endeavours to defend itself from the most overpowering and profound anxiety of all, namely, its dread of internalized persecutors and of the id. That is to say, that which is *first of all denied is psychic reality* and the ego may then go on to deny a great deal of external reality.
>
> (Klein, 1935/2011, n.p., original emphasis)

Put differently, by resorting to alcohol, drugs, or other manic behaviours, the individual deprives themselves of the opportunity for growth and emotional maturation –achievements that stem from the acceptance and integration of these feelings. In other words, the constant flight from pain only deepens the sense of inner emptiness and disconnection from the self.

At this point it is important to highlight the distinction between manic reparation and genuine reparation. The former, expressed through manic states, is a frantic and superficial attempt to mend perceived damage, driven more by an internal need to alleviate one's own anxiety than by a true impulse to relieve the suffering of the object. The omnipotence that characterises mania seeks to erase any perception of harm swiftly, without truly facing the reality of what has occurred. By contrast, genuine reparation represents a sincere acknowledgement of the damage caused and a genuine attempt to put it right.

Finally, it is worth noting that the notion of the depressive position remains a central pillar throughout Klein's body of work, acquiring further theoretical developments as her clinical practice and formulations evolved. In one of her later works, "On the Criteria for the Termination of a Psycho-analysis" (1950), she emphasises that:

> An intrinsic element of a deep and full personality is wealth of phantasy life and the capacity for experiencing emotions freely. These characteristics, I think, presuppose that the infantile depressive position has been worked through, that is to say, that the whole gamut of love and hatred, anxiety, grief and guilt in relation to the primary objects has been experienced again and again. This emotional development is bound up with the nature of defences. Failure in working through the depressive position is inextricably linked with a predominance of defences which entail a stifling of emotions and of phantasy life, and hinder insight.
>
> (Klein, 1950/2011, n.p.)

The Depressive Position According to Winnicott

Winnicott never denied the influence of Kleinian thought on his work as an analyst. In fact, it is quite misguided to treat these two authors as entirely independent from one another. In the beautiful text "A Personal View of the Kleinian Contribution" (1962), written as a posthumous tribute to Klein, he states:

> Working along Klein lines one came to an understanding of the complex stage of development that Klein called the "depressive position". I think this is a bad name, but it is true that clinically, in psycho-analytic treatments, arrival at this position involves the patient in being depressed. Here being depressed is an achievement, and implies a high degree of personal integration, and an acceptance of responsibility for all the destructiveness that is bound up with living, with the instinctual life, and with anger at frustration. Klein was able to make it clear to me from the material my patients presented, how the capacity for concern and to feel guilty is an achievement, and it is this rather than depression that characterizes arrival at the depressive position in the case of the growing baby and child. [...] This is Klein's most important contribution, in my opinion, and I think it ranks with Freud's concept of the Oedipus complex.
>
> (Winnicott, 1962/2017, pp. 329–330)

However, numerous differences in the understanding of this concept can be identified when we consider the entirety of Winnicott's work. In Klein, the movement towards the depressive position is intrinsically linked to internal factors, which as she herself emphasises: "[...] depends on love-impulses predominating temporarily over destructive impulses, leads to transitory states in which the ego synthesizes feelings of love and destructive impulses" (Klein, 1952/2011, n.p.). The notion of progress is, therefore, anchored in the individual's instinctual dynamics, with less emphasis on the external conditions that enable this transition.

Winnicott, on the other hand, takes a different path. For him, emotional maturation cannot be dissociated from the environment that supports the infant, providing a sufficiently good space for psychic integration to occur. While Klein explores the internal oscillations that either facilitate or hinder the arrival at the depressive position – based on the duality between life and death instincts – Winnicott places environmental reliability at the centre of the matter. Without such reliability, the psyche cannot develop in a healthy way. Thus, his divergence from Kleinian thought does not lie in denying the depressive position as a developmental achievement, but rather in emphasising what enables this process: namely, the essential role of the other, of the caregiving environment. In fact, Winnicott also disagrees with Klein regarding the timing at which the depressive position is achieved. Let us take a closer look:

> Study of ego development would make us unable to accept so complex a matter as the depressive position in an infant younger than six months, and indeed it would be safer to give a later date. If we found references to the depressive position as something that might be found in infants of a few weeks, this would be absurd.
>
> (Winnicott, 1958a/2017, p. 252)

Put differently, Winnicott sees the attainment of this position as a later development, which can only be established once the infant has achieved a certain degree of existential continuity. In his view, the psyche is not born ready; it must be sustained by the environment. Without a sufficiently good holding, the infant would not even be in a position to experience the guilt and the reparative drive that characterise the depressive position.

Unlike Klein, who emphasises the instinctual forces at play and draws on Freud's theory of the death instinct to explain primary anxiety and destructiveness, Winnicott moves away from this conception. For him, psychic maturation does not consist of a battle against internal destructive forces, but rather unfolds through a process sustained by environmental care, which may – or may not – enable the integration of emotional experiences. If this environment proves inadequate, the depressive position cannot be consolidated, and the infant may remain trapped in an inability to sustain the feeling of ambivalence – becoming, therefore, incapable of fusing love and hate in their relation to the object.

It is, then, a developmental phase in which the individual realises that the object towards which destructive impulses are directed is the very same object that nurtures and cares for them.

However, before reaching this higher level of maturity – which makes possible the stage of concern – the infant is not yet capable of situating themselves in time or of maintaining continuity in their experience. They live in a fragmented world, unable to connect the different emotional states they go through. As such, they do not perceive that the mother who feeds them, soothes them, and puts them to sleep is the same mother who offers her breast. To the infant, there are two distinct mothers: 1) the *environment mother*, present in moments of calm – she who cares, protects, and attends to the infant's basic needs; and 2) the *object mother*, associated with the moment of feeding, with the intense experience of hunger, and the voracious desire to suck, devour, and satisfy instinctual needs.

Likewise, the infant is not yet able to integrate the differences between the emotional states they experience. That is, periods of excitement and frustration are not connected to moments of relaxation and satiation. Everything occurs as though these were isolated experiences, lacking psychic continuity. This is why Winnicott describes the infant as *unintegrated* and *ruthless*, for at this early stage they do not yet possess the resources to perceive the other as a whole being, nor to recognise the impact of their actions on the surrounding world. In his words:

> There is a helpful approach to the problem which starts with the word 'ruthless'. At first the infant (from our point of view) is ruthless; there is no concern yet as to results of instinctual love. This love is originally a form of impulse, gesture, contact, relationship, and it affords the infant the satisfaction of self-expression and release from instinct tension; more, it places the object outside the self. It should be noted that the infant does not feel ruthless, but looking back (and this does occur in regressions) the individual can say: I was ruthless then! The stage is one that is pre-ruth.
>
> (Winnicott, 1955/2017, p. 188)

Over time, as the infant begins to integrate their experiences and to recognise the mother as a whole object – someone who exists beyond moments of satisfaction and frustration – they start to realise that their own instinctual impulsivity has effects on the other. This discovery gives rise to a sense of guilt and responsibility, especially towards the one who cares for them.

The unification of instinctual life, with all the aggressive charge it entails, is a process that requires time and the ongoing presence of a reliable personal environment. Without such support, the infant will not be in a position to process guilt – and in many cases, this feeling may not even emerge. After all, if there is no sufficiently stable other, there can be no one towards whom the infant may feel responsible for the impulses directed at them.

Upon realising that aggressiveness is part of themselves, the child tends to project it onto the external world, turning the environment into a scene of constant threats. Everything around them becomes potentially dangerous and persecutory. It is the mother's receptiveness and solidity that prevent this fear from crystallising into a worldview marked by insecurity. When the mother survives these attacks – whether real or fantasised – the child discovers that their destructiveness is not as omnipotent as they had feared, and this opens the way for the reparative impulse.

Accepting that love and aggression coexist within oneself is a vital challenge. Moreover, the possibility of repairing what has been attacked in unconscious fantasy allows the individual not only to take ownership of these contradictory aspects, but also to develop a sense of responsibility for their own impulses. This process, however, can only take root if the mother endures – if she remains a reliable object, capable of containing and transforming this dynamic. As Winnicott explains:

> When confidence in this benign cycle and in the expectation of opportunity is established, the sense of guilt in relation to the id-drives becomes further modified, and we then need a more positive term, such as "concern". The infant is now becoming able to be concerned, to take responsibility for his own instinctual impulses and the functions that belong to them. This provides one of the fundamental constructive elements of play and work.
>
> (Winnicott, 1963/2017, p. 355)

We can see, then, that the fundamental issue here is not to eliminate impulsivity, but to find a way of expressing it without guilt becoming unbearable. The fear that the damage caused to the mother may be irreversible is something that accompanies the infant throughout this process. However, if the mother remains present and allows the benign cycle to repeat itself time and again, the infant begins to believe in the real possibility of repair. Given the necessary conditions to tolerate the guilt that arises during this period, instinctual love can finally be expressed in a genuine way.

For Winnicott, this is the only *true guilt*[3] – the kind that does not paralyse, but rather gives rise to the impulse to repair and to connect with the other in an authentic way.

In other words, by neither retaliating nor disintegrating in the face of the infant's aggressive attacks, the mother allows the baby to experience their own strength without being overwhelmed by a fear of irreversible destruction. In this way, aggressiveness can be acknowledged and gradually owned, making reparation possible.

The *stage of concern* – which is how Winnicott preferred to refer to the "depressive position", as mentioned earlier – is one of the crucial phases in emotional development. Moreover, reaching this stage is essential for entering the Oedipal complex, a period in which conflicts related to ambivalence will be experienced through the triangular relationship (Almeida and Naffah Neto, 2022). Additionally, Winnicott points out that it is also at the stage of concern that the capacity to perceive the mother as a fellow human being emerges, along with the experience of *true guilt*: that is, when the infant has the "fantasy" of destroying the maternal body, already in a phase of oral sadism, during feeding.[4] In the author's words:

> It should be understood that I am not denying that each infant carries a tendency towards the development of guilt. Given certain conditions of physical health and care, walking and talking appear because the time has come for these developments. In the case of the development of a capacity for guilt-feeling, the necessary environmental conditions are, however, of a much more complex order, comprising indeed all that is natural and reliable in infant and child care. In the earliest stages of the emotional development of the individual, we must not look for a guilt-sense. The ego is not sufficiently strong and organized to accept.
>
> (Winnicott, 1958b/2017, p. 145)

It is worth emphasising that Winnicott also disagreed with Melanie Klein's view[5] regarding the existence of an early or archaic Oedipus complex, which would occur with partial objects, at a stage when the ego is not yet fully integrated. For Winnicott, the Oedipus complex can only be experienced once the infant is able to recognise both themselves and external objects as whole persons. Indeed, a triangular relationship is only possible if the child has previously achieved a state of integration.

Nevertheless, the ambivalence characteristic of the stage of concern lays the foundation for empathy. For Winnicott, this capacity does not arise from an impersonal experience or from externally imposed norms, but from a process deeply rooted in the primary mother-baby relationship (Naffah Neto, 2007). It is not the result of obedience to external rules, nor of Oedipal prohibition, but of an affective experience that allows the child to feel recognised in their existence – and, in turn, to recognise the other without needing to mould them to any ideal.

This ethical construction is not based on demands for adaptation or belonging, but on the possibility of the subject being welcomed as they are – and precisely because of this, developing the capacity to offer that same space to the other. Respect for otherness is born from this original experience of care – one that neither suffocates nor violates, but sustains and enables. It is, therefore, a psychic development free from intrusions, anchored in the child's own time and in the right to exist in their singularity.

Notes

1 If the baby is unable to appropriate their aggressive-destructive impulses due to intense feelings of guilt (which are not alleviated, owing to the impossibility of repairing the fantasised damage inflicted upon the loved object), they will tend to repress these impulses. And since these are already partially fused with erotic

impulses, a profound instinctual repression will occur, leading to a lowering of vital tone and the development of depressive pathologies (which may be avoided through the transformation of depression into mania). Alternatively, the aggressive-destructive impulses – having no psychic place – may be projected onto the object and return as paranoid anxieties, potentially spreading across the psyche-soma and resulting in hypochondria. According to Winnicott (Moraes, 2014), all these defence mechanisms constitute the wide range of depressive pathologies. In Klein, however, depressive pathologies are conceptualised along a different path, as fixations of the libido in the depressive position (Almeida, 2024).

2 It is common, in fact, for mothers to report that during this period babies become "calmer and sleep better", as well as interacting more with their caregivers. These are some of the distinctive features of the depressive position.

3 It is important to remember that Winnicott did not conceive of the superego as a phylogenetically formed structure – as Freud did – nor did he accept the notion of an early superego, as suggested by Melanie Klein. This idea will be explored in greater depth in Chapter 8 of this book.

4 At this stage, the distinction between fantasy and reality is still in its early phases, although it is present to some degree. This is because, in an earlier stage – which Winnicott (1968 [1971]/2017) referred to as the *stage of using the object* – the child had already begun to establish a difference between an internal world and an external world, starting to separate, albeit in a rudimentary way, what belongs to fantasy and what is part of reality (see, in this regard, Chapter 2).

5 See the text "Early Stages of the Oedipus Conflict" (Klein, 1928/2011).

References

Allers, R., and Minkoff, R. (1994). *O Rei Leão* [*The Lion King*]. Walt Disney Pictures.

Almeida, A. P. (2021). *Empatia na psicanálise: um enfoque na teoria de Klein e Winnicott* [*Empathy in Psychoanalysis: A Focus on Klein and Winnicott's Theory*]. *Psicanálise & Barroco em Revista*, 19(1): 162–183. https://doi.org/10.9789/1679-9887.2021.v19i1.162-183

Almeida, A. P. (2022). A depressão para Melanie Klein: quando as trevas aprisionam o ego [Depression for Melanie Klein: When Darkness Imprisons the Ego]. In A. P. Almeida and A. Naffah Neto (Orgs.), *Perto das trevas: a depressão em seis perspectivas psicanalíticas* [*Near to Darkness: Depression in Six Psychoanalytic Perspectives*], pp. 137–172. São Paulo: Blucher.

Almeida, A. P. (2024). A depressão para Melanie Klein: um estudo teórico-clínico [Depression According to Melanie Klein: A Theoretical-Clinical Study]. *Revista da Faculdade Paulo Picanço*, 4(1): 1–13. https://doi.org/10.59483/rfpp.v4n1.105

Almeida, A. P., and Naffah Neto, A. (2021). Sándor Ferenczi e Melanie Klein: a análise do analista como alicerce da formação [Sándor Ferenczi and Melanie Klein: The Analyst's Analysis as the Foundation of Training]. *Trivium – Estudos Interdisciplinares*, 13(2): 92–102. https://doi.org/10.18379/2176-4891.2021v2p.92

Almeida, A. P., and Naffah Neto, A. (2022). O estágio da concernência e a elaboração do complexo de Édipo: revisitando Winnicott e o caso Piggle [The Stage of Concern and the Elaboration of the Oedipus Complex: Revisiting Winnicott and the Piggle Case]. *Psicologia Revista*, 31(1): 27–50. https://doi.org/10.23925/2594-3871.2022v31i1p27-50

Garvey, P. (2023). *Melanie Klein: A Contemporary Introduction*. London: Routledge.

Grosskurth, P. (1992). *O mundo e a obra de Melanie Klein* [*The Life and Work of Melanie Klein*]. Rio de Janeiro: Imago.

Hinshelwood, R. D. (2018). Anxiety and Phantasy. In J. Abram and R. D. Hinshelwood, *The Clinical Paradigms of Melanie Klein and Donald Winnicott: Comparisons and Dialogues*, pp. 69–75. London: Routledge.

Klein, M. (2011). A Contribution to the Manic-Depressive States. In M. Klein. *Love, Guilt and Reparation and Other Works (1921–1945)*. London: Vintage Books. E-book. (Original work published in 1935)

Klein, M. (2011). Early Stages of the Oedipus Conflict. In M. Klein. *Love, Guilt and Reparation and Other Works (1921–1945)*. London: Vintage Books. (E-book) (Original work published in 1928)

Klein, M. (2011). Love, Guilt and Reparation. In M. Klein. *Love, Guilt and Reparation and Other Works (1921–1945)*. London: Vintage Books. E-book. (Original work published in 1937)

Klein, M. (2011). Mourning and Its Relation to Manic-Depressive States. In M. Klein. *Love, Guilt and Reparation and Other Works (1921–1945)*. London: Vintage Books. E-book. (Original work published in 1940)

Klein, M. (2011). On the Criteria for the Termination of a Psycho-Analysis. In M. Klein, *Envy and Gratitude and Other Works (1946–1963)*. London: Vintage Books. E-book. (Original work published in 1950)

Klein, M. (2011). Our Adult World and its Roots in Infancy. In M. Klein, *Envy and Gratitude and Other Works (1946–1963)*. London: Vintage Books. E-book. (Original work published in 1959)

Klein, M. (2011). Some Theoretical Conclusions Regarding the Emotional Life of the Infant. In M. Klein, *Envy and Gratitude and Other Works (1946–1963)*. London: Vintage Books. E-book. (Original work published in 1952)

Klein, M. (2011). The Importance of Symbol-Formation in the Development of the Ego. In M. Klein. *Love, Guilt and Reparation and Other Works (1921–1945)*. London: Vintage Books. E-book. (Original work published in 1930)

Klein, M. (2011). *The Psycho-Analysis of Children*. London: Vintage Books. E-book. (Original work published in 1932)

Klein, M. (2011). Weaning. In M. Klein. *Love, Guilt and Reparation and Other Works (1921–1945)*. London: Vintage Books. E-book. (Original work published in 1936)

Moraes, A. A. R. E. (2014). *A teoria winnicottiana da depressão* [*The Winnicottian Theory of Depression*]. In A. A. R. E. Moraes, *Depressão na obra de Winnicott* [*Depression in Winnicott's Work*]. E-book. São Paulo: DWWeditorial.

Naffah Neto, A. (2007). *A noção de experiência no pensamento de Winnicott como conceito diferencial na história da psicanálise* [*The Notion of Experience in Winnicott's Thought as a Differential Concept in the History of Psychoanalysis*]. *Natureza Humana*, 9(2): 221–242.

Ogden, T. (1996). *Sujeitos da psicanálise* [*Subjects of Psychoanalysis*]. São Paulo: Casa do Psicólogo.

Nietzsche, F. (2017). Beyond Good and Evil. Amazon Classics. E-book. (Original work published in 1886)

Tolkien, J. R. R. (2019a). *O Senhor dos Anéis: A Sociedade do Anel* [*The Lord of the Rings: The Fellowship of the Ring*]. São Paulo: HarperCollins Brasil. E-book. (Original work published in 1954)

Tolkien, J. R. R. (2019b). *O Senhor dos Anéis: As Duas Torres* [*The Lord of the Rings: The Two Towers*]. São Paulo: HarperCollins Brasil. E-book. (Original work published in 1954)

Veloso, C. (1976). Dom de Iludir [The Gift of Deluding]. *Caetano Veloso* [LP]. Philips.

Winnicott, D. W. (2017). A Personal View of the Kleinian Contribution. In D. W. Winnicott, *The Collected Works of D. W. Winnicott (Vol. 6)*, pp. 325–332. Oxford: Oxford University Press. (Original work published in 1962)

Winnicott, D. W. (2017). On the Contribution of Direct Child Observation to Psycho-Analysis. In D. W. Winnicott, *The Collected Works of D. W. Winnicott (Vol. 5)*, pp. 249–254. Oxford: Oxford University Press. (Original work published in 1958a)

Winnicott, D. W. (2017). Psycho-Analysis and the Sense of Guilt. In D. W. Winnicott, *The Collected Works of D. W. Winnicott (Vol. 5)*, pp. 135–148. Oxford: Oxford University Press. (Original work published in 1958b)

Winnicott, D. W. (2017). The Capacity to be Alone. In D. W. Winnicott, *The Collected Works of D. W. Winnicott (Vol. 5)*, pp. 241–248. Oxford: Oxford University Press. (Original work published in 1958c)

Winnicott, D. W. (2017). The Depressive Position in Normal Emotional Development. In D. W. Winnicott, *The Collected Works of D. W. Winnicott (Vol. 4)*, pp. 185–200. Oxford: Oxford University Press. (Original work published in 1955)

Winnicott, D. W. (2017). The Development of the Capacity for Concern. In D. W. Winnicott, *The Collected Works of D. W. Winnicott (Vol. 6)*, pp. 351–356. Oxford: Oxford University Press. (Original work published in 1963)

Winnicott, D. W. (2017). The Use of an Object and Relating Through Identifications. In D. W. Winnicott, *The Collected Works of D. W. Winnicott (Vol. 8)*, pp. 355–364. Oxford: Oxford University Press. (Original work published in 1969)

4 The Capacity to Think

A Perspective from Bion and Winnicott

Alexandre Patricio de Almeida,
Filipe Pereira Vieira, and Alfredo Naffah Neto

Thinking According to Bion: An Introduction

One of the most fundamental characteristics of the human being is the capacity to *think*. When this ability is truly integrated it proves to be extremely useful, allowing us to resolve both internal and external conflicts. However, it is important to view thinking not merely as an innate aptitude of the individual, but rather as a significant *achievement* of our psychic development. For Wilfred Bion:

> "Thoughts" may be classified, according to the nature of their developmental history, as pre-conceptions, conceptions or thoughts, and finally concepts. […] When the preconception is brought into contact with a realization that approximates to it, the mental outcome is a conception. Put in another way, the pre-conception (the inborn expectation of a breast, the a priori knowledge of a breast, the "empty thought") when the infant is brought into contact with the breast itself, mates with awareness of the realization and is synchronous with the development of a conception.
>
> (Bion, 1962b/2018, n.p.)

According to Bion, thoughts exist, at the beginning of life, in an abstract form and require an individual to process and give them *meaning*. *Broadly speaking*, we could say that Bion reverses the usual order and "proposes that thoughts may be considered as epistemologically prior to the thinker. They may be imposed upon the human being by the basic need for survival" (Sandler, 2021, p. 813). In Bion's own words: "I repeat - thinking has to be called into existence to cope with thoughts" (Bion, 1962b/2018, n.p.).

A baby, for instance, experiences sensations of discomfort, such as hunger or cold, but lacks the emotional maturity necessary to understand these sensations through thought – which, at first, exist merely as *pre-conceptions*. Put differently, the primitive thought of a breast is imposed by the reality of

DOI: 10.4324/9781003642503-5

the absent breast. The origin of such thought stems from the need to deal with an object in its absence. In this sense, the development of thinking processes involves an increasing level of sophistication in the handling of *frustration* – which becomes progressively more complex. It is true that a newborn feels discomforts that go beyond their capacity to articulate them in words – highlighting the need for a caregiver who can *interpret* such feelings and respond to these "pre-conceptions".

As these anxieties are received and contained, they acquire *meaning* (thought), which can later – in similar situations – be thought about. In other words, what was once a pre-conception becomes a conception. However, the path from a pre-conception to a conception is not an easy one for the infant, nor for the one who cares for them. Regarding the process of transformation from a pre-conception into a conception, Bion tells us:

> I shall limit the term "thought" to the mating of a preconception with a *frustration*. The model I propose is that of an infant whose expectation of a breast is mated with a realization of no breast available for satisfaction. This mating is experienced as a no-breast, or "absent" breast inside. The next step depends on the infant's capacity for frustration: in particular it depends on whether the decision is *to evade frustration or to modify it*.
>
> (Bion, 1962b/2018, n.p., emphasis added)

Put differently, the baby faces considerable difficulty in transforming a pre-conception into a thought. First, it must be felt as frustrating in order to then be properly *modified* – in other words, the frustration must be experienced before it can be transformed. According to Bion (1962b/2018), the newborn is exposed to a wide range of sensations, many of which are unpleasant, such as cold, excessive noise, or severe colic. However, when held and fed in the arms of a caregiving figure, this moment is converted into an experience of deep satisfaction and joy for the infant.

Here we introduce an important point for the development of our discussion: according to the Kleinian perspective – of which Bion is a direct heir[1] – some babies are born better equipped to deal with frustration than others. It is along this line that Klein refers to Margaret A. Ribble, quoting her: "In infants who are *constitutionally* sensitive or poorly organized, these disturbances, if they are too frequent, may permanently alter the organic and psychic development, and not infrequently they threaten life itself" (Klein, 1952/2011, n.p., emphasis added). In this sense, "If the capacity for toleration of frustration is sufficient the 'no-breast' inside becomes a thought and an apparatus for 'thinking' it develops" (Bion, 1962b/2018, n.p.). That is to say: the "internal no-breast", as Bion proposes, becomes a substituted object, provided the resolution to this enigma is properly thought – by someone who can think on the baby's behalf – helping the infant digest this raw thought.

The Alpha Function and Its Importance for Emotional Development

In the earliest stages of life, the baby does not yet know how to name what a stomach-ache is, nor hunger, for example. What the infant can do, in this context, is to communicate this discomfort to the caregiving figure through crying. This type of primitive communication, Bion (1962b/2018) – following the Kleinian framework – called "projective identification". In other words, the infant signals, through gestures and wailing, that something highly distressing is happening. The mother (or caregiving figure) then appears within the infant's field of vision, offering the appropriate care in response to this misfortune. As a result, the baby's discomfort disappears or is at least temporarily reduced. This process repeats itself over time, until the infant appropriates the image of the breast as a memory – that is, until the baby *introjects* this care into their internal world as a good object (Kirschbaum, 2017).

In some scenarios, however:

> The dominance of projective identification *confuses the distinction between the self and the external object*. This contributes to the absence of any perception of two-ness since such an awareness depends on the recognition of a distinction between subject and object.
>
> (Bion, 1962b/2018, n.p., emphasis added)

Thus, an excess of projective identification hinders the development of frustration tolerance, as it distorts the very notion of otherness.

It is along these lines that Bion emphasises: "A capacity for tolerating frustration thus enables the psyche to develop thought as a means by which the frustration that is tolerated is itself made more tolerable" (Bion, 1962b/2007, n.p.).

The author stresses that the baby must have the opportunity to properly experience frustration; however, for this to occur, the mother must offer herself as a "container" receiving and holding the infant's primitive anxieties. At this point, it is worth noting: although the capacity to tolerate frustration (or the lack thereof) is, to Bion, an innate – genetically determined – factor, it may nonetheless be enhanced or diminished due to external contingencies.

Regarding the notion of container/contained, the British author tells us in notes five and six of Chapter 27 in *Learning from Experience*:

> Melanie Klein has described an aspect of projective identification concerned with the modification of infantile fears; the infant projects a part of its psyche, namely its bad feelings, *into* a good breast. Thence in due course they are removed and re-introjected. *During their sojourn in the good breast* they are felt to have been modified in such a way that the object that is re-introjected has become tolerable to the infant's psyche. From the above theory I shall abstract for use as a model the

idea of a container into which an object is projected and the object that can be projected into the container: the latter I shall designate by the term contained.

(Bion, 1962a/2023, n.p., emphasis added)

As we can see, Bion drew inspiration from Melanie Klein's (1946/2011) concept of "projective identification", significantly expanding upon it. The idea of container/contained is, essentially, the mother's capacity to *hold* the baby's anxieties through her "continence" – a process the author refers to as the "alpha function". Metaphorically, it is as if we are witnessing a wave (beta-elements) crashing against a rock (container); the beta-elements are held by this container and transformed through its containment. The rock, to which we have alluded (the container), is named by Bion as the "alpha function" (α). By containing these "beta-elements" (β) – that is, unthinkable thoughts – they can then be digested (metabolised) by the child's primitive psyche, just as the sea eventually calms after its violent waves are held back by the rocks. Let us continue with the author's line of thought:

Alpha-function operates on the sense impressions, whatever they are, and the emotions, whatever they are, of which the patient is aware. In so far as alpha-function is successful *alpha elements are produced and these elements are suited to storage and the requirements of dream thoughts*. If alpha-function is disturbed, and therefore inoperative, the sense impressions of which the patient is aware and the emotions which he is experiencing remain unchanged. I shall call them beta-elements. *In contrast with the alpha-elements the beta-elements are not felt to be phenomena, but things in themselves*. The emoticons likewise are objects of sense. We are thus presented with a state of mind precisely contrasting with that of the scientist who knows he is concerned with phenomena but has not the same certitude that the phenomena have a counterpart of things in themselves.

(Bion, 1962a/2023, n.p., emphasis added)

Let us remember, then, that "Beta-elements are not amenable to use in dream thoughts but are suited for use in projective identification" (Bion, 1962a/2023, n.p.). In other words: the alpha function (the container) holds the baby's beta-elements (unthinkable thoughts expelled through intense projective identifications), transforming them through its alpha function into alpha-elements. This beta-element, transformed into an alpha-element by the containing function of the mother, is then re-introjected by the baby as an alpha-element.

In this context, a baby without the support of a figure capable of "digesting" its beta-elements – transforming them into alpha and enabling their re-introjection – would be fated to psychosis, all of this combined with innate factors. As Melanie Klein so clearly described in her 1946 paper "Notes on Some Schizoid Mechanisms":

> In states of frustration or increased anxiety, the infant is *driven to take flight to his internal idealized object as a means of escaping from persecutors*. From this mechanism various serious disturbances may result: when persecutory fear is too strong, the flight to the idealized object becomes excessive, and this *severely hampers ego-development and disturbs object-relations*. As a result the ego may be felt to be entirely *subservient to and dependent* on the internal object – only a shell for it. With an *unassimilated* idealized object there goes a feeling that the ego has no life and no value of its own. I would suggest that the condition of flight to the unassimilated idealized object necessitates further splitting processes within the ego. For parts of the ego attempt to unite with the ideal object, while other parts strive to deal with the internal persecutors.
>
> (Klein, 1946/2011, n.p., emphasis added)

We believe that Klein – even though she did not use Bionian terminology – vividly illustrates the torment experienced by a baby when they cannot rely on a figure capable of performing the alpha function (α). In such conditions, the baby becomes a hostage to their own internal disturbances, which are experienced as intense *paranoid and persecutory anxiety*, colouring the external world with hues of destructiveness (stemming from the death instinct).

This capacity to contain, which Bion termed *reverie*, means *dreaming the undreamt dreams* of the other (baby, patient, etc.). In other words, it is the act of dreaming dreams that have not yet been given meaning (i.e., not yet thought). *Broadly speaking, reverie* is a component of the alpha function. However, if the baby projects too many aspects of the self into the environment through intense projective identifications, they tend to destroy the alpha function of their caregiver. This generates what Bion referred to as the *beta screen*[2] (1962a/2023) – a sort of "imaginary wall" that shields the individual from the introjection of any kind of object. This screen blocks the possibility of symbolising thoughts, which remain as pre-conceptions.

There are several consequences of this psychic disturbance. For instance: the mother becomes confused in her caregiving, as her care becomes trapped in this impermeable *beta screen*, preventing the introjection of the good object.

In the clinical context, when the analyst is overtaken by projective identifications – that is, by the patient's beta-elements (β) – and feels that the sessions are not progressing, this may indicate that the analyst's alpha function (α) is not sufficiently strengthened to manage the situation.

If the analyst's mind is *saturated*, there is no space for the capacity to symbolise, as Ruggero Levy so brilliantly explains:

> [...] what is not symbolised in these patients, or is only weakly symbolised, emerges in a raw state, as beta-elements that *can only be evacuated*. These are primitive, deeply painful emotions that must be expelled before they can even be felt through the gaining of meaning, precisely because such meanings are *unbearable*. Perhaps experiences of abandonment, threat, helplessness, and mistrust. These lead to hatred of the object, felt as responsible for this suffering. [...] These proto-emotions, insofar as they are not symbolised, can neither be repressed nor worked through. They cannot be understood as something belonging to the past, nor can they be forgotten. *They are present and suffocate both the patient and their objects.*
>
> (Levy, 2022, p. 178, emphasis added)

In Bion's conception, the essence of analytic practice lies in the professional's ability to continually *contain* the expulsions of beta-elements from their patients. These expulsions occur through projective identifications that seek a *container* capable of processing them – that is, converting them into alpha-elements through interpretation – thus rendering them available for reflection (capable of being thought about).

The Imaginative Elaboration of Body Functioning: A Foreshadowing of the Capacity to Think

First and foremost, it is important to emphasise that the Winnicottian baby is born with an *innate tendency towards development*, possessing various potentialities that must be experienced in order to become an integrated part of the self – among them, *the capacity to think*. However, *tendency* is not the same as *certainty*. This means that without an environment capable of supporting these aptitudes, the baby will not be able to develop them (Almeida and Naffah Neto, 2021). In such cases, what occurs is a false maturation, entirely adapted to the demands of the environment.

In short, the newborn arrives in the world in a state of extreme environmental dependence – a state that Winnicott termed "absolute dependence". To Winnicott the baby exists in total *fusion* with the figure who performs the maternal function. In this regard, we share a historical excerpt that illustrates the foundational premise of Winnicott's thinking: during a scientific meeting of the British Psychoanalytical Society, around 1940, Winnicott shocked his colleagues by stating: "'There is no such thing as an infant', meaning, of course, that whenever one finds an infant one finds maternal care, and without maternal care there would be no infant" (Winnicott, 1960/2017, p. 157). When we speak of absolute dependence, we speak of total dependence – according to Winnicott's theory, the baby comes into the world in a kind of oceanic state. Their perception of reality is, *a priori*, entirely *subjective*. "Living merged with the environment, without any distinction between subject and object, the baby's evanescent identity is secured by maternal *holding* and *handling*" (Naffah Neto, 2023, p. 57, emphasis added). Holding and handling refer, respectively, to the physical and emotional support and the adequate handling of the baby's body and needs.

Here, then, we find a fundamental point of divergence: to Bion the baby communicates its unthinkable discomforts through projective identification; these discomforts are received and transformed by the mother through her alpha function, restoring the comfort that had been lost during a moment of unpleasure. But how does this process occur from Winnicott's perspective, given that the baby lives immersed in a *subjectively perceived reality* and remains, for a significant period, submerged in a near-oceanic experience, devoid of an ego (even a rudimentary one, as Bion proposes)?

Much like nature, the ocean is not always calm; in moments of turbulence, it becomes agitated. The same phenomenon applies to the Winnicottian baby. According to the author the baby alternates between "relaxed states" and "excited states" as Naffah Neto explains:

> [...] thus prevails, both in relaxed and excited states, what Winnicott termed *primary identification*, in which the baby is entirely identified with the other – with the *environment-mother* in relaxed states, and with the *object-mother* in excited states. The continuous alternation between excited and relaxed states, and the presence of instincts in the former and their absence in the latter, will gradually create, for the baby, a kind of distinction between the two states. This is because, in states of excitation, the baby is seized by an urgency in search of an unknown object which (with the formation of memory) will soon come to be recognised (Winnicott, 1964/1965, p. 90), whereas in states of relaxation, the baby is not seized by anything, but rather "poured out" into the environment, in a kind of oceanic experience.
>
> (Naffah Neto, 2023, p. 58, original emphasis)

Still lacking *space-time integration*, the baby depends on environmental care (the maternal function) – both in calm moments and in states of excitation. The care assimilated by the mother, through what Winnicott called *primary maternal preoccupation* (1958/2017),[3] enables her to attune herself to the baby's needs, seeking, for instance, to provide a quiet environment during relaxed states, as well as offering the object essential for satisfying the baby's needs during excited states.

This maternal adaptation is not limited to the physical dimension but extends into the psychological realm, where the baby finds a space for recognition and the emergence of identity in the reflection the mother provides – during nappy changes, bath time, or in everyday interactions (*management*).

In contrast to relaxed states, Winnicott also describes excited states, in which the baby is driven by *instinctual impulses*. In these circumstances, the individual takes on the form of the object of their need – that is: "when feeding, for example, the baby becomes, throughout the feeding process, a hungry mouth, a breast, and milk" (Naffah Neto, 2023, p. 57). Through this process – which is repeated countless times – the baby transcends the condition of a mere passive recipient, *metamorphosing into* a dynamic entity, shaped by their physiological needs.

This highlights an *evanescent identity*, one that depends on the object with which the baby identifies (the breast, the mother's arms, the image reflected in the maternal gaze, etc.). In other words, the baby has not yet achieved space-time integration, and the psyche has not yet settled into the body to form a psychosomatic unity that could provide a stable sense of self.

In excited states, the baby reaches a *momentary integration*, as this condition is necessary to move towards the breast and feed. In relaxed states, the baby returns to its oceanic experience.

In both stages (relaxed and excited), environmental predictability plays a crucial role, as it is through this predictability that the baby may feel reassured regarding their instinctual needs, thus creating space for the emergence of *primary creativity* (the spontaneous gesture) – enabling the infant to express their needs to the environment, which should respond to them at a level of sufficient adequacy.

Within this context, the baby begins to develop a relationship of trust with the world, grounded in the dynamic interaction between self and other, in which creative expression and reality come into contact. If the child can rely on an environment that is at least reasonably predictable (*good enough*) – or, put differently, if they do *not have to worry* about potential threats that force them into a defensive position – they are able to relax and, with the process of maturation, come to play. In such a scenario, the child can experience their relationship with the objective world in the best possible way. From this state of relaxation, the ability to shape the world in accordance with their subjectivity becomes the driving force that allows them to realise their creative potential. From this perspective, thinking develops spontaneously – as an achievement of the psyche.

Moreover, Winnicott presents a unique view on the integration of the "psyche-soma" unit and the development of the "mind" – which, for him, is distinct from the psyche. In his paper "Morals and Education", we read:

> In more hidden ways there starts in the infant and continues in the child a tendency towards integration of the personality, the word *integration* tending to have a more and more complex meaning as time goes on and as the child gets older. Also the infant tends to live in his or her body and to build the self on a basis of bodily functioning to which belong *imaginative elaborations* that quickly become extremely complex and constitute the psychic reality specific to that infant.
>
> (Winnicott, 1963a/2017, p. 380, emphasis added)

The *imaginative elaboration of body functioning* inaugurates a psychic dimension that assigns *meaning* to both the physiological sensations induced by maternal care and those anticipated through the baby's instinctual activation. This process enables the infant to progressively *differentiate* basic physiological satisfaction from experiences of pleasure. It is through this attribution of meaning to "bodily functions" – mediated by imagination – that the baby's experiences begin to be consolidated into *memory*, thus laying the foundation for the construction of a personal narrative and the formation of a life story (Naffah Neto, 2023).

On this rather complex psychic phenomenon, in a text entitled "Mind and its Relation to the Psycho-soma", Winnicott states: "I suppose the word psyche here means the imaginative elaboration of somatic parts, feelings, and functions, that is, of physical aliveness" (Winnicott, 1949/2017, p. 246). "The psyche encompasses everything in the individual that is not soma, including the mind, understood as a specialised mode of psychosomatic functioning" (Dias, 2003, p. 105). The psyche, while preserving its primary function, evolves throughout maturation, expanding into increasingly sophisticated functions. These include a range of mental operations that reflect the various nuances of the term "thinking". "But the central task of the psyche is the gradual construction of *human temporality* and, therefore, of a sense of history in human life" (Dias, 2003, pp. 105–106, emphasis added).

To Winnicott "There are the soma and the psyche. There is also a developing complexity of interrelationship between the two, and an organisation of this relationship coming from that which we call the mind" (Winnicott, 1988/2017, p. 39). "The mind is of an order special to itself, and must be considered as a special case of the functioning of the psyche-soma" (Winnicott, 1988/2017, p. 39).

In the best-case scenario, the following dynamic takes place: 1) the baby *experiences* the creation of the world that is there to be found; 2) through sensory experience, the *psyche* engages in the *imaginative elaboration of body functioning*, attributing *meaning* to what is being lived; and 3) through this elaboration, the memory of what has been experienced becomes a fact, thus enabling the infant to make use of their internal resources to think creatively.

In a less favourable context, we have: 1) the baby creates the object through their illusion of omnipotence; 2) the object is not found by the baby, as the environment, out of tune with their needs, fails to understand them; 3) as a result of repeated *disappointments*, the infant, who had to develop defensive resources in order to survive, does not reach the capacity to *believe in*; and 4) the infant's psyche, in order to cope with such adversities, seeks alternative strategies to protect them from further environmental failures.

In this second case may occur what Winnicott called *hypertrophy of the intellect*. This refers to a mental development that does not accompany the integration of the psyche-soma unit – in other words, the mind arises prematurely, as a wholly impersonal defence mechanism. As the author states, "The mind, then, has as one of its roots a variable functioning of the psyche-soma, one concerned with the threat to continuity of being that follows any failure of (active) environmental adaptation" (Winnicott, 1949/2017, p. 248).

It is essential to note that Winnicott does not romanticise motherhood; on the contrary, he emphasises the necessity for the maternal function to be able to "[...] provide *graduated failure of adaptation*, according to the growing ability of the individual infant to allow for relative failure by mental activity, or by understanding" (Winnicott, 1949/2017, n.p., original emphasis).

As we have seen, *experience is the opposite of adaptation*. Therefore, a good enough environment will gradually lead to the creation of a *potential space*, through the emergence of what Winnicott called the area of *transitional phenomena* (or the third area). As Almeida explains:

> [...] quite succinctly, we can think that when the totality of maternal care enables the infant to live within the subjective world they have created – one populated by imaginative life – this place will, throughout their life, serve as their primary refuge for rest and retreat. It is essential to the capacity to be alone – a capacity that begins in the presence of another. Then, after having spent sufficient time in this universe, the baby will come to inhabit the *potential space*, an area that will initially be filled with *transitional phenomena* and, later on, with play, artistic expression, and cultural activities – that is, with everything that is free from the reins of objectivity.
>
> (Almeida, 2023, pp. 87–88, emphasis added)

We can summarise the development of the Winnicottian baby in the following sequence:[4] 1) while still in the womb, the baby originates from a state of *essential solitude*; 2) upon birth, the baby inhabits a *subjectively perceived reality* – a reality shaped by omnipotent creations: "the baby creates the object that is there to be found" (referring here to one of Winnicott's most important paradoxes); 3) as the baby gradually experiences their primary environment – through adequate holding and handling – their body acquires shape and meaning through the *imaginative elaboration of body functioning*; and 4) little by little, psyche and soma achieve integration; *the psyche, now housed within the soma, can be* thought *by it.*

What was initially expressed through motor discharges is now *thought* by the psychosomatic unity.

It is important, however, to emphasise that intellectual activity develops primarily as a compensation for environmental failures – particularly during the stage of *relative dependence*. In this phase, the mother begins to frustrate the baby gradually, as she returns to her everyday responsibilities, in response to the infant's growing capacity to be without her constant and intensive presence. Winnicott tells us:

> It could be said that at the beginning the mother must adapt almost exactly to the infant's needs in order that the infant personality shall develop without distortion. She is able to fail in her adaptation, however, and to fail increasingly, and this is because the infant's mind and the

infant's intellectual processes are able to account for and so to allow for failures of adaptation. In this way the mind is allied to the mother and takes over part of her function. In the care of an infant the mother is dependent on the infant's intellectual processes, and it is these that enable her gradually to reacquire a life of her own. There are, of course, other ways in which the mind develops. It is a function of mind to catalogue events, and to store up memories and classify them. Because of the mind the infant is able to make use of time as a measurement and also to measure space. The mind also relates cause and effect.

(Winnicott, 1958/2017, p. 323)

From the stage of relative dependence onward, and with the aid of their own *mind*, the baby may move towards a greater differentiation between the internal and external world, distinguishing an *inside* from an *outside*, and gradually acquiring the capacity to use symbols, as Winnicott highlights:

The words inside and outside here refer simultaneously to the psyche and to the soma because I am assuming a satisfactory psychosomatic partnership, which of course is also a matter of healthy development. [...] In so far as the individual boy or girl has now reached to a personal organization of inner psychic reality, this inner reality is constantly being matched with samples of external or shared reality. A new capacity for object-relating has now developed, namely, one that is based on an interchange between external reality and samples from the personal psychic reality. This capacity is reflected in the child's *use of symbols* and in *creative playing* and, as I have tried to show, in the gradual ability of the child to use cultural potential in so far as it is available in the immediate social environment.

(Winnicott, 1971/2017, pp. 329–330, emphasis added)

Mental capacities encompass the diversity of processes involved in the act of thinking. In the early stages, these functions play a crucial role in organising experience, engaging in the cataloguing, comparison, and classification of perceptions (Dias, 2003). As they evolve, these mental functions *expand* their scope to include the notion of time as a measurable dimension, the exploration of spatial relationships, the establishment of cause-and-effect connections, and the development of the capacity to make provisions.

Notes on Clinical Practice: Resonances and Dissonances Between Bion and Winnicott

Bion and Winnicott approach the development of the capacity to think through distinct theoretical pathways, as previously outlined. However, there is a crucial aspect of their theories – not yet explored in this chapter – that promises to enrich our understanding: the notion of the *death instinct*.

Bion, following the Kleinian tradition, maintains that the baby, from birth, is permeated by a destructive force (*death instinct*), which is constitutional. It is along these lines that he asserts: when the death instincts prevail, a tendency towards excessive projective identification is reinforced (Bion, 1959/2018). In other words, when this destructive force is too intense within the baby's ego, it is projected outward, with the hope that the alpha function will comprehend this primitive communication.

At this point, an important distinction must be made: to Bion – following Klein's theses – the death instinct is only projected because, from the very beginning of life, there exists an archaic ego capable of carrying out such projection. This premise stands in sharp contrast to Winnicott's view, in which the baby is born in a state of fusion with the environment, lacking the ability to differentiate or situate time, space, self, and other.

From a Bionian perspective depending on the innate strength of the death instinct, the baby becomes a *hostage* to their own projections which, when not contained by the alpha function, are re-introjected as *bizarre objects*.

On the other hand, in Winnicott's conception, the nature of the baby differs significantly as the idea of a death instinct holds little meaning for him. This perspective outlines an understanding of infant development and the psyche that moves away from the notion of an inherent force of self-destruction, placing greater emphasis on other dimensions of emotional growth.

In fact, in a letter written to Roger Money-Kyrle, Winnicott expressed regret that Melanie Klein had made such a strenuous effort to align her theories with the notions of life and death instincts. He stated that perhaps this was Freud's only mistake (and, by extension, Klein's). In his opinion, the introduction of the death instinct "muddles everything up, and from my point of view [Winnicott] it is a concept which Freud introduced because he had no notion whatever about the primitive love impulse" (Winnicott, 1952/2017, p. 65, our brackets). Thus, the absence of the death instinct in Winnicott's theory radically alters his understanding of psychic functioning and, consequently, the dynamics of psychoanalytic treatment, leading to distinct strategies of clinical intervention.

To illustrate some of these central differences in practice we now turn to a clinical vignette presented by Bion in his 1953 paper "Notes on the Theory of Schizophrenia". We quote the passage in full:

Patient: I picked a tiny piece of skin from my face and feel quite empty.
Analyst: The tiny piece of skin is your penis, which you have torn out, and all your insides have come with it.
Patient: I do not understand… penis… only syllables.
Analyst: You have split my word "penis" into syllables and it now has no meaning.
Patient: I don't know what it means, but I want to say, "If I can't spell I cannot think".
Analyst: The syllables have now been split into letters; you cannot spell – that is to say you cannot put the letters together again to make words. So now you cannot think.

(Bion, 1953/2018, n.p.)

We can see from this fragment of analysis how Bion interprets processes of splitting and massive projective identifications which, in his view, the schizophrenic patient enacts within the transference relationship with the analyst.

However, we may also attempt to analyse Bion's patient from a Winnicottian perspective. Winnicott understood schizophrenia as a condition emerging from *environmental failures* during the earliest stages of emotional development.

These deficiencies arise when the environment is unable to provide the necessary support for the infant to achieve crucial developmental milestones such as *integration*, the formation of a *personal identity* (*personalisation*), and the establishment of *object relations* (*realisation*). In Winnicott's own words:

> The main point is that these failures are unpredictable; they cannot be accounted for by the infant in terms of projection, because the infant has not yet reached the stage of ego-structuring that makes this possible, and they result in the *annihilation* of the individual whose going-on-being is interrupted.
>
> (Winnicott, 1963b/2017, p. 339, emphasis in original)

Winnicott, therefore, proposed a *differentiated* psychoanalytic approach to the treatment of psychoses, insisting on the need to revise the understanding of their origins – an adjustment that, in turn, would require changes to classical technique. He acknowledged the possibility of therapeutic success but emphasised that the analyst's role must go beyond the mere interpretation of transference, splitting mechanisms, and projective identification, as Bion suggests.

From a Winnicottian perspective, the analyst who ventures into the treatment of psychoses must be willing to adapt their role as needed. One of the analyst's central functions is to *compensate for the environmental failures* that disrupted the patient's psychic development and interrupted their continuity of being. This would involve providing the necessary support for the maturation of a self that had become frozen due to failures occurring in the earliest stages of life.

In undertaking these investigations, Winnicott re-evaluated the concept of *regression* within metapsychology, distancing himself from the Freudian notion (Freud, 1905/1981) of a simple return to early instinctual phases and specific points of fixation. He argued that this traditional perspective placed excessive emphasis on the instinctual aspects of infancy, while neglecting the importance of environmental care. Through his observation of children in natural settings and the experience he gained in paediatrics, Winnicott highlighted the need to take the environment and dependency into account within the analytic setting – elements which, in turn, gave a new meaning to the term *regression*.

From this vantage point, regression is no longer seen merely as a backward movement, but rather as an attempt to restore a state of dependency. According to Winnicott, "The tendency to regression in a patient is now seen as part of the capacity of the individual to bring about self-cure. It gives an indication from the patient to the analyst as to how the analyst should *behave* rather than how he should *interpret*" (Winnicott, 1965/2017, p. 449, emphasis added).

From a Winnicottian standpoint, we can assume that when Bion offers an interpretation of the patient's gesture, such interpretation has no function for the patient, as they have not yet developed – through the *imaginative elaboration of body functioning* – the capacity to think in verbal symbols. This hypothesis is supported by the patient's immediate response: "I don't understand… penis… only syllables". In cases of psychosis, whatever may occur in terms of healing takes place at a *pre-verbal* level – that is, through the reconstruction of environmental reliability, allowing the individual to return to a point prior to the loss of hope and to re-live the original trauma, integrating it as part of their personal history. In such scenarios the most essential element is the *management* of the setting.

To Winnicott offering a classical-style interpretation is not only unnecessary – it is also potentially harmful and ill-advised. It represents a premature and invasive gesture on multiple levels:

> [...] firstly, because by referring – through interpretation – to matters the patient has not yet reached in their maturational development (unconscious conflicts, greed, ambivalence, threat of castration, etc.), the analyst not only reveals a misunderstanding of the patient's real predicament – thereby confirming the patient's despair of being understood – but also exceeds the patient's maturational capacity, likely repeating the original trauma. [...] secondly, because the patient, whose intelligence remains intact, is compelled to understand, to make use of mental functions, before being able to do what they most need: to have the experience of contact and silent communication.
>
> (Dias, 2023, pp. 57–58)

Whereas neurosis implies that the patient has reached a specific stage of emotional development in childhood, psychosis suggests a *deviation* along that path, with distinct implications for personality structure and object relations. However, Winnicott (1965/2017) emphasises that the primitive mechanisms operating in psychosis are *not exclusive* to psychotic[5] states. In Winnicott's view, what characterises psychosis is not the psychic mechanisms themselves, nor the particular kind of anxiety involved, but rather the *primitive defences* – defences that would not have needed to be mobilised at later stages of development had there been a sufficiently good environmental provision during the earliest phases of absolute dependence.

Unlike in neurosis, in such cases the individual has not yet reached the Oedipus complex, meaning that *castration anxiety* is not yet a central concern for the personality. While the work with neurosis involves exploring the meanings of the repressed unconscious, the clinical approach to psychosis dives into the most primitive stages of development – an era in which the distinction between *self* and *not-self* has not yet clearly emerged. This points to a stage preceding the establishment of the mechanisms of *projection* and *introjection*.

Returning to Bion's clinical case: on the following day, the patient begins the session with what he describes as "disjointed" associations, complaining that he cannot think. Let us take a look:

Patient: I cannot find any interesting food.
Analyst: You feel it has all been eaten up.
(Bion, 1953/2018, n.p.)

We observe that Bion insists on interpretation, even though the patient is, between the lines, communicating that he cannot find any help in that therapeutic encounter – "I can't find any kind of food that interests me", he says.

Bion, undeniably, stood out as a pioneer in the treatment of "difficult patients", revitalising Freudian theories through his work with psychotic individuals. Though his early work was heavily influenced by Klein – a trailblazer in the exploration of the complex and challenging terrain of psychosis – Bion eventually charted a singular course, developing innovative theses in this domain.

It is worth recalling that in 1930, Klein published her brilliant essay "The Importance of Symbol-Formation in the Development of the Ego", in which she offered a detailed account of the case of Dick, a four-year-old boy diagnosed at the time with childhood schizophrenia. "When faced with a child who could not express himself, the author ventured to symbolise *with* and *for* him, offering some bold interpretations of small, repetitive, mechanised gestures he performed in her consulting room" (Almeida, 2020, p. 565, emphasis added). This was, admittedly, a risky move, as the boy could have experienced these communications as an invasion of his internal world, thus breaking the analytic bond. However, the result was surprising: the interpretations mobilised anxieties in Dick that, until that moment, never had been experienced by him.

Could this be said to be Bion's very intention? To *mobilise anxieties* in order to insert something symbolic amid the patient's beta-elements?

Indeed, this seems to capture a key aspect of Bion's clinical approach. The phenomenology he proposes is remarkably distinct, especially in relation to *ego splitting* and the characteristics that personality fragments acquire for the psychotic individual through *projective identification*. Bion was extraordinarily precise in capturing the *essence of radical fragmentation*, and in elucidating the *devastating significance* of possessing a fragmented mind – that is, a reality in which the internal world is either entirely absent or has never truly existed, rendering the individual incapable of processing certain experiences.

In such a framework, the *rejected fragments* of the personality are perceived to exist in the external world, lodged in both animate and inanimate objects, constituting what Bion famously termed *bizarre objects*.

Bion observed something particularly striking in the psychotic personality: a *capacity* – however rudimentary – to make use of sensory impressions and ego functions to confront the rejected, painful aspects of experience. He noted that this part of the personality operates not solely under the *pleasure principle*, but also under the *reality principle*. In his paper "On Hallucination" (2018/1958), Bion identifies in delusion and hallucination an interaction with *whole objects*, suggesting a nascent capacity to enter depressive states. These processes, according to him, serve a certain *reality-oriented function*, challenging Freud's (1924/1981) notion of delusion as merely a "patch" covering the rupture between ego and external world.

From Bion's reflections, it becomes vital to question what *contact with reality* actually means in clinical practice – an essential dimension for understanding and working with psychotic phenomena. In this sense, his interpretations – far from being merely invasive – are deeply consistent within the theoretical framework he adopts. These interpretations do not aim at explaining, but at *containing* and *naming*, allowing the analyst to act as a psychic organ capable of metabolising the unthinkable.

By contrast, Winnicott proposes an entirely different way of understanding the human being – one grounded in the value of *personal experience* and in the essential role of the environment. In this framework, interpretations – particularly in cases of psychosis – assume a *secondary role*. The main point is the establishment of *reliability in the relationship* and the analyst's *holding* of the phenomenon of *regression to dependence*.

Reflecting on the legacy of Plato, we are reminded that the heart of the Socratic method lies in the promotion of cooperative dialogue – nurtured through questions and answers – with the aim of fostering critical thought and unveiling the underlying ideas and assumptions of one's discourse.

Inspired by this approach, it becomes increasingly evident that we must clarify the dissonances among psychoanalytic schools. Too often, practitioners from each tradition remain resistant to divergent perspectives, thereby perpetuating longstanding misunderstandings. From this angle, a *comparative study* presents itself as a valuable contribution to the future of psychoanalysis – one that not only strengthens its scientific foundations but also deepens our understanding of the various lineages and the distinctive contributions each offers to our clinical practice.

Notes

1 Even in *Attention and Interpretation*, one of the final works of his career, Bion states: "[...] the gap between what some regard as analysis and what I, as a Kleinian, regard as analysis is very wide and widening" (Bion, 1970/2018, n.p.).

2 In *Learning from Experience*, Bion defines the "beta screen" as: "the beta-element screen – I shall call it beta-screen for short in future - has a quality enabling it to evoke the kind of response the patient desires, or, alternatively, a response from the analyst which is heavily charged with counter-transference. Both possibilities require examination for their implications" (Bion, 1962a/2023, n.p.).

3 Referring to this concept, defined in the text "Primary Maternal Preoccupation", published in the book *From Paediatrics to Psychoanalysis*, Winnicott writes:

> it is often stated that the mother of an infant becomes biologically conditioned for her job of special orientation to the needs of her child. In more ordinary language there is found to be an identification – conscious but also deeply unconscious – which the mother makes with her infant. I think that these various concepts need joining together and the study of the mother needs to be rescued from the purely biological. The term symbiosis takes us no further than to compare the relationship of the mother and the infant with other examples in animal and plant life – physical interdependence. The words homeostatic equilibrium again avoid some of the relationship with the care it deserves. We are concerned with the very great *psychological* differences between, on the one hand, the mother's identification with the infant and, on the other, the infant's dependence on the mother; this latter does not involve identification, identification being a complex state of affairs inapplicable to the early stages of infancy.
>
> (Winnicott, 1958/2017, p. 184, original emphasis)

4 This chronological scheme does not always unfold in such a manner or follow the linear progression we have outlined here. For Winnicott, "Any stage in development is reached and lost and reached and lost over and over again; the attainment of a stage in development only gradually becomes fact, and then only under certain conditions" (Winnicott, 1988/2017, p. 64). Although such conditions may cease to be vital as time goes on, they never lose their significance.

5 We explore the theme of psychosis in greater depth in Chapter 10 of this book.

References

Almeida, A. P. (2020). Melanie Klein e o processo de formação dos símbolos: revisitando o caso Dick [Melanie Klein and the Process of Symbol Formation: Revisiting the Case of Dick]. *Estilos da Clínica, 25*(3): 552–567. https://doi.org/10.11606/issn.1981-1624.v25i3p552-567

Almeida, A. P. (2023). *Por uma ética do cuidado: Winnicott para educadores e psicanalistas (vol. 2)* [*For an Ethics of Care: Winnicott for Educators and Psychoanalysts (Vol. 2)*]. São Paulo: Blucher.

Almeida, A. P., and Naffah Neto, A. (2021). A teoria do desenvolvimento maturacional de Winnicott: novas perspectivas para a educação [Winnicott's Theory of Maturational Development: New Perspectives for Education]. *Revista Latinoamericana de Psicopatologia Fundamental, 24*(3): 517–536. https://doi.org/10.1590/1415-4714.2021v24n3p517-3

Bion, W. R. (2018). *Attention and Interpretation*. London: Routledge. E-book. (Original work published in 1970)

Bion, W. R. (2018). A Theory of Thinking. In W. R. Bion, *Second Thoughts: Select Papers on Psychoanalysis*. London: Routledge. E-book. (Original work published in 1962b)

Bion, W. R. (2018). Notes on the Theory of Schizophrenia. In W. R. Bion, *Second Thoughts: Select Papers on Psychoanalysis*. London: Routledge. E-book. (Original work published in 1953)

Bion, W. R. (2018). On Hallucination. In W. R. Bion, *Second Thoughts: Select Papers on Psychoanalysis*. London: Routledge. E-book. (Original work published in 1958)

Bion, W. R. (2018). Attacks on Linking. In W. R. Bion, *Second Thoughts: Select Papers on Psychoanalysis*. London: Routledge. E-book. (Original work published in 1959)

Bion, W. R. (2023). *Learning from Experience*. London: Routledge. E-book. (Original work published in 1962a)

Dias, E. O. (2003). *A teoria do amadurecimento de D. W. Winnicott* [*The Theory of Maturation by D. W. Winnicott*]. Rio de Janeiro: Imago.

Dias, E. O. (2023). *Interpretação e manejo na clínica winnicottiana* [*Interpretation and Management in the Winnicottian Clinic*]. São Paulo: DWWeditorial.

Freud, S. (1981). Three Essays on the Theory of Sexuality. In S. Freud. *The Standard Edition of the Complete Psychological Works of Sigmund Freud (Vol. 7)*, pp. 125–244. London: Hogarth Press. (Original work published in 1905)

Freud, S. (1981). The Loss of Reality in Neurosis and Psychosis. In S. Freud. *The Standard Edition of the Complete Psychological Works of Sigmund Freud (Vol. 19)*, pp. 183–190. London: Hogarth Press. (Original work published in 1924)

Kirschbaum, I. (2017). *Breve introdução a algumas ideias de Bion* [*A Brief Introduction to Some Ideas by Bion*]. São Paulo: Blucher.

Klein, M. (2011). Notes on Some Schizoid Mechanisms. In M. Klein, *Envy and Gratitude and Other Works (1946–1963)*. London: Vintage Books. E-book. (Original work published in 1946)

Klein, M. (2011). Some Theoretical Conclusions Regarding the Emotional Life of the Infant. In M. Klein, *Envy and Gratitude and Other Works (1946–1963)*. London: Vintage Books. E-book. (Original work published in 1952)

Klein, M. (2011). The Importance of Symbol-Formation in the Development of the Ego. In M. Klein, *Love, Guilt and Reparation and Other Works (1921–1945)*. London: Vintage Books. E-book. (Original work published in 1930)

Levy, R. (2022). *A simbolização na psicanálise: os processos de subjetivação e a dimensão estética da psicanálise* [*Symbolisation in Psychoanalysis: Subjectivation Processes and the Aesthetic Dimension of Psychoanalysis*]. São Paulo: Blucher.

Naffah Neto, A. (2023). *Veredas psicanalíticas: a sombra de Winnicott* [*Psychoanalytic Paths: The Shadow of Winnicott*]. São Paulo: Blucher.

Pessoa, F. (2016). *Obra poética de Fernando Pessoa (vol. 1)* [*The Poetic Works of Fernando Pessoa (Vol. 1)*]. E-book. Rio de Janeiro: Nova Fronteira.

Sandler, P. C. (2021). *A linguagem de Bion: um dicionário enciclopédico de conceitos* [*The Language of Bion: An Encyclopaedic Dictionary of Concepts*]. São Paulo: Blucher.

Winnicott, D. W. (2017). Mind and Its Relation to the Psyche-Soma. In D. W. Winnicott, *The Collected Works of D. W. Winnicott (Vol. 3)*, pp. 245–258. Oxford: Oxford University Press. (Original work published in 1949)

Winnicott, D. W. (2017). Letter to Roger Money-Kyrle, 27 November. In D. W. Winnicott, *The Collected Works of D. W. Winnicott (Vol. 4)*, pp. 63–70. Oxford: Oxford University Press. (Original work published in 1952)

Winnicott, D. W. (2017). Primary Maternal Preoccupation. In D. W. Winnicott, *The Collected Works of D. W. Winnicott (Vol. 5)*, pp. 183–188. Oxford: Oxford University Press. (Original work published in 1958)

Winnicott, D. W. (2017). The First Year of Life: Modern Views on the Emotional Development. In D. W. Winnicott, *The Collected Works of D. W. Winnicott (Vol. 5)*, pp. 319–332. Oxford: Oxford University Press. (Original work published in 1958)

Winnicott, D. W. (2017). Classification: Is There a Psycho-Analytic Contribution to Psychiatric Classification? In D. W. Winnicott, *The Collected Works of D. W. Winnicott (Vol. 5)*, pp. 445–460. Oxford: Oxford University Press. (Original work published in 1965)

Winnicott, D. W. (2017). The Theory of the Parent-Infant Relationship. In D. W. Winnicott, *The Collected Works of D. W. Winnicott (Vol. 6)*, pp. 141–158. Oxford: Oxford University Press. (Original work published in 1960)

Winnicott, D. W. (2017). Morals and Education. In D. W. Winnicott, *The Collected Works of D. W. Winnicott (Vol. 6)*, pp. 377–388. Oxford: Oxford University Press. (Original work published in 1963a)

Winnicott, D. W. (2017). Dependence in Infant-Care, in Child-Care and in the Psycho-Analytic Setting. In D. W. Winnicott, *The Collected Works of D. W. Winnicott (Vol. 6)*, pp. 333–342. Oxford: Oxford University Press. (Original work published in 1963b)

Winnicott, D. W. (2017). Interrelating Apart from Instinctual Drive and in Terms of Cross-Identifications. In D. W. Winnicott, *The Collected Works of D. W. Winnicott (Vol. 9)*, pp. 319–336. Oxford: Oxford University Press. (Original work published in 1971)

Winnicott, D. W. (2017). Human Nature. In D. W. Winnicott, *The Collected Works of D. W. Winnicott (Vol. 11)*, pp. 25–186. Oxford: Oxford University Press. (Original work published in 1988)

5 The Process of Symbolisation in Klein and Bion

Alexandre Patricio de Almeida

What We Learn from the Case of Dick

Basing herself on an essay by Ernest Jones, entitled "The Theory of Symbolism" (1916/1948), Melanie Klein described the psychoanalytic process of a psychotic child in what would become her first attempt to specify a metapsychology of schizophrenia. This was the well-known case of Dick, a four-year-old boy whose psychic functioning and intellectual development resembled that of a child barely over one year old. He appeared completely unadapted to reality and failed to form any emotional bonds with those around him. The presence or absence of his mother or nanny elicited no perceptible response. From the beginning of treatment, he showed almost no signs of anxiety – and when he did, it was mild and fleeting (Klein, 1930/2011).

Moreover, Dick did not play, showed no interest in his surroundings, and spent most of his time producing repetitive, disconnected sounds. His vocabulary was extremely limited and, even so, used imprecisely. One detail that particularly struck Klein was his apparent indifference to physical pain: when injured, he neither sought comfort nor expressed any desire for care or affection – something highly unusual in young children.

In her analysis, Klein identified that Dick had undergone early experiences of profound helplessness and frustration. From his very first weeks of life his mother had been unable to breastfeed him, resulting in a severe nutritional deprivation that placed the infant at risk. He only gained regular access to feeding around six weeks of age, when a wet nurse was finally found. By then, however, contact with the breast no longer produced the expected effects – it was as though something essential from the beginning had already been lost.

Due to these difficulties Dick began to develop digestive problems, such as constipation and, later, haemorrhoids. Although he received full attention because of his health condition, the boy never experienced the feeling of genuine love since, from the very beginning, his mother's attitude towards him was marked by extreme anxiety (Klein, 1930/2011). It is also worth noting that both the first nanny and the father appeared emotionally distant, showing no affection for the boy.

DOI: 10.4324/9781003642503-6

Using Klein's own words, we can say that Dick grew up in an "atmosphere lacking in love". However, when he turned two years old, his parents hired a new nanny, who proved to be very affectionate. In the following months, Dick spent a relatively significant amount of time with his grandmother who also gave him a great deal of attention.

Although he learned to walk at the usual age, the boy experienced severe difficulties in controlling his excretory functions. On the other hand, some activities occurred rather early in his life: at the age of four, he developed the habit of masturbating. The reprimand from his former nanny, who described his behaviour as "very nasty", contributed to the development, in Dick, of an intense sense of guilt linked to his early genital manifestations. Klein noted that this punitive intervention contributed to the emergence of a tyrannical superego (see Chapter 8 of this book and Almeida, 2022), intensifying perse-cutory anxieties and the conflicts related to his bodily excitations.[1]

The genuine affection offered by the grandmother and the nanny – both important caregiving figures – contributed to some progress in Dick's develop-ment. Even so, the damage caused by failures in early care continued to leave their mark on his psychic constitution. The boy remained unable to form emo-tional bonds with those around him – a condition which, in psychoanalysis, is understood as an absence of object relations (Almeida, 2024a; Vieira, 2025).

Through her attentive observation, Klein identified in Dick an almost total inability of the ego to manage anxiety. It is therefore possible to suggest that the early traumas he experienced made it impossible for him to internalise a good object capable of supporting and strengthening an ego still in formation and profoundly weakened (Almeida, 2024a).

Klein also observed that, following a debilitated beginning of life, the child's capacity for *symbolic formation* had become atrophied. Although he had received some basic early care, the repetition of frustrating experiences led the boy to become fixated on a single type of interest: repetitive and ste-reotyped movements with no connection to the external world. This behav-ioural pattern, in turn, made it difficult to develop new forms of sublimation (Klein, 1930/2011).

In the analytic setting, Dick appeared indifferent to the available objects and toys, unable to sustain his attention for more than brief moments. Only the trains, the toy stations and, above all, the doors and doorknobs – with their constant motion of opening and closing – were capable of minimally capturing his interest.

Klein's clinical sensitivity enabled her to perceive that Dick's fascination with trains, stations, and doors was not a mere coincidence; these elements were linked to an unconscious desire to penetrate the maternal body and seize for himself everything he believed had been denied to him in his earliest relationships. In psychoanalytic terms, this was a symbolic attempt to reclaim those lost aspects through a form of appropriation marked by omnipotence. Dick was overwhelmed by intense aggressive impulses which, rather than being worked through, were experienced as persecutory threats by an ego still extremely fragile. Unable to symbolise or to express his destructiveness within the realm of fantasy, the boy found himself paralysed in the face of annihilatory instinct – something that manifested in inhibited behaviours, such as his refusal to chew food.

Here, I would like to raise a question: how is it possible to conduct an analysis with a child whose capacity for symbolisation is so poorly developed? Klein, however, did not shy away from this challenge. She interpreted the little that Dick did (with the trains and with the doorknobs), attributing meaning to his actions. She symbolised *on his behalf* and, gradually, *with him*:

> The first time Dick came to me [...], he manifested no sort of affect when his nurse handed him over to me. When I showed him the toys I had put ready, he looked at them without the faintest interest. I took a big train and put it beside a smaller one and called them "Daddy-train" and "Dick-train". Thereupon he picked up the train I called "Dick" and made it roll to the window and said "Station". I explained: "The station is mummy; Dick is going into mummy". He left the train, ran into the space between the outer and inner doors of the room, shut himself in, saying "dark" and ran out again directly. He went through this performance several times. I explained to him: "It is dark inside mummy. Dick is inside dark mummy".
>
> (Klein, 1930/2011, n.p.)

In the third session, immediately after an interpretation by the analyst, Dick had an anxiety outburst, hid behind a chest of drawers in the consulting room and, for the first time, from his hiding place, called out Klein's name. He also began to call repeatedly for the nanny, clearly expressing insecurity and distress – feelings he had never previously shown. When the session ended, Dick ran into the nanny's arms with a joy he had never before exhibited. He also became interested in the toys and the games played with the analyst, using play to represent his aggressive tendencies: he cut, broke, dismantled, and threw various objects to the ground.

At the beginning of the fourth session, Dick cried when the nanny left the consulting room (soon calming down afterwards) – "something unprecedented and extraordinary", as Klein (1930/2011) puts it. The little boy also displayed the beginnings of curiosity as he explored the toys scattered around the room. Dick loved playing by throwing things far away – a behaviour Klein understood as an "expulsion of his intense sadism".

Over the course of the treatment, Dick began to regain the use of language, recalling words, their meanings, and how to use them appropriately. This development was accompanied by a gradual expansion of his communicative capacity, indicating progress in ego integration and, consequently, in his capacity for symbolisation. As treatment progressed, Klein observed significant changes in Dick's attitude towards his mother and his nanny, who in turn became more affectionate. The desire to be understood, previously absent or inhibited, began to emerge more clearly. Although his vocabulary remained limited, the boy made a clear effort to communicate.

By accessing Dick's unconscious world, Klein was able to alleviate the impact of intense persecutory anxieties, stemming from the un-symbolised aggression that inhabited the boy's psyche. That is, through interpretations attuned to the child's level of psychic functioning, it became possible to gradually strengthen the ego (Vieira, 2025). As a result, Dick began to recognise and work through his fantasies, becoming able to express his sadism in less threatening ways, without the fear of moral punishment.

According to Kleinian theory infantile sadism – derived from the innate death instinct – represents a significant psychic threat, as it is linked to the ego's most primitive anxieties, originating from the fear that destructive impulses directed at the object might turn back against the subject himself. In such cases, the object attacked through sadism is transformed into a threatening figure, as the individual comes to fear retaliation. Thus, the baby's archaic ego is faced with a demand for which it is not yet equipped: to contain and process persecutory anxiety.

Klein highlights the existence of an internal object relation resulting from the processes of projection and introjection. In other words, our enigmatic world of fantasy (see Chapter 2 of this book). In this light, psychic suffering may emerge as a product of these internal object relations, coloured by constitutional sadistic intensity.

Furthermore, we must not forget that, to Klein, access to knowledge and its expansion are directly linked to sadistic and destructive impulses which, when not tolerated by a holding environment, take central control of the psyche, leading to inhibition – and consequently hindering the process of symbolisation (Almeida, 2020). This situation produces intense anxiety triggered by primary sadism (death instinct), as the child believes that the destructive action projected onto objects will rebound upon the self (introjection).

Thus, the anxiety arising at this stage can be overwhelming and paralysing – as was indeed the case with Dick – resulting in an "autistic encapsulation", characterised by the absence of affective contact with objects and a deep impoverishment of symbolic capacity.

Notes on the Formation of Symbols

The individual shatters this hateful part of the ego into tiny fragments and projects it violently into the object, which, in turn, becomes equally split. The result is that the subject feels surrounded by "bizarre objects". These objects are tiny fragments of the subject's personality embedded in tiny fragments of the object and infused with intense hostility. The existence of these bizarre objects in the mind can be easily detected in the psychotic, but they may also exist in a split-off part of the mind in non-psychotic individuals, particularly in severe neurotics. [...] Bizarre objects cannot be easily removed, and the establishment of the depressive position is severely hindered.

(Segal, 1993, p. 62)

Dick's case has been the subject of research to various psychoanalytic authors, ranging from some within the Kleinian school to Jacques Lacan himself, who made this case the object of study in his *The Seminar, Book I: Freud's Technical Writings*.[2]

However, one particular article offered significant contributions to Klein's theoretical developments. I am referring to an essay by Hanna Segal (1918–1992), originally published in 1957, entitled "Notes on Symbol Formation". In this paper the author discusses the importance of understanding and interpreting unconscious symbolism, offering new perspectives on Melanie Klein's technique.

Segal begins her text by pointing the difficulty some psychotic or schizoid patients face in forming and freely using symbols. She illustrates this limitation with the case of a schizophrenic patient who gave up public violin performances because he believed that playing the instrument was equivalent to a masturbatory act. In this patient's mind, the violin did not symbolise the male genital organ – it was experienced as such. This confusion between the symbol and the thing it represents prevents symbolic mediation and makes the use of the instrument in the presence of others unfeasible (Almeida, 2020).

Building on this observation and on Klein's paper about the case of Dick, Segal states that:

> Symbol formation is an activity of the ego attempting to deal with the anxieties aroused by its *relation to the object*, and it is generated primarily by the fear of bad objects and the fear of the loss or inaccessibility of good ones. Disturbances in the ego's relation to objects are reflected in disturbances in symbol formation.
>
> (Segal, 1957/1982, p. 81, emphasis added)

According to Segal's analysis, Dick was unable to form symbolic relations with the external world due to the anxiety he experienced in relation to the persecutory or guilt-inducing object: the mother's body (in other words, "the bad breast"). As the analytic process progressed, and with the help of Klein's interpretations, the boy began to show interest in certain objects in the consulting room, initiating the process of symbolisation. For Segal, it takes a symbol in order to displace aggression away from the original object, thereby reducing guilt and the sense of loss.

The ability to mourn loved objects and to take responsibility for one's own impulses is what enables an individual to use symbols freely and creatively. While employing a substitute for the lost object, there is no total identification between the lost object and its substitute. The symbol is not confused with the original object – and it is precisely this distinction that allows its own characteristics to be recognised and valued. In this way, the symbol can be used more freely, without confusion with the real object hindering its symbolic function (Segal, 1957/1982).

Let us take children's play activity as an example. In play, children use toys to symbolise roles and reframe emotions. When playing "school", for instance, a child often takes on the role of the teacher in order to occupy an active position, reversing the passivity experienced in the role of pupil. It is common for this same child to shout at her students – usually dolls or stuffed animals – sending them to the corner or even hitting them. Such behaviour, however, does not necessarily constitute a literal reproduction of the real teacher's actions. What happens, in fact, is that through representation the child also assigns meaning to her sadism (Almeida, 2024a).

According to Segal symbolic formation governs our capacity for *communication*. Unsurprisingly when disturbances occur in object relations the capacity for communication is significantly affected: "[...] first, because the differentiation between subject and object breaks down; second, because the *means* of communication are absent since symbols are experienced in a concrete way" (Segal, 1957/1982, p. 88, original emphasis).

In this light, one of the major recurring challenges in the analysis of psychotic patients is the difficulty in establishing effective communication. This is because, in the ego's more primitive functioning, words – whether spoken by the analyst or by the patient – are not understood as symbolic representations, but rather as concrete objects or actions in themselves. That is why they fail to fulfil their communicative function, becoming charged with a real, literal value that prevents their use as mediators of thought or symbolic exchange.

Segal considers that symbols are essential not only for communication with the external world, but also for the establishment of internal communication. Under such conditions fantasies tend to be experienced as real and concrete events, without the symbolic mediation necessary to distinguish them from external reality. For this reason, the difficulty in working with psychotic patients "lies not only in their failure to communicate with us, but, above all, *in their failure to communicate with themselves*" (Segal, 1957/1982, p. 89, emphasis added).

Segal's contributions on symbolic formation deepen Klein's findings, particularly with regard to the primitive relationship between the baby and the mother. It is worth recalling that it is only when the baby is situated within a sufficiently containing environment – capable of holding his aggressive fantasies – that he can reach the depressive position, a central concept in Kleinian theory. At this stage of development the ego begins to strengthen as the child recognises the damage directed at the loved object and feels driven to repair it, gradually taking responsibility for their own impulses.

This internal shift fosters a more integrated perception of reality, allowing for the introjection of positive experiences – beneficial experiences begin to accumulate and gradually take the place of earlier persecutory experiences, previously marked by fragmentation and anxiety.

Upon reaching this developmental achievement the baby begins to feel (and perceive) that the object which received his destructive projections is the same one that provides care and love. In the *depressive position*,[3] therefore, a "psychic space" is created to process not only the anxieties linked to guilt and the desire for reparation, but also archaic conflicts that, until then, had remained unresolved.

In the schizoid-paranoid position, however – a phase in which object relations are partial and dominated by sadism – anxieties are caused by the extreme concreteness of fantasy.

In contrast, upon reaching the depressive position, the individual becomes capable of reframing their destructive instincts based on whole object relations, in which the ego is more integrated and mature. Object relations support the experience of instincts and fantasies within the symbolic realm, fostering the growth of subjectivity. I quote Segal:

> The word "symbol" comes from the Greek term meaning to join, to pair, to integrate. The process of symbol formation is, I believe, a continuous process of bringing together and integrating the internal with the external, the subject with the object, and earlier experiences with later ones.
>
> (Segal, 1957/1982, p. 91)

Let us recall, then, that in Klein's perspective internal violence is structuring; it emerges prior to the capacity to love, to think, to delay gratification, to create or to sustain any project. We are, above all, a pulsating organism of urgencies and needs, immersed in helplessness. It is within this original field that such "psychic violence" is inscribed as a point of departure – the primordial death instinct.

Symbolisation requires a process of construction. The very idea of a symbol refers to joining, to the possibility of bringing together separated parts. Something within is must already have achieved a minimum level of articulation. And this integration – far from being spontaneous – depends on the presence of sufficiently good objects which allow the psyche to withstand splitting and to process loss without collapsing. It is within such an environment that the fragments of the ego, previously dispersed, find the conditions to come together and form a more cohesive unity.

Nevertheless, it is not uncommon to find, even among psychoanalysts, the notion that Klein may have neglected the importance of the external environment in the infant's early experiences. Such a reading, however, overlooks important aspects of her work. In one of her more mature texts, the author herself clearly emphasises:

> In spite of all these internal and external difficulties, the young child normally finds a way of coping with his fundamental conflicts, and this allows him at other times to experience enjoyment and gratitude for happiness received. If he is lucky enough to have understanding parents, his problems can be diminished, and – on the other hand – a too strict or too lenient upbringing may increase them.
>
> (Klein, 1960/2011, n.p., emphasis added)

What distinguishes Melanie Klein from other post-Freudian authors, however, is the *weight* she attributes to external factors.[4] For her, constitutional aspects and unconscious phantasies have a far greater impact on the constitution of the psyche. In this regard, in her classic essay "Envy and Gratitude" (1957), she writes:

> Another factor that influences development from the beginning is the variety of external experiences through which the infant goes. This in some measure explains the development of his early anxieties, which would be particularly great in a baby who had a difficult birth and unsatisfactory feeding. My accumulated observations, however, have convinced me that the impact of these external experiences is in *proportion to the constitutional strength* of the innate destructive impulses and the ensuing paranoid anxieties.
>
> (Klein, 1957/2011, n.p., emphasis added)

In short: although Klein acknowledges the value of the infant's early relations with the external environment in the formation of the psyche, it is in the transference experience that her clinical practice finds its transformative potential – in the here and now of the sessions. The technique she developed places its faith in this space of encounter: it is when the subject comes face to face with someone who contains and translates what has not yet been symbolised that something within the internal world can begin to reorganise. Psychic change, in this context, occurs in the presence of someone who, through interpretation, takes part in the process of giving form to the unspeakable.

Phyllis Grosskurth (1986), in the biography she wrote about Melanie Klein, records her personal encounter with Dick, when he was around 50 years old. The author recounts a few details of this episode:

> "I was very fond of Melanie", he told me feelingly. In her symposium reply to Anna Freud, Klein insisted that she refrained from caressing a child but, according to "Dick", she always soothed him when he cried, which he frequently did. "Life is not all that bad", she would say.
>
> (Grosskurth, 1986, p. 205)

Finally, it is worth highlighting that, within the Kleinian tradition, one of the most important factors in the development of the psyche is the notion of *reparation*. Introduced in 1929, in her paper "Infantile Anxiety-Situations Reflected in a Work of Art and in the Creative Impulse", this idea is directly linked to the depressive position. It is a phenomenon that arises from the fear of having destroyed the loved object and from the genuine desire to restore and preserve it internally. On this subject, I wrote in another work:

> When we fail to work through the depressive position, guilt becomes entangled with the ego; which becomes entangled with manic defences;

which in turn become entangled with the space of creativity – and, ultimately, resentment fills the entirety of our psyche with pain and hatred, though these remain, paradoxically, denied and inaccessible to our consciousness. Tyrannical or monstrous aspects of an archaic persecutory superego are revived to punish us, while we continue to avoid direct contact with responsibility and ambivalence.

(Almeida, 2024b, p. 12)

From this perspective the symbol can be understood as the product of creative work: a construction that gives meaning both to the external world and to inner life. Here, the capacity for reparation plays a main role – it supports some of the subject's most fundamental functions, such as loving, working, learning, investigating, and forming bonds (Almeida, 2025). Communication itself – even when understood beyond the mere exchange of information – also depends on this very potential. To truly speak to someone else implies opening oneself to alterity and recognising the other as distinct from oneself, seeking a connection that welcomes what is not ours without erasing the richness of singularity.

The Formation of Symbols According to Bion: From the Alpha Function to the Capacity for Dream Thoughts

It is curious to consider that among all the forces that drive the psyche – derived mainly from love (L) and hate (H) – Bion (1963/2018) chose knowledge (K) as the fundamental impulse behind the formation of symbols. Not that he ignored the weight of libido (Eros) or the death instinct, but he intuited that the desire to know can only exist when these forces submit to something greater: the will to make experience thinkable. In other words: L and H are subordinate to K.

It is worth noting that this Bionian conception is, so to speak, a *product* of a lineage that includes Freud and Klein, yet it cannot be reduced to them. Bion draws nourishment from these roots and simultaneously expands them. His work cannot be understood without Klein – that seems evident to me – but it would be a naïve mistake to label him a "pure" Kleinian. What he proposes is another cartography: a mind built in the constant movement between splitting and reparation. Indeed, thinking is born not in the schizoid-paranoid position, nor in the depressive one, but in the oscillation between both (PS↔D).

I recall a patient who, when speaking about her mother, would always describe an empty room. She would *actually see*, in her mind, a room where the mother should have been – but never was. Over time, this image gained weight, colour, and texture. It was as if what had once been a brute fact – absence – slowly began to turn into a narrative. The room acquired furniture, the scent of lavender and, one day, a ray of light entered through the window. That was the point at which the pain of abandonment began to be thought about (by both of us, *together*).

Bion called this capacity to transform the raw impact of experience into something representable the *alpha function* (see Chapter 4 of this book). Sensory impressions, raw emotions, and undigested fragments of reality (*beta elements*, β): all of this must be transformed into mental images – that is, into forms one can dream, remember, and imagine. When this function fails, the subject does not think: the beta elements evacuate. They project onto the other what they cannot bear within themselves, as one might expel a poison that corrodes from within.

As we know, the clinic is full of such moments: the patient arrives with a chest heavy with nameless anguish and pierces us with a raw affect, discharged as if it were a leftover. If the analyst is not sufficiently prepared, there is a risk of becoming complicit in this evacuation, merging with it. I fully agree with Chuster (2024), who, in highlighting the analyst's *negative capability*, observes:

> Life is meant to be lived, and there is no life without thinking. Negative capability raises the fundamental question of the time of life – that is, how to tolerate mystery, uncertainty, and the infinity of time in order to make better use of it. Lost time cannot be recovered. [...] I believe it is important for the analyst to bear in mind that they are not merely opening up session time for the patient; they are offering the patient something deeply precious: their own lifetime. That is negative capability. With Bion, it became clear that the function of psychoanalysis is to preserve human thought and, through that, to preserve human and social autonomy.
>
> (Chuster, 2024, p. 48)

At this point, we can also speak of *reverie* – the analyst's psychic availability to dream what the patient is not yet able to dream for themselves. However, "dreaming" here is not daydreaming. We are speaking of a form of work – a kind of digestion, in which the strange is received without being entirely swallowed, and something new is returned: something the other can finally bear.

> In other words, from Bion onwards, the mother comes to be seen as performing structuring functions for the infant's mind. Just as she feeds the baby with milk, she also feeds it with "thoughts" by placing her alpha function at the baby's service. This is far more than simply presenting the object of the infant's need or desire.
>
> (Levy, 2022, p. 118)

Bion (1962/2018) developed a sophisticated model for thinking about this process: *beta elements* – unprocessed experiences – can only be transformed into *alpha elements* when the symbolic function is active. These alpha elements may be understood as the "building blocks of thought": images, sounds, and sensations that carry meaning and can be *linked* to one another. When this transformation does not occur, the subject lives in chaos. Things make no sense; pain has no name, fear has no shape, and time becomes confused.

There are patients who bring us dreams that resemble *hallucinations*. Images that narrate nothing, but instead seem to *explode* into meaningless fragments. In many cases, these images are not in the service of elaboration. They are ghosts that do not wish to be seen – they want to be left with the analyst, as though the analysand were saying (without saying): "Here, take this. I cannot contain it within me".

One of the great challenges of clinical work is distinguishing an image constructed in order to think from an image created to evacuate. That demands listening and, above all, patience and humility. It is recommended that the analyst, in such a position, refrain from interpreting unconscious content too quickly. One must wait. Dream with the patient, until the symbol can be born. Until anxiety finds some kind of outline. Until what was once only noise can become, at last, language. As Levy aptly points out,

> Interpretation, understood in this way – as a symbol created between analyst and patient – fulfils the criteria we have explored thus far in defining what constitutes a true symbol: it unites and at the same time distinguishes analyst and patient; it enriches both, since it adds meaning to each; it is created in the heat of the emotional experience shared between them and represents that experience; and, last but not least, it is structuring in the sense that it provokes a catastrophic reaction, forcing a reorganisation of all prior knowledge. It is the *third* born of the fertile relationship established between analyst and patient. Of course, once formulated, we must observe what the patient will do with this *third*: whether it will be received within a container where the L-link predominates, allowing for the birth of yet another new idea – and so on, endlessly; or whether it will be stripped of meaning through envy or destruction, attacked, leading to an emptying-out.
>
> (Levy, 2022, pp. 148–149)

Nonetheless, Bion proposes an intriguing image of the mind in formation: a loom onto which emotional experiences are cast as misaligned threads. The alpha function would then be the capacity to weave these threads together, giving them meaning and structure. It is this act of making that renders possible the very existence of what we call thought. And it is also what allows for the formation of the alpha screen – a kind of internal weave that separates, but also connects, the unconscious to the conscious (Levy, 2022). Without this mesh everything becomes confused. The individual cannot distinguish inside from outside, past from present, fantasy from reality. The mind becomes raw flesh.

I recall an adolescent I saw in a psychiatric outpatient clinic during the time of my first clinical placements. He always arrived exhausted. He spoke little.

His sentences were fragmented, usually accompanied by complaints of physical pain – headaches, stomach aches, muscle pain, and so on. There were no dreams, nor any stories. His body was his only mode of expression. Over the course of our sessions, I came to realise that this was not a hysterical presentation. It was something else: it seemed that every nameless emotion was inscribed directly into his flesh – beta elements circulated without rest, seeking discharge through his muscles, viscera, and bones.

Bion's theory helps us to understand such phenomena as failures in symbolic transformation. When experience cannot be metabolised by the mind, it is evacuated – into the body, into action (acting out), or into delusions (hallucinations). These are extreme attempts to deal with the unbearable. The mind, lacking an alpha screen, cannot contain or organise. And it is at this point that the greatest risk emerges: an attack upon the very functions that make thinking possible. The mind turns against that which binds, connects, and establishes relationships – the links themselves (Bion, 1957/2018).

This is why the clinical setting, in such cases, demands a particular kind of presence. The analyst must sustain what the patient is not yet able to – the "negative capability", in Chuster's (2024) terms. One must be fully present in the moments when the other is in collapse. Sometimes this simply means bearing to be alongside without rushing to produce meaning before its time.

When Bion (1962/2018) tells us that thoughts precede the capacity to think them, he is inviting us into a radical mode of listening. There are thoughts that pass through us, but which we are not yet capable of housing. They are "in suspension", waiting for something within us to transform so that they may, finally, make sense. And what determines whether a thought will be articulated or evacuated is not its origin, but the way we deal with frustration. It is a matter of learning to tolerate absence, the "no", the void – this is the true challenge of psychic maturation.

In other words, thinking is only possible when the subject can bear *not having*. The absence of the breast, in Bion's model, is what inaugurates the possibility of thought. If the breast is present, there is no need to think – there is satisfaction. However, when it is absent, one must imagine, wait, and elaborate. For Bion, thought arises from lack, not plenitude.

When this absence becomes intolerable, the object that fails to arrive – the frustrating breast – is transformed into a kind of "bad thing" – something undesirable – and must therefore be expelled. In such a scenario, the apparatus for thinking gives way to an apparatus for evacuation. The mind functions as a system for discarding. As a result, what should have become a symbol turns into substance, and what should have become language is reduced to discharge.

We can observe this phenomenon in patients who confuse external reality with internal states, who cannot distinguish what they feel from what they see. They are immersed in a sensory-emotional confusion that borders on the delusional. In such cases, the symbol does not appear as a substitute; it appears as a "hallucinated object". Thought, therefore, becomes a threat.

Bion (1962/2018) captured this movement with precision, stating that there are situations in which, instead of generating meaning, the psyche reverses its course and dismantles the symbolic capacity. Elements that previously held the potential to form mental images begin to behave as "things in themselves" – without structure or connection. He referred to this collapse as the *reversal of the alpha function*. It is as though the mind loses its ability to transform impressions into symbols and instead fragments them further, producing what he called *bizarre objects* – that is, psychic residues, unassimilable elements.

I believe it is along this path that Bion goes beyond Klein. His great turning point lies in viewing these mental states as effects of the bonding with the other. In their radical dependence, babies project into the mother what they cannot yet digest. And it is through the quality of this bond – through the way the mother receives or fails to receive these projections – that the mind begins to take form. If the mother possesses a *capacity for reverie* she receives these raw contents, transforms them, and returns them in a symbolisable form.

I must confess that this idea always moves me when I hear, in the clinical undercurrents, the implicit question asked by so many patients: "Can you digest what I am?". I refer to a doubt that emerges in the tone of their voice and materialises in eyes that either avoid or plead. In many circumstances what is at stake is not the interpretation, but the construction of the bond; the analyst is expected to contain without contaminating, to receive the horror without returning it in an amplified form.

Yet we do not always attain such competence. There are mothers – and analysts – who cannot tolerate what is projected into them. They respond with anxiety, with guilt, and/or with a need for control. And when this happens, the baby – or the patient – feels that they have deposited something unbearable and are now faced with a hostile object. The terror that follows has no name, because it has never found a symbolic form. Thus, the cycle begins anew: more evacuation, more fragmentation, and, inevitably, less capacity for thought.

Bion (1962/2023) also described how mental development depends on the oscillation between states of psychic disintegration (PS) and moments of integration (D). As I have mentioned, before thinking can occur, one must bear *not knowing*. Being in the dark. Floating in chaos. Until, at some point, a detail emerges, and the mind begins to organise itself around that nucleus. Bion called this phenomenon the *selected fact*: when something in the emotional experience attains a degree of coherence.

In clinical practice, this translates into small moments of clarity that arise after long stretches of darkness. The patient speaks, repeats, contradicts themselves, falls silent, and so on. Until, suddenly, something slips through – an image, a memory, a dream – and the session takes a different turn. The analyst, who has borne the not-knowing, can now construct a reading that is not the result of mere rationalisation.

From this perspective, Ferro (2019) argues that Bion's focus does not fall upon the symbol as a fixed content of the mind, but rather on symbolisation as a *creative function* – that is, the mind as an instance that produces symbols.

To Ferro, contemporary conceptions of the symbol are linked to how one understands projective identification. If this identification is conceived as a means of communication and if thought is formed through mediation by the other's mind, then symbolisation takes shape as a shared process.

In this light, the emphasis shifts away from the search for a "correct" symbolic meaning or one that is faithful to the patient's phantasies, and towards the intersubjective dimension of the analytic experience. The analyst's mind, with its own objects and phantasies, transforms the circulating affects, operating in resonance with the patient's mind. From this symbolic collaboration new meanings, new connections, and new ways of representing the dreaming of the psychic experience may emerge.

Nevertheless, in his book *Transformations* (1965/2020), Bion shifts the focus of psychoanalysis away from the pursuit of purely rational truths (knowledge) towards the efficacy of the analytic process itself (becoming). His interest lies less in the accumulation of knowledge and more in the transformative impact of the clinical experience. When discussing the purpose of interpretation, he proposes, "If I am right in suggesting that phenomena are known but reality is 'become' the interpretation must do more than increase knowledge" (Bion, 1965/2020, n.p.).

In other words, the interpretation should not be confined to the expansion of consciousness or the explanation of latent content; its role is to foster a movement of "transformation in O", allowing the subject to access more authentic modes of being. It is, therefore, a process that aims less at explanation and more at becoming oneself – a bridge between unformed experience and the possibility of coming into being.[5]

For these and other reasons presented here, I often say in my lectures that every session carries within itself an attempt to *form symbols*. I shall therefore conclude this chapter with the following quotation from Levy:

> In patients with impaired symbolic capacity, the first goal of treatment is to "translate" the raw experiences brought into the analytic field – through the analyst's capacity to "dream" them – into something more intelligible, to give them meaning, a symbolic representation, which in turn will allow the development of this function in the patient. In patients whose symbolic capacity is preserved, or relatively intact, the analytic experience will further enhance it, insofar as it is in the very nature of this experience to symbolically transform the emotions lived.
>
> (Levy, 2022, p. 149)

Or better yet, I turn to the brilliance of Clarice Lispector, so that we may continue thinking and, with luck, symbolising:

> ... I'm searching, I'm searching. I'm trying to understand. Trying to give someone what I've lived through and I don't know to whom, but I don't want to keep what I've lived. I don't know what to do with what I've lived, I'm afraid of this profound disorganisation. I don't trust what

happened to me. Did something happen to me which, not knowing how to live it, I lived something else instead? That's what I would like to call disorganisation, and then I would have the reassurance to take risks, because I'd know where to return to afterwards: to the previous organisation. I prefer to call it disorganisation, because I don't want to confirm what I've lived – If I were to confirm myself, I would lose the world as I had it, and I know I'm not capable of another one.

(Lispector, 2020, n.p.)

Notes

1 For further reading on censorship, repression, and the inhibition of sexuality from a Kleinian perspective, we recommend Almeida, 2024a and Vieira, 2025.
2 Lacan even remarks that, "Melanie Klein thrusts symbolism, with the utmost brutality, upon little Dick. She immediately starts imposing major interpretations on him. She subjects him to a brutal verbalisation of the Oedipal myth, almost as revolting to us as it would be to any reader – *You are the little train, you want to fuck your mother*" (Lacan, 1979/1953–1954, pp. 83–84, original emphasis). However, we must not treat the author's critique lightly, as in the very next paragraph of the same *Seminar*, he offers a sort of reparation: "This way of proceeding is evidently open to theoretical debate – which cannot be separated from the diagnosis of the case. But it is certain that following this intervention, *something happens. That's the point*" (Lacan, 1979/1953–1954, p. 84, emphasis added).
3 Regarding the notion of the "depressive position", see Chapter 3 of this book.
4 This characteristic marks a fundamental divergence between the ideas of Klein and Winnicott, given that, for the latter, the environment has a crucial impact on the individual's maturational development and is regarded as the main factor involved in psychic disturbances when it proves to be inadequate or neglectful.
5 Thomas Ogden expands on this perspective by stating:

> Bion insists that, as psychoanalysts, we must relinquish the desire to understand and instead engage as fully as possible in the experience of being with the patient. We must "cultivate a vigilant avoidance of memory", because memory is what we think we know based on what no longer exists and is no longer knowable. We must also renounce "desires for results, for cure, or even for understanding". The memory of what we think we know and the desire to understand what has not yet occurred (and is therefore also unknowable) are 'obstacles to intuiting the reality [of what is taking place in the present moment of a session] with which the psychoanalyst must be in unison' (Bion, 1967/2013, pp. 136–137). This is the hallmark of Bion's ontological thinking: being and presence have supplanted comprehension – the analyst does not come to know, understand, grasp, or apprehend the reality of what is occurring in a session; on the contrary, they *intuit* reality and become *one* with it: they are entirely present in experiencing the present moment.
>
> (Ogden, 2020, pp. 30–31, emphasis added)

References

Almeida, A. P. (2020). Melanie Klein e o processo de formação dos símbolos: revisitando o caso Dick [Melanie Klein and the Process of Symbol Formation: Revisiting the Case of Dick]. *Estilos da Clínica*, 25(3): 552–567. https://doi.org/10.11606/issn.1981-1624.v25i3p552-567

Almeida, A. P. (2022). *O superego arcaico, as redes sociais e sua relação com o burn-out na era do cansaço: revisitando Melanie Klein* [The Archaic Superego, Social Media, and Its Relationship With Burnout in the Age of Exhaustion: Revisiting Melanie Klein]. *Jornal de Psicanálise*, 55(102): 105–123.

Almeida, A. P. (2024a). *Melanie Klein além da clínica: contribuições à educação escolar* [*Melanie Klein Beyond The Clinic: Contributions To School Education*]. São Paulo: Zagodoni.

Almeida, A. P. (2024b). A depressão para Melanie Klein: um estudo teórico-clínico [Depression according to Melanie Klein: a theoretical-clinical study]. *Revista da Faculdade Paulo Picanço*, 4(1): 1–13. https://doi.org/10.59483/rfpp.v4n1.105

Almeida, A. P. (2025). Reflexões psicanalíticas sobre a separação amorosa: contribuições de Melanie Klein e Winnicott [Psychoanalytic Reflections on Romantic Separation: Contributions from Melanie Klein and Winnicott]. *Psicanálise & Barroco Em Revista*, 22(1): 14–32. https://doi.org/10.9789/pb.v22i1.14-32

Bion, W. R. (2018). *Differentiation of the Psychotic from the Non-psychotic Personalities*. In W. R. Bion, Second Thoughts. London: Routledge. E-book. (Original work published in 1957)

Bion, W. R. (2018). *A Theory of Thinking*. In W. R. Bion, *Second Thoughts: Selected Papers on Psychoanalysis*. London: Routledge. E-book. (Original work published in 1962)

Bion, W. R. (2018). *Elements of Psychoanalysis*. London: Routledge. E-book. (Original work published in 1963)

Bion, W. R. (2020). *Transformations*. London: Routledge. E-book. (Original work published in 1965)

Bion, W. R. (2023). *Learning from Experience*. London: Routledge. E-book. (Original work published in 1962)

Chuster, A. (2024). *Linguagem de alcance psicanalítico: a diferença transcendental em W. R. Bion* [*Psychoanalytically Oriented Language: The Transcendental Difference in W. R. Bion*]. São Paulo: Blucher.

Ferro, A. (2019). *Na sala de análise: emoções, relatos, transformações* [*In the Consulting Room: Emotions, Narratives, Transformations*]. São Paulo: Blucher.

Grosskurth, P. (1986). *Melanie Klein: Her World and Her Work*. New York: Knopf. E-Book.

Jones, E. (1948). The Theory of Symbolism. In E. Jones, *Papers on Psycho-Analysis*, pp. 87–144. London: Karnac. (Original work published in 1916)

Klein, M. (2011). Infantile Anxiety-Situations Reflected in a Work of Art and in the Creative Impulse. In M. Klein, *Love, Guilt and Reparation and Other Works (1921–1945)*. London: Vintage Books. E-book. (Original work published 1929)

Klein, M. (2011). The Importance of Symbol-Formation in the Development of the Ego. In M. Klein, *Love, Guilt and Reparation and Other Works (1921–1945)*. London: Vintage Books. E-book. (Original work published 1930)

Klein, M. (2011). Envy and Gratitude. In M. Klein, *Envy and Gratitude and Other Works (1946–1963)*. London: Vintage Books. E-book. (Original work published 1957)

Klein, M. (2011). On Mental Health. In M. Klein, *Envy and Gratitude and Other Works (1946–1963)*. London: Vintage Books. E-book. (Original work published 1960)

Lacan, J. (1979). *O Seminário, livro 1: Os escritos técnicos de Freud* [The Seminar, Book I: Freud's Technical Writings]. Rio de Janeiro: Zahar. (Original work presented in 1953–1954)

Levy, R. (2022). *A simbolização na psicanálise: os processos de subjetivação e a dimensão estética da psicanálise* [*Symbolisation in Psychoanalysis: Subjectivation Processes and the Aesthetic Dimension of Psychoanalysis*]. São Paulo: Blucher.

Lispector, C. (2020). *A paixão segundo G.H.* [*The Passion According to G.H.*]. Rio de Janeiro: Rocco. E-book.

Ogden, T. (2020). Psicanálise ontológica ou "O que você quer ser quando crescer?" [Ontological Psychoanalysis or "What Do You Want to Be When You Grow Up?"]. *Revista Brasileira de Psicanálise, 54*(1): 22–45.

Segal, H. (1982). Notas a respeito da formação de símbolos [Notes on Symbol Formation]. In H. Segal, *A obra de Hanna Segal: uma abordagem kleiniana à prática clínica* [*The Work of Hanna Segal: A Kleinian Approach to Clinical Practice*], pp. 77–98. Rio de Janeiro: Imago. (Original work published in 1957)

Segal, H. (1993). *Sonho, fantasia e arte* [*Dream, Fantasy and Art*]. Rio de Janeiro: Imago.

Telles, L. F. (2010). *Verão no aquário* [*Summer in the Aquarium*]. São Paulo: Companhia das Letras. E-book.

Vieira, F. P. (2025). Breves considerações sobre a clínica de Melanie Klein: o sentido das interpretações [Brief Considerations on Melanie Klein's Clinical Practice: The Meaning of Interpretations]. In F. P. Vieira, *A interpretação psicanalítica: revisitando Klein e Winnicott* [*The Psychoanalytic Interpretation: Revisiting Klein and Winnicott*], pp. 73–134. São Paulo: Blucher.

6 The Basic Function of the Mother (and of the Analyst) According to Bion and Winnicott, with a Focus on the Concepts of *Reverie* and *Holding*[1]

Alfredo Naffah Neto

Initial Considerations

Reverie and *holding* are core concepts in the English school of psychoanalysis, the first forming the cornerstone of Wilfred Bion's clinical work, while the second is the central notion of the clinical work by Donald Winnicott. It is possible that, because they are considered homologous concepts in both theories, they often appear juxtaposed – when they are not mistaken for each other – in the psychoanalytic literature, especially when the authors move in between the theories without much care, cherry-picking the concepts from their theoretical/clinical contexts and treating the notions as if they were the same or, at least, complementary, in the psychoanalytic function.

Clearly, I am not referring to those who use Bionian and/or Winnicottian concepts (or even those of other authors) in their theoretical compositions and recreate them in a new light, such as André Green or Thomas Ogden. These authors make the effort to try to build a new body of theory, in which the notions loaned from other authors come to occupy new places, but as part of a relatively coherent whole. We can identify with their writing or not, agree or disagree with their theoretical lines taken, but we cannot deny that a reconstruction is taking place, with varying degrees of rigour.

For all these purposes – with their varying degrees of justification in the use of the concepts – it is, however, necessary to ask ourselves if, in their original places, *reverie* and *holding* designate similar, or at least equivalent, processes. The fact that, for both authors, they are designations for *maternal care* – and, by extension, the core of the *analytic function* – does not necessarily make them similar.

The task I have set myself, here, is to research the meaning of these notions in the theories that endorse them, as well as how the consequences of their meaning impose on the clinical practices of their respective authors. For such, I am only considering the clinical treatment of borderline and/or psychotic patients.

This does not in any way translate into an attempt to restrict the utility of these concepts (which can be used very broadly, in different life situations, both inside and outside the practice), but simply focusing on a clinical

DOI: 10.4324/9781003642503-7

condition that is privileged in making the singularities of both concepts become more clearly explicit.[2]

Reverie and Schizophrenia

The notion of *reverie* is highly complex and connected, in Bionian theory, to the notion of beta elements (β) and alpha-function (α).

Bion's understanding is that our first experiences after birth imply sensuous elements (and, therefore, of somatic origin), denominated as beta elements that, to unfold a mental component, need to undergo a process of elaboration, analogous to digestion, which he designates as the alpha-function (α).[3] In his words: "The mental component, love, security, anxiety, as distinct from the somatic, requires a process analogous to digestion" (Bion, 1962/2023, n.p.). That is, if the baby feels a diffuse and undefined somatic discomfort that, in an adult mind could be translated as a fear of death, this obscure and terrifying feeling will depend on being digested in order to acquire a mental outline and meaning. In this example, we could say that the diffuse discomfort is a set of beta elements (β) that, when digested, transform into alpha elements, thus gaining image and verbal form: the fear of dying (that is, they acquire a symbolic dimension).

"Alpha elements can be used to think, to store in memory and to dream. Alpha-function abstracts the 'concreteness of sensory impressions'" (Sandler, 2005, p. 27). Or, in other words, "the extent that alpha function 'de-sensefies' or turns into immaterial that which was material in its origins" (Sandler, 2005, p. 643).

Bion's understanding is that the primitive mind of the baby is, initially, incapable of carrying out this kind of cleansing/transformation, thus depending on the adult caregiver. Therefore, the beta elements are, according to them, evacuated over the mother in the form of projective identifications and she returns them to the baby, digested and transformed. For him, this constitutes the most primitive form of communication in the mother-baby relationship. Sandler says:

> Infants, so to say, "borrow" from their mothers' alpha-function. Therefore, the mother detoxifies the child's beta-elements; they are returned to the infant in a digested form. "Reverie" refers to an ability of mothers to contain their own anxieties of annihilation. A continuous exposure to someone who does this may allow learning that such a state – not to become unstructured, fragmented before anxiety – may be achieved.
>
> (Sandler, 2005, p. 27)

Thus, Bion asks himself: "For example, when the mother loves the infant what does she do it with? Leaving aside the physical channels of communication my impression is that her love is expressed by *reverie*" (Bion, 1962/2023, n.p.).

Or, further, in a more precise sense:

> [...] reverie is that state of mind which is open to the reception of any "objects" from the loved object and is therefore capable of reception of the infant's projective identifications whether they are felt by the infant to be good or bad.
>
> (Bion, 1962/2023, n.p.)

Reverie therefore designates the exercising of the alpha-function on products of the projective identifications received from the loved object.

In summary, we could say that by conferring a mental constitution for the baby's somatic sensations – regardless of whether they are good or bad, calming or terrifying – the mother allows the baby to re-introject what was evacuated, but in a cleansed, dematerialised form that is able to, for these reasons, gradually provide the ability to dream,[4] store memories, and so create an apparatus for thinking (see Chapter 4 of this book). This process is necessary because only alpha elements have the capacity to relate and create bonds, to form structures. They are also what will, later on, ensure the distinction between the conscious and unconscious and train the child in the use of symbolic function, at its most varied levels.

This is how the gradual development of a normal baby proceeds, a baby who, later, may (or may not) develop a neurosis. But, how are psychotics formed, according to Bion? Do they simply lack a mother capable of *reverie*?

The question is not so simple: the lack of a mother with an open mind – to use Bion's expression – may, indeed, be one of the causes of the formation of a psychosis, but it is not normally the only one, or even the main reason (in Chapter 10 of this book, we develop a study on the origin of psychoses according to Bion and Winnicott, carrying out a broad and complex investigation).

When the pre-conditions for the emergence of schizophrenia are pointed out, Bion starts by saying: "There is the environment, which I shall not discuss at this time [...]" (Bion, 1957/2018, n.p.), which already poses the question: "Why does he not discuss it, at this time?". And the answer that becomes clear over the course of the text is: simply because it is not from the environment that the main pre-condition for schizophrenia comes. It is found:

> [...] in the personality, which must display four essential features. These are: a preponderance of destructive impulses so great that even the impulse to love is suffused by them and turned to sadism; a hatred of reality, internal and external, which is extended to all that makes for awareness of it; a dread of imminent annihilation and, finally, a premature and precipitate formation of object relations, foremost amongst which is the transference, whose thinness is in marked contrast with the tenacity with which they are maintained.
>
> (Bion, 1957/2018, n.p.)

That is, everything described above as a pre-condition for schizophrenia does not arise from a lacking environment, since Bion is not examining the role of the environment in the etiology of psychoses, in this text. Now, if they are not environmental, these pre-conditions can only be *innate, constitutional*. Bion considers them as "an endowment":

> To return now to the characteristics I listed as intrinsic to the schizophrenic personality. These constitute *an endowment* that makes it certain that the possessor of it will progress through the paranoid-schizoid and depressive positions in a manner markedly different from that of one not so endowed. The difference hinges on the fact that this combination of qualities leads to minute fragmentation of the personality, particularly of the apparatus of awareness of reality which Freud described as coming into operation at the behest of the reality principle, and excessive projection of these fragments of personality into external objects.
>
> (Bion, 1957/2018, n.p., emphasis added)

In other words, because they are poorly endowed, certain children already have a predisposition to schizophrenia, which makes them different from normal children. A baby with a schizophrenic predisposition sadistically attacks the mother's breast and splits the objects and parts of its personality – especially those linked to perception – into minimal parts, in function of its hatred for reality. Such a baby will, thus, tend to destroy all the bonds that can lead it into contact with what it hates. In this sense, it will also not tolerate the alpha elements and its immaterial capacity to produce bonds, connections, thoughts. For the baby with a propensity for schizophrenia it is very little use, in this sense, to have a mother with an open mind, one capable of *reverie*, as he will tend to destroy the elaborative work she carries out. In summary, we could say that this is about children with a very low resistance to frustration, who develop all these primitive defence mechanisms in function of the psychic pain that reality provokes in them – including all the types of frustration that it necessarily entails.

However, the question is even more complex than it may appear, as this entire process described above constitutes an *omnipotent fantasy*, the baby's *illusion*, in the terms of Bion (cf. Bion, 1957/2018). That is, it is the psychotic part of the child that believes (and, in this, *deludes* itself) it can make these splits and destroy its perceptive apparatus when, *in fact*, there is another part of it that is non-psychotic and that continues to maintain contact with reality, but which is, however, obscured by the dominion of the psychotic part. If that non-psychotic part and contact with reality did not exist, the defence mechanisms described above would not be necessary.

Schizophrenia thus describes, above all, these clashes between the psychotic and non-psychotic parts of an individual's personality, under the dominion of the psychotic part. According to Kleinian tradition, to which Bion belongs, it can be said that this preponderance of the destructive impulses, the hatred of reality, terror of imminent annihilation, etc. – associated with a low resistance to frustration – are manifestations of the dominion of the death instinct over the life instinct. And that this characterises the schizophrenic's "endowment".

Bionian Clinical Practice with Schizophrenics

To briefly analyse the clinical practice of schizophrenic patients by Bion, I will first cite a section from a session described in a paper he published in 1957. According to his description, it is about a patient who uses the psychotic part of his personality to create splits and projective identifications. He had been in psychoanalysis for six years and never tended to miss sessions. In this session, however, he arrived fifteen minutes late and lay down on the couch.[5]

> He spent some time turning from one side to another, ostensibly making himself comfortable. At length he said: "I don't suppose I shall do anything today. I ought to have rung up my mother". He paused, and then said: "No, I thought it would be like this". A more prolonged pause followed; then, "Nothing but filthy things and smells", he said. "I think I've lost my sight". Some twenty-five minutes of our time had now passed, and at this point I made an interpretation [...].
>
> I told him that these filthy things and smells were what he felt he had made me do, and that he felt he had compelled me to defecate them out, including the sight he had put into me.
>
> The patient jerked convulsively and I saw him cautiously scanning what seemed be the air around him. I accordingly said that he felt surrounded by bad and smelly bits of himself including his eyes which he felt he had expelled from his anus. He replied: "I can't see". I then told him he felt he had lost his sight and his ability to talk to his mother, or to me, when he had got rid of these abilities so as to avoid pain.
>
> (Bion, 1957/2018, n.p.)

We could continue with the description of the session in question, but it would not lead us to anything very different from what can be observed in the section above. In other words, regardless of Bion's justifications for his interpretations – in function of material previously supplied by the patient – we can clearly see that they are set in a particular conception of the psyche and psychotic defence mechanisms. This is, therefore, about interpretations that clearly describe projective and introjective projections made by the patient. They are: the patient's sight, evacuated into the analyst's body; followed by the fantasy of its defecation through the analyst's anus; that same sight, newly re-introjected due to the fear of blindness and, again, evacuated in fantasy through the patient's anus in order to avoid the pain produced by seeing

things; and all this leading to the loss of sight and the capacity to communicate with each other.

When Bion exposed the paper which contains the description of this session to the British Psycho-Analytic Society (in 1955), Winnicott was present
and, afterwards, wrote a letter to Bion, in which he talked about his comprehension of the patient's speech. He wrote:

> [...] if a patient of mine lay on the couch moving to and fro in the way
> your patient did and then said: "I ought to have telephoned my mother" I
> would know that he was talking about communication and his incapac-
> ity for making communication. Should it interest you to know, I will say
> what I would have interpreted: I would have said: "A mother properly
> oriented to her baby would know from your movements what you need.
> There would be a communication because of this knowledge which be-
> longs to her devotion and she would do something which would show
> that the communication had taken place. I am not sensitive enough or
> orientated in that way to be able to act well enough and therefore I in this
> present analytic situation fall into the category of the mother who failed to
> make communication possible. In the present relationship therefore there
> is given a sample of the original failure from the environment which con-
> tributed to your difficulty of communication. Of course you could always
> cry and so draw attention to need. In the same way you could telephone
> your mother and get a reply but this represents a failure of the more subtle
> communication which is the only basis for communication that does not
> violate the fact of the essential isolation of each individual".
>
> (Winnicott, 1987/1999, p. 91)

This comprehension shows a completely different approach to the material
from the session: Winnicott interprets the necessity of the patient to telephone
his mother as a reaction to the failure of his mother to receive his more subtle
communication in infancy, duplicated in that session through transference
(then the analyst occupying the place of the mother who fails). This means to
valorise the importance of the environment failure in the production of the
symptom of the patient's difficulty of communication.[6]

The Bionian interpretation, however, is more focused in the patient's defence
mechanisms over the session than in transference (and its origin in past time) and
its focus becomes even clearer with the second example we will be examining.

Let us now reproduce another session fragment described in "Notes on
the Theory of Schizophrenia" (1953), from the book *Second Thoughts* — a
session from the 1950s, revisited years later. This quotation has already been
used in Chapter 4 of this book, yet we consider it essential to return to it here,
given its theoretical and clinical relevance to the discussion that follows. The
author warns that the patient in question was a schizophrenic who had been
in analysis for five years, and that the account of the session is condensed

(leaving out several repetitive formulations), which may give an impression of a certain "baldness" in the interpretations:

Patient: I picked a tiny piece of skin from my face and feel quite empty.
Analyst: The tiny piece of skin is your penis, which you have torn out, and all your insides have come with it.
Patient: I do not understand…penis…only syllables.
Analyst: You have split my word "penis" into syllables and it now has no meaning.
Patient: I don't know what it means, but I want to say, "If I can't spell I cannot think".
Analyst: The syllables have now been split into letters; you cannot spell – that is to say you cannot put the letters together again to make words. So now you cannot think.

(Bion, 1953/2018, n.p.)

The section above is short, but sufficient for the purposes of this paper. We can take it that, very much despite this description being condensed and filtered of repetitions and, therefore, closer to a fictional construct than the factual reality, it is no less revealing of the *principles* of the Bionian technique (also because it corroborates what we could observe from the previous session). Moving on, then, to this second section.

The first important thing to state is that the fundamental clinical tool in the analysis of schizophrenia continues to be *interpretation*, which is very understandable, since according to Bion himself, this is about returning back to the patient – but transformed into alpha elements – the products of the splitting and evacuation processes he carried out, trying to destroy any possible form of contact with reality, maintaining the perceptive and mental data under the unknowable form of beta elements.[7] This means a form of *resistance* to the knowledge that could be provided by the analysis.

The interpretations work because, there, they are a form of *reverie*, of digestion and transmutation of the diffuse products of these operations, whose mental component needs to be cleansed. The analyst thus carries out a kind of non-violent, projective contra-identification (according to Bion), which helps the patient re-introject what was evacuated, but in a new form: one digested and capable of gradually providing him with the construction of a mental apparatus.

It should also be noted that, in the section of the session under examination – even if we include all the pauses and repetitions Bion excluded from the summarised report – the interpretations are used without much parsimony, in the best of Kleinian tradition.

However, more toward the end of his psychoanalytic trajectory, Bion would change this analytic way of operating, becoming more skeptical and, consequently, sparser in the interpretations given to psychotic patients.

In his last book, *Cogitations* (1992)[8] there is an undated text, called "The Attack on the Analyst's α-Function" (Bion, undated/1992, pp. 216–221), which contains descriptions of sessions with a patient in whom the psychotic part of his personality dominates. One can see how, in the sessions, Bion remains practically silent, only listening.[9] In the middle of relating one of the sessions, he writes, "[...] But I decide to wait" (Bion, undated/1992, p. 218). At the end of the description of another session, he comments: "There are many interpretations I could give, and have given in the past. They are apparently quite ineffectual [...]" (Bion, undated/1992, p. 219).

Here, one can notice a certain disenchantment Bion has regarding the efficacy of this analytical tool that he tried so hard to elaborate and refine in the treatment of patients who, according to his report, are truly bottomless pits, who swallow the interpretations or throw them back at the analyst without leaving, at the end, any trace of them. It is not by chance that he calls this section of the text, which contains the descriptions of the sessions, "the analyst's Odyssey", meaning, perhaps, that this is a kind of analytical voyage that meanders almost aimlessly and finds it very difficult to reach solid ground.

Nevertheless, despite the weight of all the pros and cons and all the difficulties encountered, Bion never abandoned interpretation as the go-to clinical tool in the treatment of psychotics. And this, in my opinion, is for a simple reason: if the basic analytical function is defined, for him, as *reverie*; that is, if it is necessary to distil a mental meaning from the purely sensuous forms (or from the splittings and evacuations) and this meaning has to be communicated to the patient who is lying down, denied a line of sight, it has to happen through language and, therefore, a verbal communication is needed, an *interpretation*.[10]

The main question, then, may be *how* and *when* to interpret, especially when the psychotic parts of the patient's personality are dominating. But the use of the concept of *selected fact* (borrowed from the philosophy of mathematics, from Jules-Henri Poincaré) will, then, make it possible to enlighten the precise moment when to interpret. The best definition of selected fact comes from Poincaré:

> If a new result is to have any value, it must unite elements long since known, but till then scattered and seemingly foreign to each other, and suddenly introduce order where the appearance of disorder reigned. Then it enables us to see at a glance each of these elements in the place it occupies in the whole.
>
> (Quoted in Sandler, 2005, pp. 725–726)

So, the analyst will wait for the appearance of a selected fact, along the session, in order to captivate, at a glance, the whole meaning of what is happening, and then interpret it.

In the last period of his analytic work, Bion advises that the analyst must listen to the patient with an *empty mind* (like that recommended by Zen-Buddhism), with no *wishes*, no *memory* and no *comprehension* (Almeida, 2025). He must function predominantly by intuition, in intimate resonance with the patient, in order to "become O", the Ultimate Reality that composes the patient's experience throughout the session (Grotstein, 2000, pp. 282–283).[11]

Holding and Schizophrenia

Holding is a word that, in Winnicottian psychoanalysis, condenses several meanings (see Almeida and Vieira, 2023). In Winnicott's own words:

> Holding:
>   Protects from physiological insult.
>   Takes account of the infant's skin sensitivity – touch, temperature, auditory sensitivity, visual sensitivity, sensitivity to falling (action of gravity) and of the infant's lack of knowledge of the existence of anything other than the self.
>   I include the whole routine of care throughout the day and night, and it is not the same with any two infants because it is part of the infant, and no two infants are alike.
>   Also it follows the minute day-to-day changes belonging to the infant's growth and development, both physical and psychological.
> (Winnicott, 1960/1990, p. 49)

Perhaps the most complete way of defining *holding* is by describing the mother as the baby's auxiliary ego, employed to sustain it in time and space for a long period over which the baby lives merged with its environment, having a totally evanescent and fleeting identity, while depending upon this maternal care as a way of maintaining at least a minimum of *going-on-being*. The mother as a connecting link, the maintenance and sustaining of a set of fragmentary and disperse experiences (Almeida and Naffah Neto, 2021).

Winnicott also understands that the instinctive physiological sensations that run through the baby and drive it to the vital activities need elaboration to attain a psychic condition and become able to be gradually appropriated by the *self* (including, here, the aggressive/destructive impulses and experiences of pleasure/displeasure that will come to form the child sexuality). However, unlike Bion, Winnicott believes the baby is, *on its own*, able to carry out this function since birth, initially in a very rudimentary manner, but in ever increasingly complex ways over time. It is about the *imaginative elaboration of body functioning*. I quote Winnicott:

> [...] I think we must reckon that there is being from the first a crude form of what later we call the imagination. This enables us to say that the infant takes in with the hands and with the sensitive skin of the face as well as with the mouth. The *imaginative* feeding experience is much wider than the purely physical experience. The *total* experience of feeding can quickly involve a rich relationship to the mother's breast, or to the mother as gradually perceived, and what the baby does with

the hands and eyes widens the scope of the feeding act. This which is normal is made more plain when we see an infant's feed being managed in a mechanical way. Such a feed, far from being an enriching experience for the infant, interrupts the infant's sense of going on being. I don't know quite how else to put it. There has been a reflex activity and no personal experience. [...] When an infant sucks bits of clothing, of the eiderdown or a dummy, this represents a spillover of the imagination, such as it is, imagination stimulated by the central exciting function which is feeding.

(Winnicott, 1956/2017, pp. 116–117, original emphasis)

In this concept, the entire child psyche forms itself through this process of imaginative elaboration, wholly supported on body functioning, coming to constitute, later, a psyche-somatic unit.[12] At first, the imaginative elaboration of the functioning of feeding creates, under normal conditions, what Winnicott called the young infant's *illusion of omnipotence*. When there is a *good enough mother*, one able to make the breast appear, as if by magic, when faced with the infant's instinctive urgency, there is the illusion that the infant created the object in the moment it was needed. This, here, is the *subjective object*.

The psychic functions of incorporation, evacuation, introjection, and projection are also born, further on, anchored to physiological functions and having ingestion and defecation as their models; that dynamic follows, then the pattern of functioning of the physiological model.[13]

However, the constantly working process of imaginative elaboration – the producer of the psyche – on the part of the baby necessitates a *holding* by the mother as a *sine qua non* condition, as it is thanks to this maternal sustainment that these experiences can gain a minimum of integration and coherence over a period in which the baby is not integrated (or even minimally integrated).

Along this line of thought, the psychotic child would be one who has suffered severe environmental *holding* failures during the period of absolute (or relative) dependence or who has formed, over the course of those periods, a precarious personality structure that, during the stage just before the Oedipus complex,[14] collapsed when faced with its greatest needs. In Winnicott's words:

The term *psychosis* is used to imply either that as an infant the individual was not able to reach the degree of personal health which makes sense of the concept of Oedipus complex, or, alternatively that the organization of the personality had weaknesses which became revealed when the maximal strain of the Oedipus complex had to be borne. It will be seen that there is a very thin line between the second type of psychosis and psycho-neurosis [...].

(Winnicott, 1959/1990, p. 131)

The difference, to Winnicott, between borderline and schizophrenic patients designates, above all, in my opinion, a difference of state: *latent* or *manifest*. Borderline disease can well designate this second type of psychosis, as described here, which is closer to psychoneurosis (but which, during crises, exhibits psychotic symptoms)[15] or rather a *latent schizophrenia*, in which the false self has been functioning satisfactorily, but can enter into a psychotic episode during its collapses. As I have dedicated myself quite frequently to this issue in previous papers, I will only summarise it briefly, here.

The split "false self" constitutes one of the schizophrenic's defences and is formed to protect the infant's spontaneous core from the lack of environmental care. It is formed through mimicking environmental features and functions as a protective barrier that isolates the infant's real self until better environmental conditions arise, when he can continue with his development. In these conditions, the real self remains in a fragmented state and the environmental adaptations are all ensured by the false self. When it fails and disintegrates, the individual can suffer a collapse, seeing as, in these conditions, the fragmented real self does not have the tools to deal with the environmental pressures. Thus, other kinds of schizophrenic defences can arise, such as active disintegration, a process in which the primordial splits of the psyche are multiplied and rearranged in order to protect the true self from environmental/instinctual intrusions. This occurs because, without the false self protecting it, the psyche is left completely at the mercy of such intrusions.[16]

Through this, we see that, for Winnicott, on the contrary to Bion, the innate, constitutional components present in the constitution of schizophrenia, although they are not discarded, are very far from occupying the same degree of importance. Evidently, they constitute the genetic baggage that will make one infant different to another: more or less voracious, more or less calm, more or less demanding when being cared for, etc. But in the final instance, their mental health will depend on the quality of the maternal *holding*.

Winnicottian Clinical Practice for Schizophrenia

Winnicott always postulated that, in the analysis of schizophrenics (as well as with borderline pathologies), the fundamental tool is the creation of a therapeutic environment able to build trust in the patient and provide the sustainment for a process of regression to the dependence stages, in which the environmental failures occurred. That is, with a more historical and diachronic concept of the patient – in comparison to that of Bion, which is more structural and synchronic – Winnicott believes that regression in a therapeutic setting is a second chance for, when supplied with more propitious environmental conditions, the patient to be able to revisit situations lived through that gave rise to trauma and repair them through transferential *holding*. In other words, the emphasis, there, falls upon *holding* as a basic clinical tool for repair in these situations of regression to the stages of dependence.

Bion's rationale was completely different. Regarding regression, in 1976, during a conference in Los Angeles, he said the following:

> We talk about "getting back" to childhood or infancy. It is a useful phrase, but I think it is meaningless. [...] Do you remember when you were at the breast? No, it's forgotten or got rid of. But having been forgotten these things persist in some archaic way in one's mind, so that they still continue to operate, to make themselves felt...Since they operate in this archaic way they go on affecting one's work.
>
> (Bion, 1994/2000, p. 244)

This means that, in this text, Bion is saying he believes in repression and the psychic effects of what is repressed, but does not believe in regression. In another text, however, he is less emphatic. He comments:

> Winnicott says patients need to regress: Melanie Klein says they *must not*: I say they are regressed, and the regression should be observed and interpreted by the analyst without any need to compel the patient to become totally regressed before he can make the analyst observe and interpret the regression.
>
> (Bion, 1960/1992, p. 166).

However, what does it mean when he says that patients "are regressed"? In my opinion, it is somewhat analogous to postulating the existence of childlike parts of the personality that have acted *since the beginning* on the psychic dynamic, creating a permanent state of "regression", but which has nothing to do with returning to the stages of dependence. And, here, once again, Bion reaffirms the clinical tool that he never lets go of, even in cases of "regressed patients", namely: *interpretation*.

Winnicott thought differently (Vieira, 2025). For him, regression signified an experiential return to the stages of dependence and, while patients were in that regressed state, believed that interpretations were unnecessary.[17] But, to better understand his clinical posture, let us revisit the case of Margaret Little, one of the interesting analyses he worked with, involving *schizoid*[18] patients.

Let us say that Winnicott took a while to realise his patient had schizophrenic defences. In the first session, faced with Little's withdrawal, he interpreted this as a resistance that would be made for neurotic patients: "I don't know, but I have the feeling that you are shutting me out for some reason [...]" (cf. Little, 1990, p. 42). But Little did not let him fool himself for long; in the following sessions, feeling she was not being understood, she smashed a vase of white lilacs from the waiting room, trampling them underfoot. Winnicott, who was very fond of the vase, must have gotten very angry; perhaps to protect the patient from his anger, he withdrew, returning only at the end of the session; when he did come back, however, he knew the situation. So, what did he do?

He first increased the duration of the sessions to an hour and a half; but why? To *sustain* Little's need for schizoid withdrawal and provide more time so that she could, feeling more relaxed, leave her psychic refuge and enter into a relationship with him.

And, what did Winnicott do in the moments of pure terror when Little entered into utter despair and fear of annihilation? He would hold her hands for a long while, sometimes falling asleep from exhaustion. What was happening there? Again, *holding*; more specifically, *physical holding*.

The interpretations Winnicott made were sometimes shared statements of the type: "Your mother is unpredictable, chaotic, and she organizes chaos around her (Little, 1990, p. 49), or temporal interpretations, capable of helping the patient discriminate the present from the past; for example, when he said, during a period of intense fear of annihilation – that she had been *psychically* annihilated, but had *physically* survived and was, therefore, reliving the past experience.

But we might ask, is that not *reverie*? Here, is Winnicott not revisiting the patient's diffuse somatic experience, naming it and giving a temporality and, thus, a mental condition?

We can answer emphatically in the negative as this is not about any kind of projective identification, evacuated over the figure of the analyst.[19] It is about a past traumatic experience that could be relived by Little, in the present, thanks to the *holding* offered by the analyst over the course of the process. He uses interpretation to help her discriminate the tenses, to become conscious of the fact that what she is feeling in that moment *had already happened in the past* (and, therefore, is not happening in the present); it is only being relived through a form of reminiscing.

Little's final recovery from psychosis happened over a period of hospitalisation, during which Winnicott was on vacation, but controlling the hospital environment from afar in order to provide the maximum amount of freedom while also ensuring a protective limit was in place. During this time, Little was able to regress to her dependence stages, reliving fundamental experiences and being reborn, cured. This period is described in detail in the author's book (Little, 1990) and is the reason I choose not to extend her account, here.

By Way of Conclusion

We could, perhaps and after all this journey, conclude that *reverie* and *holding* constitute very dissimilar concepts, involving equally diverse clinical practices.

It is not proper to compare or assess their value and efficacy, here, with both sides always finding their adepts and defenders.

However, when someone says that they work with both *holding* and *reverie* in their clinical practice – without revisiting and re-contextualising these concepts into a new form of theoretical elaboration – it is possible to conclude that this is, if not impossible, at least silly; similar to bringing together an aria from Italian opera with one from German opera without any musical context that gives them *meaning*.

I think that some forms of theoretical eclecticism, of the kind described above, simply destroy the rigour and singularity of the concepts, launching them into the realm of common sense, where they come to mean almost nothing. Their potency, as a theoretical tool, comes from the internal connections to the theories that they are a part of. Ripped from their habitat, they are like flowers that soon dry up and wither away.

Notes

1 A first version of this article was published (in the Portuguese language) in *Revista Brasileira de Psicanálise, 45*(3), 2011, 119–131 and, then (also in the Portuguese language) as a chapter of the book: Naffah Neto, A. (2023). *Veredas Psicanalíticas: à sombra de Winnicott*. São Paulo: Blucher. That version was translated into the English language, revised and somewhat modified (enlarged) for the present publication.

2 An analysis to discriminate the differences of these concepts has already been carried out by other authors, among them Ogden, in a very interesting paper (Ogden, 2004). However, unlike the proposal of this present paper, he does not use the analysis of schizophrenics (by both authors) as a privileged focus of investigation, which colours his discoveries in a slightly different light that is unveiled by the present paper.

3 Bion did not differentiate between the concepts of *mind* (*mental*) and *personality* (and, even *thought,* when he wanted to talk about the mind in what he considered its most important function). Winnicott, however, used *psyche* and *mind* as different terms, with the latter only applicable to a specialised part of the psychic functions: the *intellectual* ones.

4 Ogden seeks to articulate the notion of *reverie* with Bion's concept of container-contained, unfolding from it different forms of dreaming as a basic process of psychic elaboration:

> Thus, basic to Bion's thinking is the idea that dreaming is the primary form in which we do unconscious psychological work with our lived experience. This perspective, as will be seen, is integral to the concept of the container-contained. I will begin the discussion of that idea by tentatively defining the container and the contained. The 'container' is not a thing, but a process. It is the capacity for the unconscious psychological work of dreaming, operating in concert with the capacity for preconscious dreamlike thinking (reverie), and the capacity for more fully conscious secondary-process thinking. [..] The 'contained', like the container, is not a static thing, but a living process that in health is continuously expanding and changing. The term refers to thoughts (in the broadest sense of the word) and feelings that are in the process of being derived from one's lived emotional experience.
>
> (Ogden, 2004, p. 1356)

However, for these different modalities of dreaming to be possible, and for the articulations between them to form within the adult mind, it is necessary that the "the most elemental of thoughts constituting the contained" (Ogden, 2004, p. 1356), the β-elements, which are, so to speak, "the souls of thought" (Ogden, 2004, p. 1356), be transformed into α-elements. For this to happen, the newborn requires the maternal container to be fully developed and functioning.

5 However, to be able to reproduce the section of the session in question, I had to skip the parts of the text in which Bion carries out long descriptions of the patient's prior process, trying to inform the reader what leads to such interpretations. Had I not done so, it would have been necessary to reproduce entire pages from the paper, which would shift the focus from the objectives of this paper. To readers who wish to access the complete version, I would therefore recommend the reading of the paper quoted from, in its entirety.

6 It is important to note that Winnicott could have given that interpretation only because Bion's patient was not in deep regression, at that moment of the process. I will discuss this theme later on.

7 We could say that, starting with "O" (reality in itself, intangible and which, according to Bion, we can only know through its transformations), the schizophrenic tends to make *projective transformations* and *transformations into hallucinosis*. This latter, in addition to producing an evacuative movement, generates figures who in the imagination fill the lack of object and avoid psychic pain. A detailed description of these processes is given by Bion in *Transformations* (1965), a book that is difficult to read, but is worthwhile. In this regard, I recommend reading Almeida (2025), in which the author develops this Bionian notion through the discussion of a clinical case.

8 *Cogitations* is a posthumous work by Wilfred Bion, published only after his death, in 1992, with organisation and introduction by his wife, Francesca Bion. The manuscript, however, had been written during the 1950s and 1960s, a period of intense theoretical and clinical elaboration by the author, who chose not to publish it during his lifetime. The text brings together personal notes, loose reflections, aphorisms, clinical fragments, and philosophical ideas – many of which anticipate or converse with concepts later developed in his published works, such as *Transformations* (1965) and *Attention and Interpretation* (1970). The publication of *Cogitations* places the reader within a more intimate and less systematised dimension of Bion's thinking, revealing the impasses, uncertainties, and creative flashes that traversed his path as both analyst and thinker. It is, therefore, a valuable body of material not only for its theoretical content, but for the way it offers access to the living process of thought-construction – a mode of writing that closely resembles what Bion himself would later describe as the experience of *O*: the unspeakable, the formless, the raw real before it is symbolised.

9 I decided against reproducing the description of the sessions due to space constraints, as they are very detailed and this would lead to the need to include long quotes, diverting us from our objectives.

10 I will return to this question later, when discussing the difference between Bion and Winnicott as regards the use (or non-use) of *regression* in analysis, as a therapeutic tool in cases of patients with psychoses. Moreover, the notion of regression was extensively developed and discussed by the authors Alexandre and Filipe in Chapter 7 of this book.

11 "The primary but unknowable reality called O is represented by being transformed or processed in someone's mind. […] There could be many different transformations of the same O. The analyst at the commencement of a session is faced with O, with which he tries to get in touch by free-floating attention and by keeping his mind artificially blinded to his expectations so as to leave himself as open as possible to this new experience. In Bion's terms, he keeps his mind, his preconceptions, as unsaturated with premature meaning as possible, so as to be receptive to the selected fact. This in turn is bound by a name and, with further time, will gradually accrue meaning from the events in the session. These transformations – poetic, artistic, scientific, psycho-analytic – are all constructions of the mind expressed in particular ways" (Symington and Symington, 2002, p. 107).

12 In this sense, too, there is a visible difference between Winnicott and Bion. While Winnicott thinks of the body and psyche as *equally* necessary sources of vital functions, different from one another, but forming a psyche-somatic unit, Bion tends to overvalue abstract mental functioning, placing *thinking* as a more developed psychic ability – and more hierarchically important – while maintaining the body as a kind of inferior substrate, the more basic and primordial part of the system of transformations.

13 Winnicott, in *Human Nature*, his last, unfinished book (Winnicott, 1988, pp. 75–77, 80–81) ends up distinguishing the concepts of *incorporation* and *evacuation* from *introjection* and *projection*. The former designate psychic processes that take place from the beginning, as products of imaginative elaboration: in this sense, the infant incorporates the mother's care and evacuates the parts that are excessive, unnecessary to its psychic growth. The latter (introjection and projection) imply a differentiation by the infant between the interior and exterior and are laden with a more mental and defensive connotation when the environment fails. For example, the infant can produce and introject an idealised mother to tackle a real mother who is absent or invasive.

14 For an in-depth discussion of the Oedipus complex in Winnicottian theory, see Almeida and Naffah Neto (2022).

15 Winnicott says: "By the term 'a borderline case' I mean the kind of case in which the core of the patient's disturbance is psychotic, but the patient has enough psycho-neurotic organization always to be able to present psycho-neurotic and psycho-somatic disorder when the central psychotic anxiety threatens to break through in crude form" (Winnicott, 1997/1968, pp. 219–220). On this specific topic, see Almeida, Vieira, and Naffah Neto, 2025.

16 For a deeper look at this issue, see Naffah Neto, 2007 and 2011.

17 I have already discussed Winnicott's position in detail, in a previous paper (Naffah Neto, 2010a). In brief, it could be said that, when regressed to the stages of dependence, patients enter into a *psychosis of transference*, in which the dual and simultaneous position of the analyst as a subjective object and objective object, which is characteristic of *neurosis of transference*, disappears. In psychosis of transference the analyst is seen *only* as a subjective object. Here, the dual past/ present inscription also disappears: Winnicott thinks that, on these occasions, the patient *returns* to the past and the analyst effectively *becomes* his mother, instead of simply *representing* her. In this condition, interpretation has no discriminatory function at all, as object and time become unambiguous, losing all symbolic polyvalence.

18 The schizoid pathology designates, for the meaning used here, one of the forms of borderline pathology, where this latter is understood in a broad sense, described in footnote 15 of the present chapter.

19 In fact, for Winnicott, the vast majority of psychotics are unable to clearly distinguish between the internal and external world in order to be able to project, introject and make projective identifications, which are complex and sophisticated mechanisms characteristic of someone who already possesses an inside and an outside. Thus, in psychoses, in the moments the false self fails and disintegrates, we must talk about *fused and chaotic states*. And even in those schizophrenias in which it seems impossible to deny the existence of projective mechanisms, such as, in paranoid schizophrenia, for example, that is not really what it is about. In this case, the dynamic is formed by aggressive/destructive drives that have not been appropriated by the self (due to *holding* deficiencies) and remain exterior to the patient, acting like barbarous hordes, wandering around all over the place, without their own territory. Therefore, at times they are experienced as foreign powers that threaten the integrity of the self, which, to protect itself has to use *active disintegration* (multiplying its splits). The following moment, these same

drives can invade and possess the self, producing aggressive/destructive acts that are justified as a form of self-defence. That is, the drives that threaten are the same ones that defend, but this circulation from one position to the other is not a projection or introjection (or a projective identification) made by the self. The self finds itself fragmented and unprotected, functioning as a pawn in the hands of foreign powers. In its most active moments, it resembles a dog chasing its own tail.

References

Almeida, A. P. (2025). O obsceno e a homossexualidade: considerações a partir da psicanálise ontológica [The Obscene and Homosexuality: Considerations from an Ontological Psychoanalytic Perspective]. *Ide*, *47*(79): 57–70. https://doi.org/10.5935/0101-3106.v47n79.07

Almeida, A. P., & Naffah Neto, A. (2021). A teoria do desenvolvimento maturacional de Winnicott: novas perspectivas para a educação [Winnicott's Theory of Maturational Development: New Perspectives for Education]. *Revista Latinoamericana de Psicopatologia Fundamental*, *24*(3): 517–536. https://doi.org/10.1590/1415-4714.2021v24n3p517-3

Almeida, A. P., and Naffah Neto, A. (2022). O estágio da concernência e a elaboração do complexo de Édipo: Revisitando Winnicott e o caso Piggle [The Stage of Concern and the Elaboration of the Oedipus Complex: Revisiting Winnicott and the Piggle Case]. *Psicologia em Revista*, *31*(1): 27–50. https://doi.org/10.5752/P.1678-9563.2022v31n1p27

Almeida, A. P., and Vieira, F. P. (2023). O holding como uma possibilidade do vir a ser escritor: um diálogo entre Kapus e Rilke [The Holding as a Possibility of Becoming a Writer: A Dialogue between Kapuściński and Rilke]. In S. Gomes (Org.), *A atualidade do pensamento de D. W. Winnicott*, pp. 413–434. Rio de Janeiro: INM Editora.

Almeida, A. P., Naffah Neto, A., and Vieira, F. P. (2025). *A clínica winnicottiana: os casos difíceis* [*The Winnicottian Clinic: The Difficult Cases*]. São Paulo: Blucher.

Bion, W. R. (1992). Analytic Technique. In W. R. Bion, *Cogitations*, p. 166. London: Karnac. (Original work written in 1960)

Bion, W. R. (1992). The Attack on the Analyst's α-Function. In W. R. Bion, *Cogitations*, pp. 216–221. London: Karnac. (Original work undated)

Bion, W. R. (2000). *Clinical Seminars and Other Works*. London: Karnac Books. (Original work published in 1994)

Bion, W. R. (2018). Notes on the Theory of Schizophrenia. In W. R. Bion, *Second Thoughts*. London: Routledge. E-book. (Original work published in 1953)

Bion, W. R. (2018). Differentiation of the Psychotic from the Non-psychotic Personalities. In W. R. Bion, *Second Thoughts*. London: Routledge. E-book. (Original work published in 1957)

Bion, W. R. (2018). *Attention and Interpretation*. London: Routledge. E-book. (Original work published in 1970)

Bion, W. R. (2020). *Transformations*. London: Routledge. E-book. (Original work published in 1965)

Bion, W. R. (2023). *Learning from Experience*. London: Routledge. E-book. (Original work published in 1962)

Grotstein, J. S. (2000). Bion's Transformations in O. In J. S. Grotstein, *Who Is the Dreamer, Who Dreams the Dream?*, pp. 281–304. London: The Analytic Press.

Little, M. (1990). *Psychotic Anxieties and Containment – A Personal Record of an Analysis with Winnicott*. London: Jason Aronson Inc.

Naffah Neto, A. (2007). A problemática do falso *self* em pacientes de tipo *borderline* – revisitando Winnicott [The Problem of the False Self in Borderline Patients – Revisiting Winnicott]. *Revista Brasileira de Psicanálise*, *41*(4): 77–88.

Naffah Neto, A. (2008). O caso Margaret Little: Winnicott e as bordas da Psicanálise [Margaret Little's Case and the Borders of Psychoanalysis], *Jornal de Psicanálise, 41(75)*: 107–121.

Naffah Neto, A. (2010a). As funções da interpretação em diferentes modalidades transferenciais: as contribuições de D. W. Winnicott [The Functions of Interpretation in Different Modalities of Transference: Winnicott's Contributions], *Jornal de Psicanálise, 43(78)*: 79–90.

Naffah Neto, A. (2010b). Falso self e patologia borderline no pensamento de Winnicott: antecedentes históricos e desenvolvimentos subsequentes [False Self and Borderline Pathology: Historical Antecedents and Following Developments]. *Revista Natureza Humana, 12(2)*: 1–18.

Ogden, T. H. (2004). On Holding and Containing, Being and Dreaming. *International Journal of Psychoanalysis, 85*: 1349–1364.

Sandler, P. C. (2005). *The Language of Bion – A Dictionary of Concepts.* London: Karnac.

Symington, J., and Symington, N. (2002). *The Clinical Thinking of Wilfred Bion.* London: Routledge.

Vieira, F. P. (2025). *A interpretação psicanalítica: revisitando Klein e Winnicott* [*Psychoanalytic Interpretation: Revisiting Klein and Winnicott*]. São Paulo: Blucher.

Winnicott, D. W. (1988). *Human Nature.* London: Free Association Books.

Winnicott, D. W. (1990). Classification: Is There a Psycho-analytical Contribution to Psychiatric Classification? In D. W. Winnicott, *The Maturational Processes and the Facilitating Environment,* pp. 124–139. London: Karnac. (Original work published in 1959)

Winnicott, D. W. (1990). The Theory of the Parent-Infant Relationship. In D. W. Winnicott, *The Maturational Processes and the Facilitating Environment,* pp. 37–55. London: Karnac. (Original work published in 1960)

Winnicott, D. W. (1997). The Use of an Object and Relating through Identifications. In D. W. Winnicott, *Psycho-analytic Explorations,* pp. 218–227. Cambridge/ Massachusetts: Harvard University Press. (Original work published in 1968)

Winnicott, D. W. (1999). *The Spontaneous Gesture – Selected Letters of D. W. Winnicott.* (Original work published in 1987)

Winnicott, D. W. (2017). What Do We Know About Babies Who Suck Cloths? In D. W. Winnicott, *The Collected Works of D. W. Winnicott (Vol. 5),* pp. 115–118. Oxford: Oxford University Press. (Original work published in 1956)

7 Regression in Psychoanalysis

Contrasts Between Klein and Winnicott

*Alexandre Patricio de Almeida
and Filipe Pereira Vieira*

A Few Introductory Words

One of the most significant differences between the Kleinian and Winnicottian schools is, undoubtedly, the use of *regression* in the analytic process. To Klein, there is no sense in a patient regressing since, according to her theory, regression would symbolise a return to the *paranoid-schizoid position* – which, to her, represents an even more pronounced stage of psychic suffering. One of the major achievements of the Kleinian psychoanalytic treatment is the attainment and working through of the *depressive position*, which enables the individual to take responsibility for their instincts and to deal with ambivalence, indicating a certain degree of psychic maturity.

Such a movement between positions, however, requires significant psychic work, as it implies a new perception of reality in contrast to the previous position. This transformation, in turn, involves the integration of painful aspects of experience, promoting a more complex and balanced understanding of the self and the other – what Klein referred to as *whole object relations*. It is this confrontation that enables the patient to break free from the cycle of splitting, thereby achieving a greater capacity for reparation and symbolisation.

For Winnicott, however, regression represents an opportunity to recover a line of development that was *interrupted* at some stage in life due to the impact of severe environmental failures. Through such a return the individual may relive a specific traumatic event – but this time, supported by the presence of the analyst within a safe and reliable environment.

To begin this exploration, we shall now outline the Kleinian conception of psychic maturation, highlighting the reasons why, according to the author, regression cannot be regarded as something positive within the analytic treatment.

Kleinian Psychic Development and the Notion of Regression

Klein developed much of her theory based on the analysis of very young children. Through observation she perceived that from the very beginning of life, our psyche is permeated by sadistic and voracious impulses. To her, the baby is already marked by this destructive force that Freud (1920/1981) referred to

DOI: 10.4324/9781003642503-8

as the *death instinct*,[1] leading the infant to perceive the external world as a threat to its existence. In her text "On the Theory of Anxiety and Guilt", Klein (1948/2011) asserts: "Thus in my view the danger arising from the inner working of the death instinct is the first cause of anxiety" (n.p.).

In this sense, there exists the notion that "The vital need to deal with anxiety forces the early ego to develop fundamental mechanisms and defences" (Klein, 1946/2011, n.p.). Among these defences, the most important and fundamental is *splitting*. Through this mechanism, the baby preserves its ego by projecting outward the overwhelming and unsymbolised range of emotions. The truth is: "The helpless little baby wishes, above all, to return to the comfort of the maternal womb; therefore, its fragile ego cannot withstand the tension caused by the death instinct, which, to Klein, *is potentially destructive*" (Almeida, 2022, p. 145, emphasis added). This mode of early functioning is what our author termed the *paranoid-schizoid position*.

Due to frequent sensations of discomfort – such as hunger, pain, tiredness, excessive stimulation, and so on – caused by contact with the environment, the newborn constantly feels persecuted by hostile forces. This is a direct result of ego-splitting and, consequently, of the fragments that are projected onto the external world as a form of primary defence.

Now, if the infant's first defence is the splitting of the ego, which projects parts of itself outward, we are faced with an imbalance, as pointed out by Almeida (2022):

> On the other hand, as the saying goes, we are left with "double standards". In other words, if the ego splits and is itself shattered by projecting its annihilating anxieties outward, the external object will also become split as a result of these painful projections. In this way, the baby perceives the mother who nurtures and soothes as a *good object*, to the extent that the intensity of its projections diminishes – what the author [Klein] referred to as the *good breast*. Simultaneously, when the projections occur in an overwhelming and chaotic manner, the mother is felt to be *bad*, even if she is, in fact, providing care for the baby – here, we encounter the *bad breast*.
>
> (p. 145, bracket and emphasis added)

Thus, *splitting*, to Klein, is a powerful defence mechanism of our psychic life. The author attributes to it an importance comparable to that of *repression* in Freud's thinking (Klein, 1946/2011). At the same time, it is important to recall that splitting is a crucial resource employed by the still immature psyche, given that the baby is *unable* to cope with the ambivalence of feelings – they lack the necessary maturity to perceive that they both "love and hate" the same object (the maternal figure). On this point, Thomas Ogden (2017) offers an interesting analogy:

> Although Klein does not employ ethological analogies, I would draw a comparison between splitting and the unlearned response of a chick

when perceiving the pattern of a falcon's wings. The chick's reaction is to flee rather than attack the falcon (except when cornered) – that is, to separate itself from danger. [...] Each of the primitive psychological defences can be seen as a construction rooted in the mode of dealing with danger observed in splitting – namely, built upon the biologically determined effort to generate safety by creating distance between the threatening and the threatened.

(pp. 53–54, emphasis added)

Ego splitting tends to be the result of intense anxiety, which is related, among other factors, to a frustrated need for control. The newborn is unable to *organise* this new reality – experienced by them as threatening. What they can do, within this split mode of functioning, is simply *react*. In this regard, Klein (1946/2011) points out: "The destructive impulse is partly projected outwards (deflection of the death instinct) and, I think, attaches itself to the first external object, the mother's breast" (n.p.).

A significant aspect of the Kleinian approach is the emphasis placed on the *constitutive factor*. This does not mean, however, that the author disregards the role of the environment in emotional development. In other words, to Klein (1946/2011) the impact of innate instinctual forces carries greater weight in the formation of the self. Let us now examine her ideas:

We are, I think, justified in assuming that some of the functions which we know from the later ego *are there at the beginning*. Prominent amongst these functions is that of dealing with anxiety. I hold that anxiety arises from the operation of the death instinct within the organism, is felt as fear of annihilation (death) and takes the form of fear of persecution. The fear of the destructive impulse seems to attach itself at once to an object – or rather it is experienced as the fear of an uncontrollable overpowering object.

(Klein, 1946/2011, n.p., emphasis added)

Given the overwhelming power of death instinct, the baby inevitably begins to perceive the caregiving figure as something persecutory. Due to immaturity and the absence of a developed symbolic capacity, the infant projects their own internal anxieties onto the maternal figure, perceiving her in a confused and fragmented way – in Kleinian terms, that constitutes a *partial object relationship*.

This is why it takes the baby some time to understand that the mother who cares (*good breast*) is the same mother who fails (*bad breast*). We cite Klein:

The question arises whether some active splitting processes within the ego may not occur even at a very early stage. As we assume, *the early ego splits the object and the relation to it in an active way, and this may imply some active splitting of the ego itself*. In any case, the result of splitting is a dispersal of the destructive impulse which is felt as the source of danger. I suggest that the primary anxiety of being annihilated by a destructive force within, with the ego's specific response of falling to pieces or splitting itself, may be extremely important in all schizophrenic processes.

(Klein, 1946/2011, n.p., emphasis added)

Thus, the dilemma of the *paranoid-schizoid position* arises when the subject projects their hostile fragments outward, making the internal threat appear as a free-floating presence in the external environment – the world and its objects begin to be perceived as equally hostile by the fragmented individual, generating what Klein (1946/2011) refers to as *persecutory anxiety*. We quote the author:

Introjection and projection are from the beginning of life also used in the service of this primary aim of the ego. Projection, as Freud described, originates from the deflection of the death instinct outwards and in my view it helps the ego to overcome anxiety by ridding it of danger and badness. Introjection of the good object is also used by the ego as a defence against anxiety.

(Klein, 1946/2011, n.p.)

However, a significant shift occurs in babies when their experiences are predominantly satisfying: by consistently meeting the infant's needs, the maternal figure comes to be perceived as a *good object* – one of the first fully gratifying experiences is breastfeeding, which links a physiological need to a positive psychic experience.

Here, we observe a connection between the body (hunger) and the psyche (feeling of satiety). In short, upon receiving the nurturing breast, the baby directs all their gratification towards this object, perceiving it as the *good breast*. In the same way, the baby projects their destructive impulses onto the *bad breast*, which tends to intensify as the caregiving figure frustrates them. Let us take a closer look:

Therefore, in addition to the divorce between a good and a bad breast in the young infant's phantasy, the frustrating breast – attacked in oral-sadistic phantasies – is felt to be in fragments; the gratifying breast, taken in under the dominance of the sucking libido, is felt to be complete. This first internal good object acts as a focal point in the ego.

(Klein, 1946/2011, n.p.)

According to Klein (1946/2011) the processes of splitting, omnipotence, and idealisation of the *good breast* – along with the hatred of the *bad breast* – predominate approximately until four months of age. Initially she referred to this dynamic as the *paranoid position;*[2] however, in 1946 she introduced the definitive term that would become established in psychoanalysis: the *paranoid-schizoid position*.

In summary, while the baby's ego remains *fragmented* it projects its destructiveness – originating from the death instinct – onto the only object with which it maintains contact. This object, still perceived in a partial way at this early stage of life, remains disintegrated, as the child and the maternal figure continue to be fused due to the ongoing use of *projective identifications*.[3] As a consequence of these attacks, the baby begins to fear retaliation from the object, imagining being persecuted and threatened with destruction to the same extent as their own initial aggression. That dynamic constitutes a significant part of the core anxieties of the paranoid-schizoid position.

In this position two types of anxiety predominate: 1) annihilation anxiety, resulting from the action of the death instinct; and 2) persecutory anxiety, which emerges when the baby feels threatened and persecuted by the external object – the target of its destructive projections.

Due to the extreme fragility of the archaic ego, "[...] these experiences too are from the beginning felt as being caused by objects. Even if these objects are felt to be external, they become through introjection internal persecutors and thus reinforce the fear of the destructive impulse within" (Klein, 1946/2011, n.p.). In other words, everything is deeply confusing in the early life of the infant, who – if not making use of splitting (and thereby perceiving reality in divided terms, between good and bad) – might easily go mad. As Ogden (2017) aptly states:

> The baby *must be able to split* in order to feed safely, without the intrusion of the anxiety that he is harming his mother and without the anxiety that she will harm him. It is necessary for the baby to feel that the mother who is caring for him is entirely loving and has no connection whatsoever with the mother who "hurts" him by making him wait. The anxiety that arises from the thought that the nurturing mother and the frustrating mother are one and the same would rob the baby of the reassurance he needs in order to feed safely.
>
> (pp. 62–63, emphasis added)

Paradoxically, the infant needs to split the ego in order to trust the *good breast* – perceiving it as a safe object that offers comfort amidst their intense paranoid-schizoid terror. However, the excessive use of this splitting impairs the individual's capacity to deal with ambivalence. When a person feels a constant need to protect themselves through splitting it indicates a relatively low level of trust in the external environment. On this matter, let us consider what Petot (2016) has to say:

> In the absence of this separation, the good object cannot be considered as such, making it impossible for the infant to protect and ensure, in and through a relationship of trust with the ideal object, the security of the ego.

Without this primitive splitting of the good and bad breast (including the extreme form that opposes the "ideal breast" to the "very bad breast"), there can be no construction of the good object, and therefore nothing with the suitable nature to constitute the organising *core* of the ego and, subsequently, of the superego.

(pp. 109–110, original emphasis)

Broadly speaking, according to the Kleinian school, from the very first moments of life, the baby introjects the breast in various forms, as if constructing a mosaic made up of multiple pieces. Thus, if the breast is *felt* as a representation of the baby's internal world, it follows that the newborn is never truly encountering the same breast until their perceptual capacities expand and the archaic ego matures.

When care is predominantly satisfying, the baby is finally able to internalise what Klein (1946/2011) termed the *good object* – associated with memories of a nurturing experience of care – which contributes to the integration of the ego. Around the sixth month of life, a period often coinciding with weaning, the baby begins to experience anxiety in a different way, as object relations – formerly partial – become whole. In other words, the child begins to recognise that the mother who cares (good) and the mother who frustrates (bad) are one and the same person. At this point a conflict emerges: in attacking the *bad breast*, the baby fears they may also be harming the *good breast*.

This moment marks a new stage in psychic development. Upon reaching a certain degree of integration – recognising the object as whole – the baby begins to take responsibility for the attacks directed at the *good breast*, previously the target of aggressive phantasies. This new perception transforms the infant's relationship with the object, awakening the need for reparation and strengthening the loving and gratifying bond. In this way, the baby achieves what Klein, as early as 1935, referred to as the *depressive position*. In the author's own words:

With the introjection of the complete object in about the second quarter of the first year marked steps in integration are made. This implies important changes in the relation to objects. The loved and hated aspects of the mother are no longer felt to be so widely separated, and the result is an increased fear of loss, states akin to mourning and a strong feeling of guilt, because the aggressive impulses are felt to be directed against the loved object. The depressive position has come to the fore. The very experience of depressive feelings in turn has the effect of further integrating the ego, because it makes for an increased understanding of psychic reality and better perception of the external world, as well as for a greater synthesis between inner and external situations.

(Klein, 1946/2011, n.p.)

At this stage of maturation, the individual begins to experience external reality in a more complex and cohesive way. While in the *paranoid-schizoid position* their perception of the world was rigidly divided into good and bad, with external objects seen in a fragmented manner, lacking nuance. It is important to emphasise that this *simplified division* of the inner world functions as a defence mechanism against feelings of fear and helplessness (anxiety). By projecting destructive and aggressive impulses onto specific objects, the baby is able to preserve other objects as sources of safety and gratification. This process – characteristic of the paranoid-schizoid position – allows the initial organisation of psychic experience, although it later demands the integration of good and bad aspects of the object in the transition to the *depressive position*.

With the transition to a more integrated perception the individual ceases to view the external world in rigid extremes and begins to recognise that the same objects can both frustrate and satisfy. This capacity to perceive objects as a *whole* – that is, containing both good and bad aspects *simultaneously* – marks a significant developmental step: the individual begins to manage ambivalence, understanding that the maternal figure, for instance, can care for and frustrate at the same time without ceasing to be the same person. This new understanding enables the formation of more realistic and lasting bonds, as external figures are no longer idealised or demonised, but perceived with their proper imperfections and qualities.

In the Kleinian approach, it is essential to explore the patient's early primitive life, as it manifests primarily in the transference relationship – in the *here and now* with the analyst. This is the only way to understand the roots of transference, which reflect persecutory anxieties, feelings of guilt, and aggression. Klein (1952/2011) emphasises the importance of interpreting both positive and negative transferences. To her, just as life and death instincts (love and hate) are deeply intertwined, ambivalence dominates the transference dynamic – at times in a split form, at others in an integrated one. As the author herself states:

> Altogether, in the young infant's mind every external experience is interwoven with his phantasies and on the other hand every phantasy contains elements of actual experience, and it is only by *analysing the transference situation to its depth* that we are able to discover the past both in its realistic and phantastic aspects.
>
> (Klein, 1952/2011, n.p., emphasis added)

The figure of the analyst can therefore represent both the good and bad introjected objects of the patient, embodying both nurturing and frustrating aspects of their early experiences. It is only through the continuous connection between present and primitive experiences that past and present can truly be integrated, fostering a more structuring connection within the analytic relationship.

By reducing persecutory anxiety – characteristic of the *paranoid-schizoid position* – and by working through the guilt associated with the responsibility for destructive impulses, arising from the *depressive position*, the individual begins to manage ambivalence more effectively. This process strengthens the ego and enables a gradual integration, achieved through the interpretation of unconscious phantasies, the central axis of the Kleinian technique.

Given the meticulous work involved in the elaboration and traversal of the *depressive position*, it is not possible, from this perspective, to view regression to the *paranoid-schizoid position* as a gain. Ego splitting naturally occurs in moments of great threat, when the psychic apparatus cannot withstand the stress. However, if the ego is able to reintegrate after the impact, progress is made towards psychic maturity. This maturity is achieved when the individual takes responsibility for their position in the world, that is, when they speak in the first person, in an implicated and accountable manner. Thus, regression to the paranoid-schizoid position is viewed as an undesirable setback.

Other Kleinian analysts have also contributed important reflections on analytic regression. A notable example is the text by Paula Heimann and Susan Isaacs (1952/1969), entitled "Regression". In it the authors argue that the collapse of the genital phase – which represents an achievement of psychic maturity – simultaneously affects libido, destructive instincts, and ego's accomplishments. That regressive process therefore involves a kind of deterioration of character and weakening of sublimations, which may interfere with the acquisition of reparative impulses, essential to mental health.

As long as the individual is able to keep their destructive impulses under control and repair any damage done, they are capable of operating within the genital phase, tolerating real frustration and directing their libido towards new objects. When sublimation is sustained the pursuit of new sources of gratification supports the individual in coping with frustration.

However, if reparation and sublimation fail, the ego's defences collapse. Libido-linked gratifications are lost, destructive impulses intensify, and early pre-genital anxieties resurface. In this scenario, despair and fear of persecution render frustrations unbearable, triggering a vicious cycle in which archaic impulses and their associated anxieties return with force, while sublimation and reparation break down. For Heimann and Isaacs (1952/1969), this is one of the significant harms attributed to regression.

Jan Abram (2018), in a recent work, supports our observations:

My impression is that Melanie Klein must have been observing many of these developments. Winnicott was writing about holding and interpretation from the mid-1950s when she was still alive, and his work on regression, as you know, was very much disapproved of by Klein, Segal, and Joseph. I have a sense that Klein would never have gone along with many of the developments after she died because the evidence suggests that it is unlikely she would have changed her mind about her formulations. Therefore, while recognising the difference in age between Klein and Winnicott, I consider it important and valuable to compare their perspectives despite the age and epoch discrepancy.

(Abram, 2018, p. 152)

On the other hand, we shall now explore how regression, in the Winnicottian approach, can be understood as a positive element within the analytic process.

To Be and *To Go On Being*: Regression as an Act of Hope

Winnicott is, without a doubt, a thinker of human nature. His training in paediatrics enabled him to closely observe the challenges of infant maturation (see Almeida and Naffah Neto, 2021). The experience he gained through working with mothers, babies, children, adolescents, and families broadened his understanding of the complex interactions between environment and individual from the very earliest moments of life. He observed that personal development does not follow a linear trajectory; on the contrary, we tend to regress to earlier stages of life when faced with crises or difficulties.

In applying psychoanalytic theory and method to his patients, Winnicott validated several foundational discoveries in psychoanalysis, while also identifying important differences between his day-to-day clinical observations and certain claims made by Freud and Klein. In his reinterpretations of classical texts, he revisited the roles of sexuality and the Oedipus complex in both healthy and pathological emotional development. Although he continued to value these phenomena, Winnicott highlighted other factors that, to him, were equally central to psychic illness.

Winnicott (1945/2017) also introduced a new vision of the human being, grounded in the idea of *being*. For him, the individual evolves from a state of *non-being* to *being*; this state of being implies living from within oneself, without being pressured or shaped by the demands of the external world. Such a conception represents a new ontology, which is also connected to a theory of health and the individual's integration into cultural life.

In a lecture delivered to the Psychotherapy and Social Psychiatry Section of the Royal Medico-Psychological Association on 8 March 1967, entitled "The Concept of a Healthy Individual", Winnicott stated:

The life of a healthy individual is characterized by fears, conflicting feelings, doubts, frustrations, as much as by the positive features. The main thing is that the man or woman feels he or she *is living his or her own life*, taking responsibility for action or inaction, and able to take credit for success and blame for failure. In one language it can be said that the individual has emerged from dependence to independence, or to autonomy.

(Winnicott, 1967b/2017, pp. 69–70, original emphasis)

We can say that Winnicott is a psychoanalytic author who distinguishes himself from others precisely by having developed a *theory of emotional development* – or *maturational theory*, as some prefer to call it. As such, the entire Winnicottian clinical approach revolves around this theoretical framework.

In the classic essay "Primitive Emotional Development" Winnicott (1945/2017) lays the groundwork for some of his main theses which would later be developed throughout his scientific work. He identifies three processes that begin in the earliest moments of life: 1) *integration*; 2) *personalisation*, and, as a consequence of those; 3) *realisation* – which involves the perception of time, space, and other properties of reality, as well as the construction of a unified experience of psyche and soma.

Let us begin with the first process: *integration*. According to Winnicott (1945/2017), we are born with an innate tendency toward integration which develops primarily through the care provided by the environment to the infant. Such care involves *holding* (to hold, contain, keep warm) and *handling* (to bathe, change, and physically care for the infant). During this phase of intense dependence and vulnerability, it is essential that the mother be completely attuned to the baby's needs, as both exist in a kind of fused state. The baby does not yet distinguish between "me" and "not-me" – an idea that inspired Winnicott's well-known phrase "there is no such thing as a baby"[4] – for, at this early stage of life, the maternal figure is perceived by the infant as an extension of the self.

Winnicott (1945/2017) uses the term *integration* both to denote the innate disposition towards maturation and to refer to the various partial integrations that occur progressively throughout life, beginning from an initial state of non-integration. Integration in time and space constitutes a fundamental task in the baby's early emotional development. This process, however, does not occur spontaneously; it depends on a *good enough* environmental provision, one that offers the baby a sense of safety and continuity.

Without environmental reliability and security, the baby runs the risk of becoming lost in a sense of discontinuity – as if immersed in a bottomless abyss where reality fails to present itself in a structured form. Although integration begins in the earliest period of life it is a process that extends throughout childhood, taking on new forms and connections that may either support or hinder the child's perception of space and time.

Integrating the child into time and space, however, does not mean placing them directly into the external world; at the earliest moments of life no one is sufficiently mature to sustain – or even perceive – the sense of reality (Naffah Neto, 2023).

In the earliest moments of life, the newborn does not perceive itself as a separate entity, but rather as part of an existential continuity extended towards the other – especially the mother (or maternal figure). This experience of continuity is sustained by primary rhythms reminiscent of intrauterine life, such as the mother's heartbeat, breathing, and movements. These elements provide a sensory and auditory background that anchors the baby in a state of *continuity of being*, essential for the development of a sense of existence. Thus, this initial contact with time is, first and foremost, a *continuity of being* – subtly perceived. Therefore, precisely because the infant inhabits a subjective world, introducing the notions of time and space involves offering these experiences in an equally subjective manner (see Almeida, 2023). As Naffah Neto aptly observes:

> However, this subject does not yet exist as a fully constituted being – that is, we could say that no person exists at all, or that only the *first person* exists (from the baby's perspective). That becomes less complex if we recall that, in those early times, the baby merges with the environment during states of relaxation, entering a kind of *oceanic experience* – and therefore, in their perception, no person exists. However, in moments when the infant is overtaken by instinctual urgency and undergoes fleeting spatiotemporal integrations (which may lead them in search of the breast), an *evanescent subject* emerges, only to disappear again shortly afterwards – thus, in these fragments of time, only the *first person* exists.
>
> (Naffah Neto, 2019, p. 214, emphasis added)

Thus, the baby's first sense of time is deeply connected to the continuous presence of the mother and the regularity with which she responds to their many needs – needs that go beyond purely physiological ones. At this early stage, the infant is not yet aware of the mother's existence, but feels the effects of her presence and gradually begins to build a bodily memory of that companionship. For the continuity of their being to be sustained and for their subjective world to remain alive, the baby must feel assured by that constant presence.

It is this constancy that makes possible what Winnicott (1967b/2017) called the *illusion of omnipotence*: a sensation that their needs are met immediately, reinforcing their sense of safety and unity. In his words: "I am referring to the two-way process in which the infant lives in a subjective world and the mother adapts in order to give each infant a basic ration of the *experience of omnipotence*" (Winnicott, 1967b/2017, p. 67, original emphasis).

Acting that way, the mother enables the baby to be introduced to the periodicity of time, using her own bodily rhythm as the template. Naffah Neto (2023) states that, through the repetition of experience, a sense of future, however rudimentary, begins to emerge: the baby becomes able to anticipate what is to come based on their own needs made real through the mother's response. If the mother (or the environment) imposes upon the baby a rhythm that is external to them, their subjective temporality and "psyche-soma cohesion"[5] may be compromised – if not altogether obstructed.

Equally important, alongside integration, is the development of the feeling of being within one's own body – that is, the stage of *personalisation*. "Again it is instinctual experience and the repeated quiet experiences of body-care that gradually build up what may be called satisfactory personalization" (Winnicott, 1945/2017, p. 362). At this stage, through the *imaginative elaboration*[6] of bodily experience, the baby gradually begins to *locate the psyche within the soma*. This is a complex and delicate process that must be sustained by the presence of the caregiving figure. In Winnicott's own words:

> I suppose the word psyche here means the imaginative elaboration of somatic parts, feelings, and functions, that is, of physical aliveness. We know that this imaginative elaboration is dependent on the existence and the healthy functioning of the brain, especially certain parts of it. [...] Gradually the psyche and the soma aspects of the growing person become involved in a process of mutual interrelation. This interrelating of the psyche with the soma constitutes an early phase of individual development.
>
> (Winnicott, 1949/2017, p. 246)

"The *soma* is the living body, which becomes personalised as it is imaginatively elaborated by the psyche" (Dias, 2003, p. 104). "Human nature is not a matter of mind and body – it is a matter of inter-related psyche and soma, with the mind as a flourish on the edge of psycho-somatic functioning". (Winnicott, 1988/2017, p. 53). The imaginatively elaborated body is the body that breathes, moves, rests, suckles, plays, etc. Everything that is experienced by the baby through their body will be personalised through imaginative elaboration.

Broadly speaking, the gradual conquest of the body is closely linked to the baby's process of spatialisation. Throughout the period in which psychosomatic cohesion is taking place – through maternal care – the mother's arms and the baby's body are one and the same: such one could say that *"the baby's first dwelling is their own body in the mother's arms"* (Dias, 2003, p. 209, emphasis added).

At the stage of *realisation,* the baby begins to establish *object relations* in the proper sense (see Almeida and Naffah Neto, 2024). However, for any sense of reality to take shape, this experience must be offered to the baby within the only reality available to them: *subjective reality*, built upon the reliability of the environment.

In this context, the important process of the mother's (or maternal figure's) gradual *disadaptation* becomes the key to triggering the baby's disillusionment – not as a negative experience, but as an essential step forward. Over time the infant needs to recognise the existence of an external world in which their control is limited. If, at this early stage, they are offered a creative and subjective interaction with the environment they will gradually develop the capacity to adapt to this new reality. At the same time, they will preserve their ability to trust and to believe, finding a healthy balance between the subjective and the objective world.

Let us recall, then, that it is only from the *primary illusion* that one can expect the child to eventually accept the independent existence of an external world and to assimilate future disillusionments. "Adaptation to the reality principle arises naturally out of the experience of omnipotence, within the area, that is, of a relationship to subjective objects" (Winnicott, 1963/2017, p. 434). When illusion is well established, the child comes to learn, over time, of the separate existence of external reality, now understanding that the world has always been there, regardless of their perception. However, the feeling that the world is personally created does not vanish, "If the individual remains alive, their personal root remains grounded in the imaginative world, and it is only from there that acceptance of the external world does not amount to annihilation" (Dias, 2003, p. 217).

Among the various aspects that constitute the process of disillusionment, *weaning* is a significant achievement. If the baby does not initiate it themselves, it must be carried out by the mother. At the same time, the separation process must be gradual and carefully managed. The child needs to be released from the mother's arms without the risk of falling into an empty space; they must move towards a broader area of control – something that can metaphorically symbolise the place they have relinquished.

Thus emerges the concept of *transitional phenomena* and *transitional objects* – one of the most well-known and widely disseminated of Winnicott's contributions.

The transitional area follows a paradoxical logic, which goes beyond the simple opposition between being and non-being; from the child's perspective, these objects, although created, are not exactly what they represent. It is within this *intermediate space* – between non-being and being – that the subject's existence unfolds, allowing the construction of their subjectivity. Acceptance of reality is never complete, as the tension between internal and external reality always remains, and the relief for this tension arises precisely in this transitional area of experience, where there's no need for challenging or confrontation.

Transitional phenomena do not reach a final resolution and constitute a fundamental part of the baby's life, remaining present throughout adulthood. They stay alive in the intense experimentation found in the arts, religion, imagination, and creative scientific work. In other words, these phenomena are not confined to childhood or the early moments of subject formation but instead form an intermediate area that enables creative living throughout one's entire life.

Following this brief outline of Winnicott's theory, we can observe that psychic maturation, to him, is nothing less than a strenuous process of *coming into being* – marked by highs and lows, comings and goings. We once again cite Naffah Neto:

But what happens when early environmental failures produce a *freezing* of the baby's maturational process through the creation of a pathological false self which, by means of the mechanism of splitting, begins to cover over the true self, still in an embryonic state, as a kind of protective shield? What occurs is what we might describe as an *alienation of the first person into alterity*, that is, into the second person. Thus, the baby ceases to act in the first person – from their own needs – and instead re-acts to the intrusions of a traumatising environment, mimicking its traits in the formation of this pathological false self (Winnicott, 1960b/1990, pp. 146–147). With the concealment of the true self, the first person becomes eclipsed, and what takes its place is a mimicry of the other. For this reason, in regressions to dependence, the task is precisely to *restore functioning in the first person*, enabling the patient to take an active role in the construction of their own destiny.

(Naffah Neto, 2019, p. 215)

This is the main point of Winnicottian psychoanalysis. To Winnicott (1955/2017) we all have the *right* to regress to the earliest stages of development when our psychic integrity is under threat. The reliability of the environment, therefore, must guarantee that possibility of return – a need that accompanies the individual throughout their entire life (see Almeida and Vieira, 2023).

Although exact ages cannot be defined for the stages of maturation, Winnicott (1945/2017) suggests that around the age of one to one and a half years children begin to establish personality integration, which is consolidated between the ages of two and three. At some point in childhood the subject achieves self-awareness as a unitary existence, developing a sense of identity.

If they could express this feeling in the early stages of life, the child would say "I AM". That "I" is the result of a long and complex process of integration that began in the earliest moments of experience. However, this unity of the self is not entirely homogeneous or free of conflict; it is a state of spatio-temporal integration in which parts of the identity are connected and organised, in contrast to a state of fragmentation and dispersion.

To reach this awareness of *being* represents, paradoxically, both an end and a beginning; the achievement of "I AM" – the feeling of being real and existing as an identity – is not an end in itself, but rather a foundation from which life can be lived. The child now feels more anchored in their own body, perceiving themselves as bounded by the skin, which separates them from what is external – the *not-me*. At the same time, they come to possess an *interior*, a personal psychic space where experiences are registered and a vast repertoire of memories and fantasies is constructed, including repressed unconscious formations that enrich the psychic structure.

Unlike the Kleinian theory, Winnicott's approach focuses on the multiple phases of individual development and the process of constructing an *authentic identity*. According to him, the goal is for the individual to attain a state of "being" grounded in the feeling of being real, of experiencing life as worth living. If this condition is not fulfilled, the subject is condemned to a *false existence*, governed only by "doing".

According to Winnicott (1955/2017), then regression can be a legitimate therapeutic goal, allowing the individual to discover their *true self* and to assume their own narrative in the first person. This perspective also contributes to thinking about different clinical approaches when working with *difficult cases*. Let us consider:

> More severe psychopathological conditions certainly require a differentiated treatment approach, guided by the analyst's management and by *holding*, which may facilitate the patient's process of regression to dependence, through a relationship of trust rooted in the essence of the analytic encounter. When well supported, such a process can recover stages of life that remained frozen due to environmental failures and intrusions. It is worth emphasising, however, that it is the patient themselves who regresses, relying on their *spontaneous gesture*, when the conditions for doing so are in place.
>
> (Almeida and Vieira, 2023, p. 276, emphasis added)

Klein and Winnicott: Convergences and Divergences in Psychoanalytic Practice

Throughout this chapter, we have seen that, according to Winnicott (1955/2017), the baby must go through various achievements in order to attain healthy integration, with the environment playing an essential role in this process. Early experiences, lived before the integration of certain ego capacities, can be profoundly damaging to the individual's development.

It is no coincidence that the British paediatrician and psychoanalyst emphasises:

> Psychotic illness is related to environmental failure at an early stage of the emotional development of the individual. The sense of futility and unreality belongs to the development of a false self which develops in protection of the true self.
>
> The setting of analysis reproduces the early and earliest mothering techniques. It invites regression by reason of its reliability.
>
> The regression of a patient is an organized return to early dependence or double dependence. The patient and the setting merge into the original success situation of primary narcissism.
>
> Progress from primary narcissism starts anew with the true self able to meet environmental failure situations without organization of the defences that involve a false self protecting the true self.
>
> To this extent psychotic illness can only be relieved by specialized environmental provision interlocked with the patient's regression.
>
> Progress from the new position, with the true self surrendered to the total ego, can now be studied in terms of the complex processes of individual growth.
>
> (Winnicott, 1955/2017, p. 209)

This Winnicott excerpt synthesises the goals of analytic work – depending on the degree of ego integration – and highlighting the importance of regression in the treatment of severely traumatised patients. That aspect also distinguishes his technique from Klein's approach, which does not work with the concept of trauma, but rather with *instinctual force* – particularly the *death instinct* – as the central factor in the origin of psychic illness. We quote Klein:

> The strength of the ego – reflecting the state of fusion between the two instincts – is, I believe, constitutionally determined. If in the fusion the life instinct predominates, which implies an ascendancy of the capacity for love, the ego is relatively strong, and is more able to bear the anxiety arising from the death instinct and to counteract it. To what extent the strength of the ego can be maintained and increased is in part affected by external factors, in particular the mother's attitude towards the infant. However, even when the life instinct and the capacity for love predominate, destructive impulses are still deflected outwards and contribute to the creation of persecutory and dangerous objects which are reintrojected. Furthermore, the primal processes of introjection and projection lead to constant changes in the ego's relation to its objects, with fluctuations between internal and external, good and bad ones, according to the infant's phantasies and emotions as well as under the impact of his actual experiences.
>
> (Klein, 1958/2017, n.p.)

Klein (1957/2011) observed that, at any stage of life, when the relationship with the good object is profoundly disturbed – with envy playing a central role – not only are inner security and peace affected, but there is also a deterioration of character. The predominant presence of persecutory internal objects intensifies destructive impulses; conversely, when the good object is well established, identification with it strengthens the capacity to love, constructive impulses, and the feeling of gratitude.

Klein (1957/2011) also emphasised the importance of the archaic persecutory object, symbolised by the breast experienced as retaliatory, devouring, and poisonous. When the baby projects their envy, it intensifies anxiety both in the early stages and in later phases of development. The "envious superego" then emerges as a force that sabotages all attempts at reparation and creation, imposing on the individual a constant and exhausting demand for gratitude.

That persecutory state is accompanied by feelings of guilt, as the individual recognises that their persecutory internal objects are the result of their own envious and destructive impulses which originally damaged the good object. The need for punishment is fuelled by the persistent devaluation of the self, resulting in a vicious cycle that reinforces psychic suffering.

To Klein (1957/2011) the ultimate goal of analysis is to integrate the patient's personality. Freud's (1923) statement that "where id was, there ego shall be" reflects this orientation. Splitting processes emerge in the earliest stages of development and, when excessive, are associated with paranoid and schizoid traits which may underlie the origins of schizophrenia. In healthy development these tendencies – the *paranoid-schizoid position* – are largely overcome in the phase marked by the *depressive position*, which fosters successful integration. This developmental advance prepares the ego to operate repression, which Klein believes becomes increasingly consolidated from the second year of life onwards.

In light of this, we can highlight a few fundamental considerations which, for the sake of clarity, we present as a list below:

1 Winnicott did not work with the concept of the death instinct, nor did he believe in an archaic ego capable of projection and introjection from birth. This difference alters his entire conception of psychopathology and, consequently, his clinical interventions.
2 Although Klein developed her theory based on instinctual duality, she never ignored the importance of the environment. However, her understanding of primitive phantasies directs her analytic stance in a different direction from that proposed by Winnicott. In the Kleinian tradition, analysis aims to facilitate the introjection of the good object, made possible through symbolisation and the working through of the *depressive position*, while also seeking to reduce the force of the destructive instinct through the interpretation of unconscious content. By contrast, Winnicott argues strongly that:

> *Psychotherapy is not making clever and apt interpretations*; by and large it is a long-term giving the patient back what the patient brings. It is a complex derivative of the face that reflects what is there to be seen. I like to think of my work this way, and to think that if I do this well enough the patient will find his or her own self, and will be able to exist and to feel real. Feeling real is more than existing; it is finding a way to exist as oneself, and to relate to objects as oneself, and to have a self into which to retreat for relaxation.
>
> (Winnicott, 1967a/2017, p. 217, emphasis added)

We must say that Klein sought to transform primitive phantasies through interpretation, thus reducing the proliferation of splittings. Winnicott, in other hand, aimed to provide an environment capable of returning to the patient their own experience of being, thereby facilitating the integration of the psyche-soma.

What follows is a clinical vignette which, in our view, may practically illustrate these fundamental differences.

One Case: Two Readings

João,[7] a 35-year-old man, bears in his body and psychic life the marks of overwhelming anxiety. Insomnia and incessant and distressing thoughts reveal a psychic functioning dominated by primitive defences that distance him from intimate contact with both himself and others, trapping him in a state of constant, almost unreal, emptiness.

His childhood memories are marked by experiences of absence and silence: an emotionally distant mother, consumed by overwork, and a critical and cold father, whose presence was felt more as a judging gaze than as affective support. These parental objects, internalised in a persecutory way, may have contributed to João's psychic organisation around the *paranoid-schizoid position*, in which persecutory anxieties and a splitting between good and bad objects predominate.

The Kleinian approach would allow us to analyse how João projects these hostile aspects onto figures of authority, and how his anxiety is rooted in unconscious phantasies related to fears of destruction and the action of the death instinct. The analytic work, through precise interpretations, would aim to help him recognise and integrate these internal elements, thereby reducing the impact of destructive impulses.

This process could allow a shift towards the *depressive position*, in which psychic reality becomes more cohesive. Through the introjection of a good object, João could begin to develop a greater capacity for reparation, building a more integrated sense of self and forming relationships less defined by the fear of loss and the threat of annihilation.

Here, however, a remark is worth noting: although Klein (1957/2011) does not associate the following quotation directly with the idea of regression *per se* – since, as we have mentioned, in her theory regression tends to lead back towards the *paranoid-schizoid position* – she states:

> In taking the analysis back to earliest infancy, we enable the patient to *revive fundamental situations* – a revival which I have often spoken of as "memories in feeling". In the course of this revival, it becomes possible for the patient to develop a different attitude to his early frustrations. There is no doubt that if the infant was actually exposed to very unfavourable conditions, the retrospective establishing of a good object cannot undo bad early experiences. However, the introjection of the analyst as a good object, if not based on idealisation has, to some extent, the effect of providing an internal good object where it has been largely lacking. Also, the weakening of projections, and therefore the achieving of greater tolerance, bound up with less resentment, make it possible for the patient to find some features and to *revive pleasant memories* of the past, even when the early situation was very unfavourable.
>
> (Klein, 1957/2011, n.p., emphasis added)

In other words, from a Kleinian perspective, by reliving "memories in feelings" (Klein, 1957/2011) during analytic treatment, we are given the chance to feel once more what had remained hidden – like a memory imbued with sensations – almost as though we were revisiting a forgotten childhood that still pulses within us. Along this path of return, the patient may finally learn to face those primitive frustrations in a new way, with a gaze less marked by the original pain.

This new encounter with a *good object* cannot erase the marks left by the earliest experiences of suffering. However, by receiving the analyst as this new good object – and not merely as an idealised figure – something genuine is established within the patient. As a result, the old projections that had cast resentment onto the world begin to lose their intensity, allowing for greater tolerance and a softening of the hurt. This movement opens the space for the patient to reconnect, however tentatively, with parts of their story that may have contained moments of light – even within a darkened past. It is, therefore, a kind of reconciliation: with the other, with the world, and, gradually, with oneself.

In the Winnicottian approach the emphasis would fall on the creation of a *good enough* therapeutic environment, in which João could find the safety and holding that had been insufficient during his emotional development. The analyst, guided by this perspective, would understand that the early environmental failure had generated a trauma that needed to be imaginatively worked through within the analytic setting. In order to achieve it the clinical environment would need to allow João to *re-experience* – or perhaps experience for the first time – the trust and dependence essential to the development of the *true self*. Interpretations, in this context, would be employed sparingly, with clinical management prioritising the loosening of the defences associated with the *false self*. In Winnicott's view, the predominance of the false self equates to a life lived on the margins – without authenticity and marked by a sense of unreality.

The core of the technique, therefore, would reside in *holding* and emotional containment, providing the patient with a relational experience capable of sustaining a potential regression to states of primary dependence. That is, regression here would allow João to (re)experience, in safety, the earliest stages of his emotional development with the aim of fostering greater cohesion in the *psyche–soma* unity.

It is important to realise, however, that Winnicott (1960/2017) highlights the existence of different levels of false self, ranging from a healthy social adaptation – in which there is a relinquishment of omnipotence to enable social coexistence and preserve mental health – to more extreme forms of total submission, in which the true self remains hidden, resulting in a lack of spontaneity. In the most severe cases this gives rise to a sense of emptiness and a feeling that life has lost its meaning. In less serious cases the individual maintains this defensive organisation while awaiting more favourable conditions that may allow them to set aside this defence.

This is the hypothesis underlying the concept of regression in Winnicott. In the theory of emotional development regression is linked to environmental failures in the earliest stages and to the way the individual responds to such failures. Regarding the false self, it is also essential to recognise that, although it constitutes an obstacle to ongoing maturation, this defensive organisation simultaneously serves as a protection for the true self, which remains safe-guarded, waiting for a new opportunity to emerge – depending on the quality of environmental provision – and to continue its development.

Winnicott's theory teaches us that it is natural – and even healthy – for the individual to protect the self in the face of significant environmental failures, by "freezing" the original situation. Simultaneously, there remains an uncon-scious (and eventually conscious) hope that, at some point, the opportunity will come to relive and work through that failure within a safe and holding environment. Within this framework, regression is understood as part of a natural healing process – one that can be meaningfully observed even in individuals considered psychologically healthy.

However, for regression to dependence to take place it is necessary that the individual has previously achieved a sufficient level of ego organisation, allowing the development of a false self while still maintaining the belief that the original failure can, one day, be repaired. In more severe cases, the analyst may need to actively "go to" the patient, offering a "good enough mothering" – an experience the patient, on their own, would not be able to expect or imagine (Winnicott, 1955/2017).

In Conclusion

In light of the reflections developed throughout this chapter, arising from a rigorous theoretical and conceptual study combined with clinical practice, it becomes possible to recognise the contributions of Klein and Winnicott as distinct paths which, although traced across different terrains, ultimately con-verge towards the same horizon of relief and reconstruction in psychoanalytic treatment. In Klein, analysis takes the form of an expedition, so to speak, into the core of primitive fantasies; that is, a careful and profound excavation in which interpretations carve out the way for understanding, transformation, and the lessening of ego-splitting.

Although Klein (1957/2011) does not employ the concept of regression as an explicit clinical device, her approach nevertheless makes use of a revival of early childhood. She speaks of a return to the most primitive experiences, in which the patient is able to re-live "memories in feeling" – those recollec-tions which, more than thoughts, are vivid emotions condensed into sensory and affective fragments. For Klein, enabling access to these deeper layers of-fers the patient possibility to re-signify archaic frustrations, transforming what was once pain or loss into a source of ego integration.

Winnicott, in turn, offers us an almost artisanal perspective of the clinic, in which the analyst crafts, piece by piece, a "good enough" environment that enables the patient to loosen the defences of their false self and embark on the reconstitution of their true self. It is no coincidence that this author, alongside Sándor Ferenczi, is regarded as one of the major forerunners of what some scholars have termed the "ethics of care" in psychoanalysis (see Almeida, 2023). Within this protected space, regression is not merely a return to childhood, but a return to the psychic home – a place where the original self may, for the first time, rest and feel at ease in its own skin. This is a space that, depending on the individual's level of maturity, does not seek to interpret "non-integration" but rather to provide the patient with a sufficiently secure experience in which they may be and continue to be, from within themselves. More than decoding, it is about sustaining an environment that nurtures the continuity of first-person existence, enabling the development of a more spontaneous and integrated self.

These distinctions – between Klein's clinic of fantasies and Winnicott's clinic of regression – reflect the internal diversity of psychoanalysis: a craft wherein multiple voices resonate, each offering distinct responses to the sufferings of the human psyche. Klein offers us the rigour of interpretation, the challenge of confronting and transforming instinctual conflicts, including the death instinct. Winnicott, on the other hand, reminds us of the primacy of the environment, of the need to create a "therapeutic nest" in which the patient may reconstruct their existence from within themselves.

This multiplicity is what lends breadth to our science. It compels us to adopt a plural and engaged mode of listening; that is, a polyphonic psychoanalysis, in which each theory not only deepens our understanding of the origins of psychic suffering but also expands the scope of possible pathways towards healing.

Notes

1 We would like to inform the reader that we have replaced the original Portuguese translation of *pulsão* with *instinct*, as the term *pulsão* (Freud's *Trieb* in German) does not exist in the English psychoanalytic tradition.

2 In a footnote to the article *Notes on Some Schizoid Mechanisms*, Klein states that up to the date of that publication (1946), she used the term *paranoid position* as a synonym for the *schizoid position*, as proposed by W. R. D. Fairbairn (Klein, 1946/2011).

3 According to Almeida (2024), "projective identification" is a defence mechanism originating in the schizoid-paranoid position, which takes place from the very beginning of an infant's life. At such an early developmental stage, when the ego is still immature and overwhelmed by a veritable avalanche of instinctual pressures, the archaic ego resorts to a viable strategy: it expels fragments of itself into the environment – primitive parts that are not yet clearly differentiated between ego and id (what Klein refers to as the self) – in the hope that the other can receive and process these elements which, for the baby, are simply unbearable to contain internally. Projective identification can thus be understood as a kind of "cry for help": when faced with unmanageable anxiety, splitting becomes the only available route for the psyche to expel such inner turbulence. Once these bad parts of the ego are projected outward the individual experiences a sense of relief. However, it is essential to bear in mind that every act of projection entails a depletion of the ego, since a portion of it is cast outside – resulting in its weakening and a consequent blurring or fusion between subject and object.

4 In the text "Anxiety Associated with Insecurity", Winnicott (1958/2017) writes that around ten years earlier, he had caused quite a stir within the British Psychoanalytical Society by stating, "There is no such thing as a baby". He goes on to clarify

what he had meant by this: "[...] if you show me a baby you certainly show me also someone caring for the baby, or at least a pram with someone's eyes and ears glued to it. One sees a 'nursing couple'" (Winnicott, 1958/2017, p. 57).

5 Winnicott (1988/2024) uses precisely this spelling with the intention of indicating the *psyche* and *soma* as distinct units.

6 See Naffah Neto (2023).

7 The patient's name and other identifying details have been altered to preserve ethical confidentiality. In fact, this is a device of *autofiction*, as "João" embodies characteristics drawn from several patients treated by the authors of this chapter.

References

Abram, J. (2018). Holding and the Mutative Interpretation. In J. Abram and R. D. Hinshelwood, *The Clinical Paradigms of Melanie Klein and Donald Winnicott: Comparisons and Dialogues*, pp. 141–147. London: Routledge.

Almeida, A. P. (2022). A depressão para Melanie Klein: Quando as trevas aprisionam o ego [Depression According to Melanie Klein: When Darkness Imprisons the Ego]. In A. P. Almeida and A. Naffah Neto (Orgs.), *Perto das trevas: A depressão em seis perspectivas psicanalíticas* [*Near to Darkness: Depression in Six Psychoanalytic Perspectives*], pp. 137–172. Blucher.

Almeida, A. P. (2024). As diversas faces da identificação projetiva [The Many Faces of Projective Identification]. In A. P. Almeida, *Melanie Klein além da clínica: contribuições à educação escolar* [*Melanie Klein Beyond the Clinic: Contributions to School Education*], pp. 129–148. São Paulo: Zagodoni.

Almeida, A. P. (2023). *Por uma ética do cuidado: Winnicott para educadores e psicanalistas (vol. 2)* [*For an Ethics of Care: Winnicott for Educators and Psychoanalysts (Vol. 2)*]. São Paulo: Blucher.

Almeida, A. P., and Naffah Neto, A. (2021). A teoria do desenvolvimento maturacional de Winnicott: Novas perspectivas para a educação [Winnicott's Theory of Maturational Development: New Perspectives for education]. *Revista Latinoamericana de Psicopatologia Fundamental*, 24(3): 517–536. https://doi.org/10.1590/1415-4714.2021v24n3p517-3

Almeida, A. P., and Naffah, A. (2024). Um estudo comparativo entre as teorias de Klein e Winnicott: Analisando o conceito de fantasia [A Comparative Study of Klein and Winnicott's Theories: Analysing the Concept of Fantasy]. *Revista Latinoamericana de Psicopatologia Fundamental*, 27, e230636. https://doi.org/10.1590/1415-4714.e230636

Almeida, A. P., and Vieira, F. P. (2023). Nem tudo é holding na clínica winnicottiana [Not everything is holding in the Winnicottian clinic]. In S. Gomes (Org.), *Winnicott: seminários mineiros (ambiente e holding)*, pp. 273–286. Rio de Janeiro: INM Editora.

Almeida, A. P., Naffah Neto, A., and Vieira, F. P. (2024). A construção do pensar: Um estudo comparativo entre Bion e Winnicott [The construction of thinking: A comparative study between Bion and Winnicott]. *Natureza Humana – Revista Internacional de Filosofia e Psicanálise*, 26(1): 40–59. https://doi.org/10.59539/2175-2834-v26n1-692

Dias, E. O. (2003). *A teoria do amadurecimento de D. W. Winnicott* [*The Theory of Maturation of D. W. Winnicott*]. Rio de Janeiro: Imago.

Freud, S. (1981). Beyond the Pleasure Principle. In S. Freud, *The Standard Edition of the Complete Psychological Works of Sigmund Freud (Vol. 18)*, pp. 3–64. London: Hogarth Press. (Original work published in 1920)

Freud, S. (1981). The Ego and the Id. In S. Freud, *The Standard Edition of the Complete Psychological Works of Sigmund Freud (Vol. 19)*, pp. 3–66. London: Hogarth Press. (Original work published in 1923)

Heimann, P., and Isaacs, S. (1969). Regressão [Regression]. In M. Klein et al., *Os progressos da psicanálise* [*The Progress of Psychoanalysis*], pp. 185–215. Zahar. (Original work published in 1952)

Klein, M. (2011). A Contribution to the Psychogenesis of Manic-Depressive States. In M. Klein, *Love, Guilt and Reparation and Other Works (1921–1945)*. London: Vintage Books. E-book. (Original work published in 1935)

Klein, M. (2011). Envy and Gratitude. In M. Klein, *Envy and Gratitude and Other Works (1946–1963)*. London: Vintage Books. E-book. (Original work published in 1957)

Klein, M. (2011). Notes on Some Schizoid Mechanisms. In M. Klein, *Envy and Gratitude and Other Works (1946–1963)*. London: Vintage Books. E-book. (Original work published in 1946)

Klein, M. (2011). On the Development of Mental Functioning. In M. Klein. *Envy and Gratitude and Other Works (1946–1963)*. London: Vintage Books. E-book. (Original work published in 1958)

Klein, M. (2011). On the Theory of Anxiety and Guilt. In M. Klein, *Envy and Gratitude and Other Works (1946–1963)*. London: Vintage Books. E-book. (Original work published in 1948)

Klein, M. (2011). The Origins of Transference. In M. Klein, *Envy and Gratitude and Other Works (1946–1963)*. London: Vintage Books. E-book. (Original work published in 1952)

Lispector, C. (2020). *A paixão segundo G. H.* [*The Passion According to G.H.*]. E-book. Rio de Janeiro: Rocco.

Mezan, R. (2024). O método psicanalítico no texto acadêmico: Três exemplos e algumas observações [The Psychoanalytic Method in Academic Writing: Three Examples and Some Observations]. *Jornal de Psicanálise, 57*(106): 187–214. https://doi.org/10.5935/0103-5835.v57n106.13

Naffah Neto, A. (2019). Em primeira pessoa [In First Person]. *Natureza Humana, 21*(2): 211–219.

Naffah Neto, A. (2023). *Veredas psicanalíticas: À sombra de Winnicott* [*Psychoanalytic Paths: In Winnicott's Shadow*]. São Paulo: Blucher.

Ogden, T. (2017). *A matriz da mente: Relações objetais e o diálogo psicanalítico* [*The Matrix of Mind: Object Relations and the Psychoanalytic Dialogue*]. São Paulo: Blucher.

Petot, J.-M. (2016). *Melanie Klein II: O ego e o bom objeto* [*Melanie Klein II: The Ego and the Good Object*]. São Paulo: Perspectiva.

Winnicott, D. W. (2017). Anxiety Associated with Insecurity. In D. W. Winnicott, *The Collected Works of D. W. Winnicott (Vol. 4)*, pp. 55–58. Oxford: Oxford University Press. (Original work published in 1958)

Winnicott, D. W. (2017). Communicating and Not Communicating Leading to a Study of Certain Opposites. In D. W. Winnicott, *The Collected Works of D. W. Winnicott (Vol. 6)*, pp. 433–446. Oxford: Oxford University Press. (Original work published in 1963)

Winnicott, D. W. (2017). Ego Distortion in Terms of True and False Self. In D. W. Winnicott, *The Collected Works of D. W. Winnicott (Vol. 6)*, pp. 159–174. Oxford: Oxford University Press. (Original work published in 1960)

Winnicott, D. W. (2017). Human Nature. In D. W. Winnicott, *The Collected Works of D. W. Winnicott (Vol. 11)*, pp. 3–183. Oxford: Oxford University Press. (Original work published 1988)

Winnicott, D. W. (2017). Living Creatively. In D. W. Winnicott, *The Collected Works of D. W. Winnicott (Vol. 9)*, pp. 213–224. Oxford: Oxford University Press. (Original work published in 1970)

Winnicott, D. W. (2017). Metapsychological and Clinical Aspects of Regression Within the Psycho-Analytical Set-Up. In D. W. Winnicott, *The Collected Works of D. W. Winnicott (Vol. 4)*, pp. 201–218. Oxford: Oxford University Press. (Original work published in 1955)

Winnicott, D. W. (2017). Mind and Its Relation to the Psyche-Soma. In D. W. Winnicott, *The Collected Works of D. W. Winnicott (Vol. 3)*, pp. 245–258. Oxford: Oxford University Press. (Original work published in 1949)

Winnicott, D. W. (2017). Mirror-Role of Mother and Family in Child Development. In D. W. Winnicott, *The Collected Works of D. W. Winnicott (Vol. 8)*, pp. 211–218. Oxford: Oxford University Press. (Original work published in 1967a)

Winnicott, D. W. (2017). Primitive Emotional Development. In D. W. Winnicott, *The Collected Works of D. W. Winnicott (Vol. 2)*, pp. 357–368. Oxford: Oxford University Press. (Original work published in 1945)

Winnicott, D. W. (2017). The Concept of a Healthy Individual. In D. W. Winnicott, *The Collected Works of D. W. Winnicott (Vol. 8)*, pp. 65–78. Oxford: Oxford University Press. (Original work published in 1967)

8 The Concept of the Superego According to Klein and Winnicott

Alfredo Naffah Neto and
Alexandre Patricio de Almeida

Some Notes on the Superego in Freud

In "The Ego and the Id" (Freud, 1923/1981), the most important text in which Freud describes the formation of the superego – or *super-ego*, depending on how one chooses to translate the German term *Über-Ich* – he does not draw a clear distinction between the concepts of ego ideal and superego, treating them virtually as synonyms. Later on, it became customary to distinguish between these concepts: the ego ideal as "[…] the outcome of narcissism (the ego's idealisation) and the identifications with the parents, with their substitutes, and with collective ideals" (Laplanche and Pontalis, 1970, p. 259), with the superego being reserved as the critical, censoring agency.

Around the 1920s, Freud was deeply influenced by phylogenetic thinking, often seeking the ontogenesis of the human being in its phylogenesis. Thus, he describes the formation of the ego ideal (or ego-ideal):

> This leads us back to the origin of the ego ideal; for behind it there lies hidden an individual's first and most important identification, his identification with the father in his own personal prehistory.[1] This is apparently not in the first instance the consequence or outcome of an object-cathexis; it is a direct and immediate identification and takes place earlier than any object-cathexis. But the object-choices belonging to the first sexual period and relating to the father and mother seem normally to find their outcome in an identification of this kind, and would thus reinforce the primary one.
>
> (Freud, 1923/1981, p. 31)

Since ego ideal and superego are treated as synonyms in that text, we can already see in this statement the phylogenetic origin of the concept of the superego. And, as Freud conceives the ego as a differentiation of the id, and the superego as a differentiation of the ego, he affirms this phylogenetic origin by linking the superego to the id, through the mediation of the ego:

> The experiences of the ego seem at first to be lost for inheritance; but, when they have been repeated often enough and with sufficient

DOI: 10.4324/9781003642503-9

strength in many individuals in successive generations, they transform themselves, so to say, into experiences of the id, the impressions of which are preserved by heredity. Thus in the id, which is capable of being inherited, are harboured residues of the existences of countless egos; and, when the ego forms its super-ego out of the id, it may perhaps only be reviving shapes of former egos and be bringing them to resurrection.

(Freud, 1923/1981, p. 38)

When Freud describes the formation of the ego ideal – or superego – as the result of identification with the parental figure during the resolution of the Oedipus complex, he is, in fact, reinforcing a process that transcends individual history. This identification with the actual parents reactivates, through phylogenesis, an ancestral bond with the primordial parental figures of prehistory. More than that, it involves the incorporation of the superegos of countless egos across generations whose experiences have been hereditarily[2] transmitted, significantly and enduringly shaping the psyche.

Here we quote Freud in describing the constitution of the ego ideal or superego on the level of personal history, but it is important to emphasise that this formulation represents only the final stage of a much broader formative process:

The broad general outcome of the sexual phase dominated by the Oedi-pus complex may, therefore, be taken to be the forming of a precipitate in the ego, consisting of these two identifications in some way united with each other. This modification of the ego retains its special position; it confronts the other contents of the ego as an ego ideal or super-ego.
(Freud, 1923/1981, p. 34, original emphasis)

It is perhaps to highlight the importance of this phylogenetic inheritance in the formation of the superego that Laplanche and Pontalis state, quoting Freud:

"The establishment of the superego may be regarded as a successful instance of identification with the parental agency", writes Freud in *New Introductory Lectures on Psycho-Analysis* (*Neue Folge der Vorlesun-gen zur Einführung in die Psychoanalyse*, 1932) [...]. The expression "parental agency" in itself indicates that the constitutive identification of the superego should not be understood as an identification with actual persons. In a particularly explicit passage, Freud made this idea clear: "The child's superego is not formed in the image of the parents, but in the image of their superego; it takes on the same content, becoming the representative of tradition, of all the judgments which have thus persisted through the generations".

(Laplanche and Pontalis, 1970, p. 646)

We do not intend to dwell on this subject, since the superego in Freud is not the central focus of this chapter. Our aim in this brief introduction was merely to highlight that this psychic agency carries phylogenetic inheritances that form its principal foundation upon which the combined superego of the parents is added – it is not about identification with their personal figures. The superego, in Freud, possesses a transgenerational character.

The Archaic Kleinian Superego

As highlighted in the previous chapters, Melanie Klein challenged classical Freudian theory and, through the analysis of very young children, observed that they suffered from intrapsychic threats arising from internalised parental imagos from a very early stage. We quote her:

> The analysis of little children reveals the structure of the super-ego as built up of identifications dating from very different periods and strata in the mental life. These identifications are surprisingly contradictory in nature, excessive goodness and excessive severity existing side by side. We find in them, too, an explanation of the severity of the super-ego, which comes out specially plainly in these infant analyses. It does not seem clear why a child of, say, four years old should set up in his mind an unreal, phantastic image of parents who devour, cut and bite. But it is clear why in a child of about *one year* old the anxiety caused by the beginning of the Oedipus conflict takes the form of a dread of being devoured and destroyed. The child himself desires to destroy the libidinal object by biting, devouring and cutting it, which leads to anxiety, since awakening of the Oedipus tendencies is followed by introjection of the object, which then becomes one from which punishment is to be expected. The child then dreads a punishment corresponding to the offence: the super-ego becomes something which bites, devours and cuts.
>
> (Klein, 1928/2011, n.p., original emphasis)

To Klein the origin of superego lies much earlier than suggested by Freudian hypotheses, and is therefore not a product of the Oedipus complex as described by Freud. It is a terrifying and persecutory figure that haunts the earliest stages of infantile psychic life, emerging from various projections and introjections which, in turn, are powerfully driven by the presence of the death instinct – an instinct that, to Klein, always bears a destructive quality.

Although Klein accepted Freud's description of the superego, she did not agree with its emergence only around the fourth or fifth year of life; her clear evidence of archaic feelings of guilt pointed to the superego arising by, at the latest, the second year of life (Spillius et al., 2011). Moreover, because it is predominantly composed of split-off partial objects, the Kleinian superego is far more unyielding than the Freudian one. This principle is justified by the fact that, for Klein, the superego is linked to the pre-genital phases of sadism, as described by Abraham (1924/1970) – namely, sadistic-oral, sadistic-anal, and sadistic-urethral phases.

As her hypotheses developed, Klein came to define the archaic superego as being formed by various internalised figures based on both the mother and the father (or those who perform such roles). These *imagos* – internalised representations of fragments of the parents – represent to the child a series of internal relationships that can be understood as the outcome of sadistic-oral *fantasies*, which essentially consist of sucking, devouring, and biting the object; the same applies to sadistic-anal impulses, namely the fantasy of expelling and inserting faeces into the object. Klein described such phenomena in detail through her analysis of young children's play (Almeida, 2022).

Therefore, the Kleinian superego can be understood as an immense constellation of internal objects, each endowed with specific fantasy functions; and psychoanalysis inspired by Klein, in practice, becomes increasingly an analysis of these *intrapsychic contents*.

In a simplified and highly didactic form, we can summarise that:

> Whereas Freud's superego contains the values and ideals the child acquires from their parents and inherited legacy, Klein's archaic superego appears to be its more primitive predecessor. While Freud's superego, initially conceived as the ego ideal (Freud, 1913, 1914), reacts with *guilt*, Klein's superego reacts at first with *persecutory anxiety* while the child is in the schizoparanoid position, and only later responds with guilt once the child reaches the depressive position. She proposed that the archaic superego develops from the child's projection of various aspects of their personality (hatred, love, greed, envy, neediness, sadism, and so forth) – onto the object, along with omnipotence, omniscience, and intentionality or will. When the image thus composed is internalised and the child identifies with it, it becomes an uncontrollable, pernicious archaic superego.
>
> (Grotstein, 2017, pp. 401–402, original emphasis)

According to the Kleinian perspective this extremely harsh superego can be the source of profound psychic suffering, shaping a wide range of forms of subjectivity. In this regard, Spillius et al. affirm that:

> An internal structure or part of the self that, as the internal authority, reflects on the self, makes judgments, exerts moral pressure, and is the seat of conscience, guilt, and self-esteem. In Kleinian thinking, the superego is composed of a split-off part of the ego into which the death instinct is projected, fused with the life instinct and the good and bad aspects of both primary and later objects. It acquires both protective and threatening qualities. The superego and the ego share different aspects of the same objects; they develop in parallel through the processes of

introjection and projection. If all goes well, the internal objects in both the ego and the superego – initially extreme – gradually become less so, leading to a progressive reconciliation between the two structures.

(Spillius et al., 2011, p. 147)

This metapsychological conception leads us to a fundamental reflection on the ways in which the psyche is organised from the very first experiences with the other. Unlike the classical Freudian view, which situates the formation of the superego at the resolution of the Oedipus complex, Klein relocates this construction to a far more primitive moment – at the very origins of psychic life. That is to say, from the earliest moments, the infant introjects not only the care and protection offered by the environment but also its persecutory aspects, projecting into the superego an amalgam of life and death instincts, good and bad aspects of the primary objects – forming a kind of internal tribunal that constantly oscillates between punishment and containment. The Kleinian superego, then, is not merely the agency that judges and imposes moral standards, but also the one that may either destroy the self or, conversely, protect it from more intense disintegration.

This construction, at once threatening and protective, finds echoes in literature and cinema, where characters often struggle against this relentless internal agency. *Black Swan* (2010), directed by Darren Aronofsky, can be seen as a cinematic representation of this dynamic. Nina, the protagonist, is haunted by a merciless superego that embodies not only maternal and societal demands, but also an internal split between her idealised self and the part that carries destructive (and transgressive) impulses.

The split between ego and superego, characteristic of the schizo-paranoid position described by Klein, is manifested in the fragmentation of Nina's identity. She projects her internal conflict into hallucinations and the feeling of being pursued by a darker version of herself. The distorted and threatening reflection she sees in the mirror can be understood as the materialisation of a ferocious superego – one incapable of integration or mediation.

If throughout development the good and bad objects are not sufficiently worked through, this internal structure may become persecutory, trapping the subject in an endless cycle of guilt, fear, and self-sabotage. In the best-case scenario, however, the psychic life moves toward a balance in which the superego and the ego – once in opposition – find a space for reconciliation, allowing the individual to bear their own ambivalence without being destroyed by it.

Marion Minerbo (2019), in her research on the cruel superego, highlights that this psychic agency attacks and disorganises the ego through three distinct psychopathological configurations: 1) in *melancholic functioning*, where the conflict between the superego and the ego unfolds on an intrapsychic level; 2) in *paranoid functioning*, in which the subject identifies with the superego and places the other in the position of the ego, treating them with the same cruelty; and 3) in *masochistic functioning*, where the individual, through projective identification, induces the other to identify with the cruel superego and, consequently, to persecute them.

These modes of superego operation can be observed in our everyday lives, beyond the more severe manifestations encountered in the clinical setting. In melancholic functioning, for instance, the subject's inner voice becomes a *relentless tribunal*. They are excessively self-demanding, intolerant of mistakes, and reduce any error – however minor – to irrefutable proof of their inadequacy. Consider someone who, after making a slight mistake during a work presentation, spends days mentally punishing themselves, reliving the moment and reinforcing the belief that they are simply not good enough. Here, the superego acts as an unforgiving judge, leaving no room for self-compassion or for learning from failure.

In paranoid functioning, this same cruel logic *is projected outward*. Rather than internalising the aggression, the subject displaces it onto others, transforming their surroundings into a hostile, persecutory environment. This might be someone who, feeling insecure within a social group, assumes they are being judged and, in defence, adopts a critical and merciless stance towards others. The suspicious gaze, the distorted interpretation of others' intentions, and the need for control are all expressions of a superego which, instead of attacking the ego, is externalised and directed toward those around them.

In masochistic functioning, the dynamic becomes even more complex. The subject, unable to cope with the violence of their own superego, enlists the other to take on this role. This may be someone who repeatedly enters abusive relationships, accepting humiliation and disdain, as they find a certain familiarity in this place of suffering. It is as if, by recreating the internal dynamic of attack and punishment within the relational field, there is a temporary relief from anguish – even if it comes at the cost of emotional integrity.

The hypothesis of an archaic superego was present throughout Melanie Klein's work, but it was in 1957, with the publication of "Envy and Gratitude", that this conception underwent a fundamental shift. While previously the superego had been conceived predominantly as the result of the introjection of fragments of parental figures, at this point Klein begins to emphasise the role of primary envy in the formation of this psychic agency. Thus, superegoic cruelty no longer stems solely from the severity of the paternal function – as Freud had proposed – but from a more primitive movement: the projection of one's own envy onto the object, which then returns to the ego in the form of persecution.

This formulation helps understanding psychic manifestations that go beyond guilt, bringing to light dynamics of resentment, hostility, and self-annihilation. To Klein, this envy projected onto the object prevents the individual from finding satisfaction in reparation, thereby intensifying guilt and suffering. It is within this context that she introduces the idea of the envious superego:

> In her important paper "Envy and Gratitude", Klein introduces the idea
> of the envious super-ego, a superego based on "the earliest internalized

persecutory object – the retaliating, devouring, and poisonous breast" (Klein, 1957, p. 231). The "envious super-ego" is described as containing projected envy and does not allow the child the satisfaction of repair. It increases guilt and persecution. This concept was later expanded upon by Bion and others.

(Spillius et al., 2011, p. 156)

Finally, it is worth noting that Klein does not dismiss the formation of the superego as described by Freud – emerging from the elaboration of the Oedipus complex, during the phase of relations with whole objects. However, this second superegoic formation does not occur in isolation; it bears the marks of the earlier path – or of the impasses – established in the primary configuration, reflecting both the pathways and the distortions inherited from that initial structure.

Winnicott: A Psychoanalytic Theory Without a Superego?

To many, it may seem that Winnicott's theory of infant maturation dispenses with describing something as important and fundamental as the formation of the child's superego, given the scarce references made to the subject.

It is true that Winnicott considered morality to be innate in the infant, having written an article on this topic (Winnicott, 1949/2017), and developed the idea further in later works. By *innate*, he meant the capacity for morality to develop spontaneously – from within – when supported by a sufficiently good environment. According to the author, this would occur during what he termed the *stage of concern*.

We are, then, dealing with a baby whose maturation has reached the point of distinguishing between inner and outer reality and who, therefore, is able to relate to whole objects. Winnicott tells us:

At this stage to which I refer now there is a gradual build-up in the child of a capacity to feel a sense of responsibility, that which at base is a sense of guilt. The environmental essential here is the continuous presence of the mother or mother-figure over the time in which the infant is accommodating the destructiveness that is part of his make-up. This destructiveness becomes more and more a feature in the experience of object relationships, and the phase of development to which I am referring lasts from about six months to two years, after which the child may have made a satisfactory integration of the idea of destroying the object and the fact that of loving the same object. The mother is needed over this time and she is needed because of her survival value. She is the environment-mother and at the same time an object-mother, the object of excited loving. In this later role she is repeatedly destroyed or damaged. The child gradually comes to integrate these two aspects of the mother and to be able to love and to be affectionate with the surviving mother at the same time.

This phase involves the child in a special kind of anxiety which is called a sense of guilt, guilt related to the idea of destruction where love is also operating. It is this anxiety that drives the child towards constructive and actively loving behaviour in his limited world, reviving the object, making the loved object better again, rebuilding the damaged thing. If the mother-figure is not able to see the child through over this phase than the child fails to find or loses the capacity to feel guilt, but instead feels crudely anxious and this anxiety is merely wasteful.

(Winnicott, 1962/2017, pp. 385–386)

This emerging morality, throughout infant development, translates into the acquisition of a sense of responsibility for the other, grounded in a feeling of guilt. During what Winnicott called *oral sadism* the baby, while feeding, fantasises about causing harm to the mother's body – which, paradoxically, is also their object of love. The guilt, described by Winnicott as unconscious, awakens in the infant a need to repair this imagined destruction through loving and constructive gestures. However, this process can only unfold if the mother – or any maternal figure performing that role – is able to withstand the child's destructive fantasies, remaining present and emotionally available, without retaliating or becoming fragile in the face of them.

We are speaking here of the child's discovery of the other as a fellow being, someone who shares their world and on whom they depend – or, more profoundly, we might say that, at this stage, the child is forming what Merleau-Ponty (1968)[3] would call their "intersubjective worldly dwelling" in which coexistence with the other and responsibility for their well-being becomes essential. We are all dependent on one another – this is the great truth – since the independence each person achieves through personal maturation is never absolute.[4]

It is for this reason that, rather than referring to the formation of a "morality" – a term derived from the Latin *moralis*, meaning "proper behaviour of a person in society", and literally "related to manners" – we prefer to consider the acquisition of the *stage of concern* as the development of an "ethics". This is because the word *ethics* comes from the Greek *éthos*, which originally meant "dwelling" or "protective shelter". As we have already mentioned, this refers to the infant's assumption of responsibility for the other upon whom their dependence rests: the mother, their "protective shelter", or, more deeply, the acquisition of their intersubjective worldly dwelling.

It is possible that, had he reflected on these etymological roots, Winnicott might well have agreed with us.

On a broader level, this is the ethics that underpins the possibility of all human coexistence and cooperation, as it is upon this foundation that, later, in the maturation process, the possibility of cross-identifications[5] will be built.

Based on Winnicott's considerations, Elsa Oliveira Dias comments:

It is worth noting that, in Winnicott, morality is constituted in a non-Oedipal context; it is not referred to law or prohibition. What is essential to it is not defined in terms of conformity or transgression – *except secondarily, for the already socialised individual* – but rather in terms of the care involved in allowing the child to be herself, so that she, in turn, may also acquire the capacity to let the other be as a self. Morality is said to be innate, according to Winnicott, in the sense that each individual possesses a tendency to develop a feeling of responsibility for their actions; however, this achievement must still be integrated into the personality through personal experience.

(Dias, 2014, p. 254, emphasis added)

The commentary, as a whole, is well constructed; the issue, however, lies precisely in the part of the statement we have emphasised: *except secondarily, for the already socialised individual*, about which Dias offers no further commentary in the book. We would argue that after passing through the stage of concern the child – if successful – has laid the groundwork for the socialisation process. However, the full process of socialisation also involves the constitution of a healthy superego, which occurs during the elaboration of the Oedipus complex (Almeida and Naffah Neto, 2022). Beyond the development of responsibility for the other, the child must also acquire what morality concretely signifies: namely, the customs, norms, laws, and prohibitions that characterise the familial and social culture in which they are embedded. It is noteworthy that in such a careful, rigorous, and fundamental book as that of Dias, there is no mention of the constitution of the superego from a Winnicottian perspective. This omission leads many readers to assume that Winnicott's theory does away with the notion of the superego altogether.

The same situation can be observed in the book by Cláudia Dias Rosa on fatherhood in Winnicott (Rosa, 2022). In section 2.3 of the book, "Direct paternal failures in the stage of triangular relationships", there is no reference to the formation of the superego, nor to the paternal failures that might hinder such formation. Once again, that may lead the uninitiated reader to assume that Winnicott never regarded the superego as a significant concept.

It is important to highlight that the aforementioned works hold great relevance within the Brazilian psychoanalytic field, influencing the research of numerous analysts dedicated to the study of Winnicottian psychoanalysis. Both the book by Dias and that of Rosa are widely referenced in academic and clinical works, contributing significantly to the dissemination of Winnicott's thought and its impact on our understanding of psychic constitution.

However, the lack of a deeper discussion on the superego within these texts ends up reinforcing the mistaken impression that Winnicott dismissed this Freudian psychic agency. This issue becomes even more significant when we consider that Winnicott's theory not only acknowledges the formation of the superego but also proposes a rather *innovative* perspective – so to speak – on its origin and functioning. To counter this mistaken assumption, we turn to Winnicott himself who, when commenting on a paper by Joseph Sandler,

"On the Concept of Superego", clarifies the relevance of the superego within his theory:

> I find the statement of the development of the idea of the superego in Freud's mind very useful and I am always grateful to anyone who will take the trouble to do this sort of research and to make this sort of statement.
>
> (Winnicott, 1960/2018, p. 465)

To justify that statement, Winnicott goes on to describe one of his clinical cases:

> One can be told by a patient, as I have been told recently by a boy of 19, just the sort of things that Freud wrote down that are quoted by Sandler. To some extent this boy of 19 was influenced by the thought of his decade which is of course much influenced by Freud's work. Nevertheless, it was this boy himself who worked out in a self-analysis that he had an institution in his mind which was all time influencing him. This was partly based on the idea of his father and of his parents in combination, and here he found he could manage by defiance. Part was based, however, on a very personal analysing and observing self, which studied everything that was happening in his life, and enabled him to get through without too much suffering. This which could be called a superego could be sadistic, and he recognised that his own sadism had gone into the sadism of the superego; he also recognised the masochistic perversion which was a way of dealing with the sadistic superego. He told me that he had tried to use the sadistic superego by turning it on to the part of himself that he loathed, which was a false self. He did not call this a false self because he was talking in his own language. He spoke of a very nice child which everyone thought he had been, but he had come to see was not by any means his true self. He had been haunted, for instance, by the myth of Doppelgänger,[6] and he was all the time looking for the other self which would turn up at the moment of death when he would no longer be alive to keep the split operative. What he suffered from was the lack of spontaneity, and the only way that he could regain the spontaneity that he had lost was through the agency of alcohol which for a few hours would deal with the superego and release the spontaneity and his capacity to make relationships and to reach out towards heterosexuality.
>
> (Winnicott, 1960/2018, pp. 465–466)

Thus, we observe that even in a clinical case Winnicott makes significant use of the concept of the superego. One could argue, in contrast, that he employs the term merely to accompany the patient's narrative – one shaped by a cultural context heavily influenced by Freudian thought. This would explain why the patient describes their inner experiences using such a framework. However, if that were the case, we would expect Winnicott to quickly move away from the term, replacing it with a concept more aligned with his own theoretical model. The opposite occurs: he continues to use the concept of the superego throughout the case description, which suggests a tacit recognition of its clinical relevance.

It is important to note, however, that while Winnicott retains the Freudian notion of the superego he associates it with a sadistic and pathological version – one that is closely linked to an equally pathological false self, dissociated from the rest of the personality. It is something imposed from the outside inwards, disconnected from the patient's true self, yet tormenting them in a cruel manner. At times this superego compels the patient into a masochistic position; at others it drives them to seek refuge in alcohol, allowing repressed aggression to surface – an aggression that challenges this oppressive agency and, in doing so, opens the way for spontaneity and the potential for a more authentic experience of sexuality.

The Superego in Winnicott

To Winnicott, first and foremost, any suggestion of phylogenetic transmission disappears. In this sense, he may be considered the most empiricist of all psychoanalysts, since to him the entire psyche-soma of the newborn is completely formed through experience – experience that always takes place within the real world the infant inhabits. In this context, *experience* means "[…] a constant trafficking in illusion, a repeated reaching to the interplay between creativity and that which the world has to offer" (Winnicott, 1987/1999, p. 43).

To understand this definition, we must first characterise the newborn as conceived by Winnicott. The Winnicottian infant is not born already marked by a conflict between the life instinct and the death instinct – as in Freud and Klein – since Winnicott did not work with these concepts. To him only what is elaborated through the infant's experience possesses psychic reality. So, there is no direct contact in his theory with any drive towards the inorganic. According to Winnicott the infant emerges from a state of non-being into a state of being, already while in the maternal womb, and their most primitive experience is that of essential aloneness (Winnicott, 1988/2017). This is in no way akin to the Freudian concept of the death instinct. In this light, he understands any wish for death as a longing to return to the peace of that essential solitude, from which one might then be reborn.

Since the notion of the death instinct proves itself unhelpful, its counterpart, life instinct, also disappears. Accordingly, Winnicott always speaks of *instincts* in the plural and without classifications.

In addition to instincts, the Winnicottian newborn is also born with something he calls *primary creativity* – a term that designates the capacity to *create* the object upon encountering it, within an *illusion of omnipotence*. This illusion is based on the infant's experience that the object is "magically created" whenever needed – since, at this stage, the infant lives in a state of fusion with the environment and therefore has no awareness of its independent existence.[7] This illusion only begins to fade much later (around 12 months of age), when the infant creates or discovers the shared world, distinguishing between an inner and an external reality.

Even so, the child – and later the adult – continues to "create" the world throughout life, for only that which bears the subjective mark of one's own creation is felt to be true and one's own. As the Brazilian poet Manoel de Barros once wrote, "Everything I don't invent is false" (Barros, 2005, p. 5).

It is precisely in this sense that, to Winnicott, experience is a "trafficking in illusion", an "interplay between creativity and that which the world has to offer". Constitutionally the Winnicottian baby inherits only an innate tendency towards integration in time and space – gradually coming to establish a sense of spatiality and temporality of its own – and an equally innate sense of morality, as previously defined. However, all these tendencies can only come into being if the baby is supported by a sufficiently good environment, one that ensures some degree of *going-on-being* while the infant remains in a state of non-integration. At this early stage, experience is marked by discontinuous moments, with no connection between them, in which the baby temporarily borrows the spatial identities of surrounding objects – at times merging with the breast from which it feeds, at times with the maternal arms that sustain it. This process continues until the baby is able to form a psychosomatic unit, allowing the psyche to take up residence in the body – what Winnicott calls *personalisation* – thereby achieving a spatial identity of its own.

For those instincts to acquire psychic reality they must undergo a process known as the *imaginative elaboration of body functioning*, which is responsible for the constitution of the baby's psyche – one that is entirely created from bodily functions – as well as for the psyche's location within the body, gradually forming a psychosomatic[8] unity. It is also through this process that infantile sexuality will emerge – throughout the course of maturation – along with the appropriation of aggressive-destructive impulses and their fusion with loving/erotic impulses. This enables the child to sustain ambivalent feelings during the stage of concern, which – as previously mentioned – prepares the ground for the elaboration of the Oedipus complex.

Thus, to Winnicott, since there is no phylogenetic transmission of any kind there are no *proto-fantasies* as proposed by Freud and Bion, nor *phantasies* present from the outset of life, as conceived by Klein (see Chapter 2). Fantasies, in Winnicott's view, are formed through the baby's maturing capacity for imaginative elaboration, along their developmental trajectory, and only emerge once the baby becomes capable of distinguishing an external world, full of *reality*, from an internal world, populated by *fantasy*, which typically occurs around 12 months of age. Only then can the baby begin to repress fantasies that generate excessive anxiety, thus initiating the formation of the repressed[9] unconscious – everything at its own time.

Accordingly, the Winnicottian superego must, without doubt, differ from both the Freudian and the Kleinian conceptions of the superego. From the

Freudian model, Winnicott borrows only the developmental timing – the elaboration of the Oedipus complex around the age of four or five – while discarding any reference to phylogenesis. As for the Kleinian superego, Winnicott rejects its archaic version, arguing that one cannot speak of superego formation while the child is still relating to part-objects – at least in the context of a healthy maturational process. Nevertheless, he does inherit certain influences from both authors, as we shall see below.

To describe more precisely what Winnicott understood by the constitution of the superego, let us now turn to his own words:

> Surely it is in health only that the classical superego belonging to the passing of the Oedipus complex can be observed. By health I mean that the emotional development of the individual has taken place satisfactorily in the earliest stages of dependence, and the family exists, and the parents are present and playing their part in a fairly good way. It is a great relief for a child to be able to experience the anxieties that belong to the Oedipus complex. We have to say, this child is well enough to be one whole person among three, to experience the triangular situation, and to be able to work through in the presence of the parents all that is meant by the passing of the Oedipus complex and the setting of a superego which has some relationship to the parents as perceived and as conceived of. A very large number of children never have this relief. What happens in such case is not that there is no superego but that the superego formation never becomes humanised and will remain rather like polytheism before monotheism. It is then as if there are forces and mechanistic agencies that are feared and that must be magically countered, and that certainly cannot be defied. Every possible kind of frightening mechanism belongs to the lack of health in this area. In health the child may (to be sure) develop psychoneurosis, but nevertheless he or she has the great relief of a superego which is related to human beings in fact, the father and the mother. The analysis can cash on this. These human beings can be loved and hated, obeyed and defied, in the ordinary way that is well known.
>
> (Winnicott, 1960/2018, pp. 470–471)

Later on, Winnicott states:

> Perhaps [...] we may find some value in the idea of the "representing" and "guiding" functions of introjects, building up to the human superego formation which relates to the passing of the Oedipus complex in children who are healthy and who get that far.
>
> (Winnicott, 1960/2018, p. 472)

Let us begin, then, by noting that this is no longer a matter of *identification* with the parents' superegos – as in Freud – but rather a process of introjection, or more precisely, the *introjection of the human figures of mother and father*, who then become internal objects that can be loved, hated, obeyed, and challenged. In other words, we may assume here a certain Kleinian legacy – more specifically, the notion of mother and father as *internal objects* used as guides.

In pathology, instead of personal superegos – those formed by whole persons, total objects – we find superegos composed of threatening, mechanistic forces and actions, with which it becomes far more difficult to reach any kind of compromise.

In an earlier text, though from the same period, Winnicott even refers to this pathological formation as "[...] a *false* superego development based in an abnormal way on the intrusion of a very powerful authoritarian influence derived from the environment of early years" (Winnicott, 1958/2017, p. 139, emphasis added). He then goes on to associate this type of superego with two pathologies: obsessive neurosis and melancholia.

We do not intend here to delve into the characterisation of these pathologies within Winnicott's framework, as doing so would require too much time and space, ultimately diverting us from the main aim of this study. However, for those interested, we recommend the text "Winnicottian Contributions to the Characterisation and Clinical Approach to Obsessive Neurosis" (Naffah Neto, 2023).

The concept of a *false superego* – which appears only in this particular text by Winnicott and in no other, and about which he offers no further commentary – evokes the articulation he previously established between the sadistic superego of the 19-year-old patient (as described earlier) and a pathological false self created as a psychotic defence.

Since it consists of authoritarian moral inculcations imposed by the environment during the early years of life – a period in which the baby still relates to part-objects – this superego is formed by "anonymous forces", rather than by whole persons. As it is constituted by external impositions rather than by something arising from the infant's spontaneous gesture or primary creativity, it cannot be regarded as authentic within Winnicott's framework. What does not emerge from subjective experience and is not created by the individual is, by definition, false – as Manoel de Barros so aptly reminds us. It is for this reason that Winnicott refers to it as a *false superego*.

It is, therefore, quite plausible to consider this type of superego as a distinct part of certain kinds of pathological false selves. In clinical practice, we may encounter such formations not only in severe obsessive neuroses and in melancholia, but also in patients with various types of borderline personalities. At times, they present as a tormenting moral conscience; at others, as a rigid ego ideal, imposing near-impossible demands in an imperious and exacting manner.

As an example, we refer to the case of José, a schizoid patient with a pathological false self structured around an intellectual hypertrophy, split off from the rest of his personality. José suffers greatly from insecurity and an elevated level of self-demand, as he frequently compares himself to acquaintances of a similar age and, when doing so, often feels like a "failure". This points to a particularly harsh *ego ideal*, one that imposes performative demands he is unable to meet. In our view, this ego ideal belongs to his false self, being shaped by mimicry and environmental introjections. We are not certain whether José ever elaborated Oedipal issues, but if he did, we suspect it occurred in a highly fragmentary manner. Indeed, he appears to lack a healthy *superego*, one formed through the introjection of parental figures, the sort of superego that arises from a more complete working through of the Oedipus complex. Thus, we assume, based on the Winnicottian framework, that his superegoic formation is of an impersonal kind, formed by anonymous forces, and therefore more difficult to confront in the ordinary course of life.

Among the performative demands imposed by this ego ideal is the need to constantly present himself in public through the creation of a persona quite distinct from his true self – which he consistently experiences as *inadequate*. This persona is livelier, more "cool", seemingly capable of eliciting admiration from others by exhibiting *false* characteristics that do not genuinely belong to him. This compels him to maintain a level of performance that he is generally unable to sustain, and the looming expectation of failure gives rise to intense paranoid anxieties.

In the analytic process, it is essential that the analyst offers support so that the patient may develop a truer form of self-acceptance, one that is rooted in their own experience. This involves helping the patient to recognise, again and again, that people cannot be compared to one another. Each individual carries a unique history, with singular challenges and experiences, and any attempt to comparison disregards this trajectory, resting on the illusion of a homogeneous starting point. Moreover, it is vital to emphasise that self-acceptance should not be contingent upon the gaze of the other, since external judgements are always filtered through the speaker's own ghosts and projections, rather than reflecting the true singularity of the one being observed.

That said, we know that this kind of analysis unfolds over years, passing through layers of guilt, demands, and imperatives that echo like a sentence within the patient. The analyst's unconditional, silent, and steadfast acceptance gradually wears down the sharp edges of a superego that is both merciless (in Klein's sense) and false (in Winnicott's), like the sea that, unhurriedly, sculpts the cliffs. There is something crafty about this process: to carve, through time and attentive listening, a terrain in which rigidity may give way, where the weight of internal demands no longer feels like an inescapable verdict. And if there is any task that falls to us, it is this: to sustain the wait, to endure the pauses, to trust that, in the folds of time, harshness may, at last, *lose its grip*.

Notes

1 In a footnote, Freud adds: "Perhaps it would be safer to say 'with the parents'; for before a child has arrived at definite knowledge of the difference between the sexes, the lack of a penis, it does not distinguish in value between its father and its mother" (Freud, 1923/1981, p. 31).

2 It is worth remarking that, to Freud, the Oedipus complex is always dual, involving both father and mother simultaneously as objects of desire and as rivals – although one form may predominate over the other. Its resolution therefore always entails a simultaneous identification with the combined parental figures of both father and mother.

3 Merleau-Ponty (1968) emphasised that our experience of the world is intrinsically intersubjective; that is, our perception and understanding of the world are always mediated by our interactions with others. He argued that there is no such thing as a "raw world" separate from our shared experience, but rather a "constructed world" shaped through our relationships and collective perceptions. To Merleau-Ponty the body plays a central role in the formation of this intersubjectivity. In other words, corporeality enables us to connect with others and with the surrounding world, establishing a shared "dwelling" in which our existences are intertwined.

4 Moreover, this cycle of destruction, guilt, and reparation – when adequately supported by the maternal figure – enables the child to appropriate their aggressive-destructive impulses without experiencing overwhelming guilt, as what is "destroyed" can be repaired. In this way, aggressive-destructive impulses may gradually fuse with loving/erotic ones, allowing the child to sustain ambivalent love-hate feelings, which will be essential in working through the Oedipus complex. When this cycle is disrupted – either by the disappearance of the maternal figure or by retaliation in response to the child's destructiveness – the child begins to fear their own instinctual impulses and resorts to repressing or inhibiting them. This can result in a lowering of vital energy and the emergence of depressive pathologies.

5 We can define *cross-identification* as the capacity to place oneself within the other and to feel what they are feeling, without losing one's own sense of self – while simultaneously allowing the reverse movement to occur. It is the Winnicottian version of the notion of *projective identification*, understood here in its healthy form.

6 *Doppelgänger*, in the myth referred to, designates a double or look-alike of a ghostly nature, who accompanies the person in question.

7 This paradox of creating/finding is something that, according to Winnicott, should not be questioned or resolved. I personally understand this *creating* as something akin to selecting and making use of exactly what the real object can offer that meets the infant's needs – thus imprinting the object with the infant's subjective mark.

8 An example of this constitution of the psyche grounded in bodily functioning is food intake, which gives rise to the psychic function of *introjection*, and defecation, which gives rise to the psychic function of *projection*, according to Winnicott.

9 The processes, which are constitutive of the baby's psyche-soma, are all unconscious – though not in the sense of a repressed unconscious, but rather as states that are incapable of reaching consciousness, since consciousness itself has not yet even formed.

References

Abraham, K. (1970). *Breve estudo da libido visto à luz das perturbações mentais* [A Short Study of the Libido Viewed in the Light of Mental Disturbances]. In K. Abraham, *Teoria psicanalítica da libido* [Psychoanalytic Theory of the Libido], pp. 81–160. Rio de Janeiro: Imago. (Original work published in 1924)

Almeida, A. P. (2022). O superego arcaico, as redes sociais e sua relação com o burnout na era do cansaço: revisitando Melanie Klein [The Archaic Superego, Social Media, and Its Relationship With Burnout in the Age of Exhaustion: Revisiting Melanie Klein]. *Jornal de Psicanálise*, 55(102): 105–123.

Almeida, A. P., and Naffah Neto, A. (2022). *O estágio da concernência e a elaboração do complexo de Édipo: revisitando Winnicott e o caso Piggle* [The Stage of

Concern and the Elaboration of the Oedipus Complex: Revisiting Winnicott and the Case of Piggle]. *Psicologia Revista, 31*(1): 27–50. https://doi.org/10.23925/2594-3871.2022v31i1p27-50

Aronofsky, Darren (director). (2010). *Black Swan*. Searchlight Pictures.

Barros, M. (2005). *Memórias inventadas para crianças* [*Invented Memories for Children*]. São Paulo: Planeta Jovem.

Dias, E. O. (2014). *A Teoria do Amadurecimento em D. W. Winnicott* (3ª. Ed.) [*The Theory of Maturation in D. W. Winnicott* (3rd Ed.)]. São Paulo: DWWeditorial.

Freud, S. (1981). The Ego and the Id. *The Standard Edition of the Complete Psychological Works of Sigmund Freud (Vol. 19)*, pp. 3–68. London: Hogarth Press. (Original work published in 1923)

Grotstein, J. S. (2017). *… no entanto, ao mesmo tempo e em outro nível…: teoria e técnica psicanalítica na linha kleiniana/bioniana (vol.1)* [*…But at the Same Time, and on Another Level…: Psychoanalytic Theory and Technique in the Kleinian/Bionian Tradition (Vol. 1)*]. São Paulo: Blucher.

Klein, M. (2011) Early Stages of the Oedipal Conflict. In M. Klein, *Love, Guilt and Reparation and Other Works (1921–1945)*. London: Vintage Books. E-book. (Original work published in 1928)

Klein, M. (2011). Envy and Gratitude. In M. Klein, *Envy and Gratitude and Other Works (1946–1963)*. London: Vintage Books. E-book. (Original work published in 1957)

Laplanche, J., and Pontalis, J.-B. (1970). *Vocabulário da Psicanálise* [The Language of Psycho-Analysis]. São Paulo: Martins Fontes.

Merleau-Ponty, M. (1968). *The Visible and the Invisible*. Evanston: Northwestern University Press.

Minerbo, M. (2019). *Novos diálogos sobre a clínica psicanalítica* [New Dialogues on Psychoanalytic Clinic]. São Paulo: Blucher.

Naffah Neto, A. (2023). *Contribuições winnicottianas à caracterização e à clínica da neurose obsessiva* [Winnicottian Contributions to the Characterisation and Clinical Approach to Obsessive Neurosis]. In A. Naffah Neto, *Veredas Psicanalíticas: à Sombra de Winnicott* (2ª ed.) [*Psychoanalytic Paths: In the Shadow of Winnicott* (2nd Ed.)], pp. 213–236. São Paulo: Blucher.

Rosa, C. D. (2022). *A paternidade em Winnicott* [*Fatherhood in Winnicott*]. São Paulo: DWWeditorial.

Spillius, E. et al. (2011). *The New Dictionary of Kleinian Thought*. London: Routledge.

Winnicott, D. W. (1999). *The Spontaneous Gesture – Selected Letters of D. W. Winnicott*. London: Karnac Books. (Original work published in 1987)

Winnicott, D. W. (2017). The Innate Morality of the Baby. In D. W. Winnicott, *The Collected Works of D. W. Winnicott (Vol. 3)*, pp. 299–302. Oxford: Oxford University Press. (Original work published in 1949)

Winnicott, D. W. (2017). Psycho-Analysis and the Sense of Guilt. In D. W. Winnicott, *The Collected Works of D. W. Winnicott (Vol. 5)*, pp. 135–148. Oxford: Oxford University Press. (Original work published in 1958)

Winnicott, D. W. (2017). Human Nature. In D. W. Winnicott, *The Collected Works of D. W. Winnicott (Vol. 11)*, pp. 3–186. Oxford: Oxford University Press. (Original work published in 1988)

Winnicott, D. W. (2017). Morals and Education. In D. W. Winnicott, *The Collected Works of D. W. Winnicott (Vol. 6)*, pp. 377–388. Oxford: Oxford University Press. (Original work presented in 1962)

Winnicott, D. W. (2018). Joseph Sandler – Comments on "On the Concept of the Superego". In D. W. Winnicott, *Psycho-Analytic Explorations*, pp. 465–473. London: Routledge. (Original work published in 1960)

9 The Body as the Support of the Psyche-Soma in Winnicott Versus the Body as the Raw and Sensory Basis of Thought in Bion (Somatic Reverie)[1]

Alfredo Naffah Neto and
Alexandre Patricio de Almeida

Some Opening Remarks

Clarice Lispector, with her unique literary style, wrote with precision:

> And within it dwells an "I". A body set apart from others – and this is what is called "I"? It is strange to have a body in which to dwell, a body where wet blood runs without end, where the mouth knows how to sing, and the eyes must have wept so many times. She is an "I".
>
> (Lispector, 2018, p. 303)

Before we delve properly into pshychoanalytic theory – particularly the contributions of Winnicott and Bion to our understanding of the bodily (psychosomatic) dimension – it is worthwhile to cast a lateral and sensitive glance at the thoughts of Merleau-Ponty. We do not seek to do a phenomenological exercise. The present text is not a work of philosophy and does not seek to engage fully with the phenomenological tradition. Rather, our interest lies in how certain intuitions from Merleau-Ponty regarding bodily experience allow us to rethink the body as *expressive matter*, that is, as a living field of meaning that precedes reflective thought.

Merleau-Ponty (1945/1994) insists that there can be no perception without the body, and that consciousness cannot be conceived as separate from the flesh that feels, acts, touches, and is touched. Subjectivity, in this sense, is not confined to a mere mental abstraction; it involves a body formed through the interweaving of time, history, world, and sensoriality. Far from being a machine the body is the first mode of being in the world – it is through the body that we hear before we understand, that we cry before we explain, that we tremble before we know why.

Merleau-Ponty (1945/1994) introduces the concept of *intercorporeality*, suggesting that our bodily experiences are inherently intersubjective. To him subjectivity is shaped through relationships with others, in which the body serves as a tool of expression and communication. That perspective highlights the construction of subjectivity unfolds through bodily and social interactions, underscoring the interconnection between self and other in lived experience.

DOI: 10.4324/9781003642503-10

Within this framework, freedom, for Merleau-Ponty, is not an arbitrary choice but a situated experience, originated from the encounter between the inside and the outside, between what passes through us and what we choose to do with it. As the body moves through the world, it does not merely react – it interprets, sets a rhythm, shifts meanings. Perception then ceases to be somewhat taken for granted and becomes language, affect, thought in its earliest state.

This background is relevant to our discussion because it invites us to reconsider the relationship between body and subjectivity beyond the psyche–matter dichotomy. Merleau-Ponty reminds us that there is a form of bodily knowledge that precedes conceptual formulation – a sensitivity that takes part in the constitution of the individual even before it is symbolised. Psychoanalysis, in turn, adds a crucial dimension to this discussion: before becoming inhabitable, it takes the body to be dreamed of, invested in, and elaborated by the psychic apparatus. It is in this crossing – between the sensible and the imagined – that the body comes to be felt as one's own, as a container and expression of the self.

Throughout this chapter, we will interweave these philosophical insights with two fundamental concepts from contemporary psychoanalysis: *holding*, in Winnicott, and *somatic reverie*, a notion developed by Bion and further expanded by Civitarese (2021).

Imaginative Elaboration of Bodily Functions

Imaginative elaboration of bodily functions is one of the main concepts in D.W. Winnicott's theory, although it has been curiously underexplored in contemporary psychoanalytic literature. Our aim in this chapter is precisely to revisit this notion through a theoretical-clinical articulation – we will present a clinical case, which clearly illustrates the importance of this function in the constitution of the psyche-soma.

The case concerns a patient with a typically borderline functioning who, at the outset of the analytic process, presented a marked split between his mind (intellect) and his feelings. His thinking, though highly developed, seemed disconnected from any embodied affection experience. His body, in turn, was scarcely appropriated, almost a foreign ground. During this period, he often dreamed of flying, performing aerial acrobatics before imaginary audiences. These flights brought him a certain narcissistic pleasure, as though he could display his lightness and superiority in a space without weight, gravity, or emotion.

As the analysis progressed and the process of personalisation advanced – a movement through which the self gradually comes to inhabit the body – dreams began to change. Images of flying still appeared, especially during times of heightened environmental stress, but they gradually gave way to dreams in which the patient was walking, stumbling, feeling the ground beneath him. The dream world started to gain weight, density, and contour. It was as if the body had finally begun to take part in psychic life.

To interpret those dreams through the lens of classical Freudian theory – as mere fulfilments of infantile sexual wishes – would entirely distort their function and clinical meaning.[2] In order to understand them in depth it is necessary to turn to Winnicott's notion of the *imaginative elaboration of bodily functions*, in which dreaming is one of the most significant manifestations.[3]

In the example presented, we might say that "flying" and "walking on the ground" are dream metaphors that express distinct ways of inhabiting the world. The former is marked by a dissociated mind, devoid of affective anchoring, launching into omnipotent flights stripped of corporeality. The latter reflects the emergence of an embodied subjectivity, capable of bearing its own affects and establishing a minimal unity between thought and sensation – a nascent experience of psychosomatic integration.

It was precisely the scarcity of in-depth studies on this concept – which is both clinical and poetic – that prompted us to develop the present reflection. We believe that, by bringing it back into focus, we can expand our listening to more primary forms of suffering in which the body is not yet a place inhabited, but a field still in the making.

The Body, as the Substrate of the Psyche

Among the various theoreticians within psychoanalysis, Winnicott could be counted as one of those who allocate the greatest importance to the body, both as a substratum of the psyche and as an integral part of it.

For Winnicott, the newborn counts solely on a genetic inheritance – one which is biologically transmitted by kinship and constitutes a biological body that, in turn, undergoes a long process before it becomes a human body inhabited by a psyche. On the psychic plane, the baby defines itself as a void loaded with possibilities that can come to be, which Winnicott denotes as *primary creativity*: pure potentiality, guaranteed on one hand by the greater or lesser spectrum of possibilities provided by this biological inheritance, but depending on the other on the environmental support that the newborn is furnished with in order to eventually give form to them. There are no inheritances in the psychic plane: neither primal phantasies, phylogenetically transmitted, as per Freud; nor phantasies as unconscious translations of Eros and Thanatos (instincts of life and death), and characteristic of the human species, as per Klein[4] – see Chapter 2 of this book. Nor are there any others.

In this respect, Winnicott behaves, philosophically speaking, as an empiricist: every psyche is born from the experience of being a child, which unrolls in the interaction between this group of possibilities provided by the biological inheritance and linked by the baby's primary creativity and the environmental configurations available. And, just as at this beginning of life the baby's primary creativity is oriented by the body's biological needs and functions, so the psyche must be created supported by them.

We might therefore think that, so far, there is nothing ground-breaking in psychoanalytic terms: Freud himself introduced child sexuality as being born supported on physiological functions. The Freudian thinking in question is widely known: the feeling of pleasure, as that "something extra" than the purely physiological satisfaction of breastfeeding, which arises supported on it, but which is only set into motion by its absence, through a hallucination of the breast – the creation of sexual desire as separate from physiological necessity, although supported by it. With Winnicott, however, *this is not the case*.

This is so because, in first place, Winnicott thinks that the issue at the beginning of life is not actually the creation of child sexuality, which will in effect constitute itself over the span of the child's development, but which will also require a longer time. Winnicott understands that first there is the need for a minimal existence of a child's self that is able to appropriate this "some-thing extra" that accompanies the physiological satisfaction and to imprint an erotic sense on it, thus allowing a sexuality to take form. It is nowhere as immediate and automatic as for Freud.[5]

For Winnicott, if the Id exists since the beginning, it is in practical terms as if it did not, for it is completely exterior to the infant's experience of existing, so much so that the instinctive drives that it feels – such as hunger – need to be satiated within a limited time for the infant to avoid being occupied with them, to avoid reacting to them. The infant who has had to react to hunger will take it in as something as threatening and traumatic as an extremely intense epidermal sensation, one that overwhelms its capacities to integrate it – tearing its being – or as a feeling of being crushed by a falling physical object. Overly intense hunger and epidermal sensation on one hand, and the feeling of being crushed by a physical object on the other, meet in an equivalent relationship external to the baby's existence, as they exceed its capacity to absorb them. In this sense, the only benign forms of hunger, epi-dermal sensation, or "external" threat are those which fail to achieve a level of sensibility that is intense enough to make them appear to the infant as enti-ties in themselves – in other words, those which remain as sensations able to melt and disappear within the baby's area of omnipotence, guaranteed and sustained by a sufficiently good environment. Any excess is always traumatic and, beyond a certain level, leads the infant to create a psychic protection against these threats.

One of these protections is the split false self as a premature differentiation of the primary creativity nucleus, created with the sole purpose of functioning as the infant's protective shield against the threats of environmental intrusions and overly intense instinctive drives that have still not been appropriated by the self. However, the constitution of this splitting in the heart of infant exist-ence will mark the start of borderline disease, the so-called latent schizophre-nias, as it interrupts the experience and thus the constitution of the psyche. The false self will therefore occupy the place of the true self, which fails to develop and remains covered.[6]

In order for the instinctive drives which, at the beginning of life, possess only a biological existence to acquire a psychic existence, it is necessary that they undergo the imaginative elaboration of body functioning. It is also this function that will gradually create the infant sexuality, first by giving a human sense to purely physiological movements and transforming them into searches for pleasure or aggressive discharge; and then by attaching these instincts to discriminate objects and melting the erotic and the aggressive/ destructive elements into ambivalent feelings (of attraction/repulsion, love/ hate), constituent of all human desire.

But what is it that comes to be, exactly, the imaginative elaboration of body functioning as Winnicott conceives it? Let us look at his own words:

> This enables us to say that the infant takes in with the hands and with the sensitive skin of the face as well as with the mouth. The *imaginative* feeding experience is much wider than the purely physical experience. The *total* experience of feeding can quickly involve a rich relationship to the mother's breast, or to the mother as gradually perceived, and what the baby does with the hands and eyes widens the scope of the feeding act. This which is normal is made more plain when we see an infant's feed being managed in a mechanical way. Such a feed, far from being an enriching experience for the infant, interrupts the infant's sense of going on being. I don't know quite how else to put it. There has been a reflex activity and no personal experience. [...] Have you ever seen an infant sucking a finger at the same time as happily breastfeeding? I have. Have you ever seen a dream walking? When an infant sucks bits of clothing, or the eiderdown or a dummy, this represents a spillover of the imagination, such as it is, imagination stimulated by the central exciting function which is feeding.
>
> (Winnicott, 1956/2017, pp. 116–117, original emphasis)

Based on these descriptions, we are able to see how the *imaginative elaboration of body functioning* describes a very basic form of imagination, one active since birth and which makes use of exploratory relations with objects, even before the infant discovers the existence of objects. They are, as Winnicott says, "odd habits" – ones that exceed and overflow the physiological functions, giving them a dimension that makes them standard for future psychic functions.

At first, the imaginative elaboration of the feeding function creates, under normal conditions, what Winnicott called the young infant's illusion of omnipotence. When the infant can count on a mother who is good enough, one who can make the breast appear, as if by magic, when faced with its instinctive urgency, the baby forms the illusion of having created the object at the moment in which it was needed. This description formulates the creation of the subjective object.

Within this process, as the infant still lives dispersed over time and space, having a completely vanishing identity that passes through various forms, it will be, at different moments, pure instinctive urgency, the nipple that is suckled, and the milk that is swallowed. This primary identification with the object will allow, as part of the process of imaginative elaboration, the infant to be able to incorporate its properties. Thus, a supportive mother will serve as a model that will, later on, become a psychic function and enable the child itself to hold the complexity of its emotional universe. Winnicott called this primary identification with the mother the female element, given this capacity to create psychic functions shaped in maternity, and distinguishes two kinds of mother's breast: one that is – allowing the infant the illusion of omnipotence and primary identification; and a second kind of breast that is not, but which does – imposing external standards on the infant and making it discover the existence of a world outside its area of omnipotence, during a period in which it is still not mature enough for this. Only the first kind of breast allows the infant to come to be; the second kind originates the formation of the split false self, as mentioned above.

The psychic functions of incorporation, evacuation, introjection, and projection are also born, later on, anchored to physiological functions, modelled on ingestion and defecation. Their dynamics will, therefore, follow the pattern of the physiological functions in question.

Internalising good environmental objects happens as a natural part of growth, whether it is in a more spontaneous or a defensive manner. In *Human Nature*, his last, unfinished, book (Winnicott, 1988/2017), Winnicott distinguishes incorporation from introjection. Incorporating good objects in the form of care, in this distinction, is a spontaneous process that takes place from the beginning, as a natural part of growth and with no defensive connotations. In the same manner, a student can incorporate the teachings of a professor (Almeida, 2023). *Introjecting* "good objects", on the other hand, implies a magical idealisation of the internalised objects, as a defence mechanism against anguish, when the environment becomes threatening.

The same reasoning applies to evacuation and projection: we evacuate the remains of that which we incorporate and has no psychic use to us, but we project persecutory internal objects that produce unbearable psychic pain in us, to magically rid ourselves of them. In any case, introjection and projection are processes that come later, subsequent to the distinction between the internal and the external world (Almeida and Naffah Neto, 2024), and have a more mental connotation – one linked to a defence against environmental storms.[7] But they are also useful for normal development, for they allow a transition between inside and outside that generates many psychic functions, one of which is learning to place oneself in the other's position in *crossed identifications* (Almeida, 2021).

Right from the start, through the act of sucking a thumb or blanket, the infant exercises a form of omnipotent control over the object, capable of generating enough confidence in the environment that, later on, it may come to lose the primary object for short periods without feeling threatened, and being able to substitute it for transitional objects such as a thumb, comfort blanket, teddy bear etc. Winnicott tells us:

> These phenomena cannot be explained except on the basis that the act is an attempt to localize the object (breast, etc.), to hold it half-way between – in and out. This is either a defence against loss of object in the external world or in the inside of the body, that is to say, against loss of control over the object. I have no doubt that normal thumb-sucking has this function too. The auto-erotic element is not always clearly of paramount importance [...].
>
> (Winnicott, 1945/2017, p. 368)

Later on, it will also be through the imaginative elaboration of body functioning that the infant will create the externality of the world by means of an already constituted infant sexuality, under the form of oral sadism.

Through the imaginative elaboration of the survival of the "breast object", destroyed by its sadistic attacks, the infant may gradually discriminate a real, objective object – independent of its area of omnipotence – from a subjective object, which it continues to destroy in its fantasies. This stage marks the appearance of fantasies as constituents of the internal world, and therefore in an area separated from reality, from the external world. Thus, a more complex form of imaginative elaboration will arise, one populated by fantasies. The possibility of repressing these fantasies, eliminating them from the conscience, will also appear whenever they generate unbearable anguish. This then gives rise to the *repressed unconscious*.[8] Henceforth, the infant can make use of real objects and, whenever necessary, protect itself in its internal world, like a weary traveller under the shade of a tree.

This distinction between inside and outside, and the capacity to act on the world pursuing the aims of its own desire, designates the constitution in the child's personality of that which Winnicott called the male element. If the female element constitutes, for the infant, the possibility of being, the male element formats its capacity to do.

In the following stage, the infant will already distinguish its mother as a being similar to itself, and will become able to feel sorry for her every time it attacks her breast sadistically. Through a (generally unconscious) feeling of guilt, it then experiences desires of reparatory movements, which create the first ethical values in the intersubjective relationship. If the mother is good enough to receive both the infant's sadistic attacks and reparatory acts again and again during this whole stage – without retaliation and without leaving the scene – the infant will gradually appropriate the aggressive/destructive impulses that pass through its body, without intense feelings of guilt, since it obtains confidence in being able to repair what it destroys. In this stage, then, imaginative elaboration has already spread to the constitution of human values.

The period of the *Oedipus complex* makes the psychic dynamic much more complicated, as it introduces a third element (Almeida and Naffah

Neto, 2022). Until then, the father is experienced by the child as a mother substitute. However, imaginative elaboration in this period is of crucial importance not only for the child to internalise cultural interdictions (such as those regarding incest, for example), but primarily to allow it to be able to sustain feelings of ambivalence when faced with objects that generate love and hate simultaneously – such as the father and mother – during this period.

This stage is also of crucial importance for the formation of a sexual identity, through the imaginative elaboration of the phallic phase with a view to the conquest of genital sexuality, and also through the advent of secondary identifications with the father, mother, and other important figures in the child's education.

For example, the manner in which Winnicott conceives the imaginative elaboration that marks the passage from the phallic phase to the genital phase in girls is very interesting. Let us look at his description, in which he simulates, step by step, the process of elaboration of castration until the discovery of the vagina, over succeeding discoveries:

> I have a penis. Of course I shall grow a penis. I had a penis, I am traumatized (punishment for excitement). I shall use a penis by proxy, let a male act for me. I shall let the male use me. In this way I get a deficiency made up but acknowledge a dependence on the male for completeness. Through this I discover my true female genital.
>
> (Winnicott, 1988/2017, p. 70)

And, for those who consider this description to be loaded with sexist culture – I, myself, have had some female students who thought so – he adds a footnote: "At the phallic phase a boy is complete, and at the genital he is dependent on the female for completeness" (Winnicott, 1988/2017, p. 74).

Passing through the Oedipus complex results in the formation of the superego. Winnicott also has some interesting things to say about this subject, even though this part of his theory is generally forgotten by most "Winnicottians". In the section reproduced below, he assesses the relief a child feels on being integrated as a whole person, when arriving at the Oedipus complex process and who, through having parents present, is able to form a normal superego:

> We have to say, this child is well enough to be one whole person amongst three, to experience the triangular situation, and to be able to work through in the presence of the parents all that is meant by the passing of the Oedipus complex and the setting up of a superego which has some relationship to the parents as perceived and the parents as conceived of. A very large number of children never have this relief. What happens in such cases is not that there is no superego but that the superego formation never becomes humanized and will remain rather like the polytheism before monotheism. It is then as if there are forces and mechanistic agencies that are feared and that must be magically

countered, and that certainly cannot be defied. Every possible kind of frightening mechanism belongs to the lack of health in this area. In health the child may (to be sure) develop psychoneurosis, but nevertheless he or she has the great relief of a superego which is related to the human beings in fact, the father and the mother. The analysis can cash in on this. These human beings can be loved and hated, obeyed and defied, in the ordinary way that is well known.

(Winnicott, 1960/2017, pp. 131–132)

In other words, here too, imaginative elaboration operates in different ways, whether or not it can count on the child's healthy development in the previous stages and with the effective presence of the parents, incorporating human images with which the child is able to dialogue internally – either obeying or challenging them. When this is not possible, the cultural interdictions are internalised through the introjection of anonymous, magical, and powerful forces, ones far distant from everyday life, creating a kind of fantastical world to which the child must submit, or which, generally, doles out severe punishment when it is disobeyed. Melancholy (Naffah Neto, 2022), although a psychosis, can constitute one of these typical cases, as can some grave obsessive neuroses.[9]

In general terms, we can say that the imaginative elaboration of body functioning operates, from the very beginning of life, by exploring and enjoying the objects in a way that foretells the playful relations with them that come later and differentiate a space for mediation between the inside and outside – the so-called *potential space* that constitutes the region of the psyche to which Winnicott allocates all and any processes of creation of, and relations with, cultural objects.

The Constitution of the Psyche-Soma, Made Possible Through Maternal Holding

It is extremely important, once again, to emphasise that the normal development of the *imaginative elaboration of bodily functions* depends, during the so-called periods of absolute and relative dependence, *entirely* on the support provided by the mother or a substitute figure.

Holding is a broad term that refers to the totality of maternal care, capable of supporting the baby's *primary creativity* throughout the constitution of the psyche. This must be clearly stated: the process of imaginative elaboration is carried out *by* the baby's primary creativity, although it requires the *sustaining* presence of maternal care. In that process the mother does not assume the role of principal *interpreter*, as conceived by Bion in the activity of *reverie*. Let us follow this further:

In the conception of Bion, the infant is incapable of elaborating, on its own, the raw material – of a sensory nature – of its constitution, which emerges in the form of β elements and needs to eject these elements outside itself, in the form of projective identifications on the mother, such that she can digest them, through the function of *reverie*, and return them transformed into α elements. These α elements are suitable for use in the function of thinking. This makes the Bionian psychoanalyst very accustomed to, in clinical practice, being the one who exercises the *alpha function* – the donor of form and sense – using interpretation for this purpose, even when dealing with borderline or psychotic patients.

For Winnicott, the infant is not primarily dependent on *reverie*, but on *holding*, on support, which means that if it has its *going on being* guaranteed through maternal care, it will be able to – through the use of its primitive and rudimentary tools – gradually give meaning to the functioning of its body in its relationship with the environment. Through this, it will gradually conquer a psyche, in which the capacity to think is included.[10] This means that psychoanalysts of a Winnicottian inclination, especially when treating borderline or psychotic patients, will favour *holding* and the processes of regression to the stages of dependency, in large part giving up interpretation.

(Naffah Neto, 2012, pp. 69–70)

Supporting the infant's primary creativity means, above all, for the mother, a vote of confidence in the life and the right of her child to be singular. However, according to Winnicott, this is guaranteed through the process of *primary maternal preoccupation*, originating from the mother's regressive movement, which allows her both an identification with the infant's basic needs and the ability to respond to her gradual conquests in a confident manner.

It would, therefore, be imprecise to base ourselves on the philosophical notion of *intersubjectivity* to designate this kind of mother-infant relationship – one that is so peculiar and unique – especially because, in those first moments, the infant is effectively unable to designate a constituted subjectivity in the strong sense of the word. It is about a relationship in which both subjects are not centered on themselves: the mother being fundamentally present as a body/breast identified with the infant, and the latter emerging as a vanishing and amorphous body identified with, in turn, this maternal body/breast. They suggest two mutually overlapping planes that pass one inside the other, in the form of a reversible *chiasm*.

Perhaps, in this sense, the notion that best expresses this state of things would be what Merleau-Ponty called *chair* in his unfinished book *Le visible et l'invisible* (Merleau-Ponty, 1964), and which would be best translated as *flesh*. Below, we can see how evocative Marilena Chauí's words are when seeking to describe this Merleau-Pontyan notion:

The reversibility and transitivity of the colours, surfaces, and movements – the *flesh of things* – of our senses among themselves – the *flesh of our body*, of them, and of things in resonance and reverberation without beginning and without end – is the unveiling of the sentience as "the medium that contains the Being, without needing to be placed." This is the sentient experience.

The fundamental narcissism of the body in synergy, that propagates between the bodies in an unfinished intercorporal reflection or permanent incarnation in the *community of Narcissus*, is the experience of *intercorporeality* as originating the existence of the self and the other.

(Chauí, 1981, p. 276, original emphasis)

This, however, is a very complex topic that would require a different reflexive journey. Thus, we leave it here simply as a suggestive title for future incursions into the subject.

In any case, we can say that, thanks to maternal *holding*, the infant's primary creativity is capable of imaginatively elaborating the biological functions in its relations with the world and creating a psyche that is effectively supported by the body – thus (obviously as long as we separate any mystical sense from the term *spirituality*) constituting its spiritual counterpart. Thus, the infant will gain a psychosomatic unit in which body and psyche constitute two components of a single structure.

However, Winnicott never reached a true monism of pure identification between the body and the psyche, because his clinical practice never allowed him to make such a postulation. He tells us:

Another psychotic patient discovered in analysis that most of the time she lived in her head, behind her eyes. She could only see out of her eyes as out of windows and so was not aware of what her feet were doing, and in consequence she tended to fall into pits and to trip over things. She had no "eyes in her feet". Her personality was not felt to be localized in her body, which was like a complex engine that she had to drive with conscious care and skill.

(Winnicott, 1945/2017, p. 361)

It is also essential to distinguish between the notions of *psyche* and *mind*, as the latter, to Winnicott, refers to a specialised function of the psychosomatic unit, entirely dedicated to intellectual operations. The *mind* differentiates itself, first and foremost, to provide the baby with some predictability regarding environmental events. It thus emerges as a zone directly in contact with the external world, tasked with transforming subjective temporality into *Chronos*, measuring space, analysing and categorising events, storing and organising memories, establishing causal relationships, and making predictions (Winnicott, 1949/2017).

Psychic health presupposes an integrated functioning of psyche, mind, and body – and that may be the most precise meaning of the term *psychosomatic unity*. It must be said that what Winnicott defines as a true psychosomatic disorder arises in pathological cases in which that unity *psyche-soma* has not happened, due to a split caused by severe environmental failures. In those cases the process or personalisation does not take place – what Winnicott defines as a *true psychosomatic disorder* arises. In such cases, the body enacts a series of disturbances in an attempt to draw attention to its very existence (Laurentiis, 2016). The task of analysis, then, is precisely to resume, through regressions to earlier stages of dependence, the maturational process that had remained frozen, awaiting an environment sufficiently capable of providing holding. Only then may psychosomatic unity be constituted, becoming, at last, the true seat of existence.

The Question of the Body According to Bion

Throughout his extensive body of work Bion seldom addresses the body directly. His writings, marked by a rigorous search for the origins of thought and the elaboration of the most primitive mental states, prioritise the *internal world* of the mind – its functions, its defences, its impasses. The body, when it does appear, is usually relegated to the background, functioning as a kind of "silent support" to the processes unfolding within the mental field. It is no coincidence that, in searching his work for any explicit formulation regarding the bodily dimension of psychoanalytic experience, we encounter more gaps than assertions.

That absence, however, should not be interpreted as indifference. Perhaps the body to Bion is not absent, *but veiled* – like an enigma running through his formulations, eluding easy capture. Indeed, it is only in his later work – especially from *Transformations* (1965) onward, and more intensively in his notion of "transformations in O" – that we begin to see him become more open-minded about the idea of an experiential field that transcends the representational mind. Here, the notion that the analyst must *become* – and not merely interpret – begins to take shape. The encounter with ultimate reality, which Bion names "O", demands a state of presence so radical that, at times, it is the analyst's own body that becomes the instrument of listening, affectability and transformation.

In Bion's early writings he focuses on the way the mind handles the raw elements of emotional experience (the so-called beta elements). Yet it is only later that we begin to glimpse the radical implications of what is at stake when these elements find no means of metabolisation. When this occurs, the body ceases to be a silent support and instead becomes the very site where pain takes root – without translation, without language, without dream.

It is at this juncture that the following clinical case arises, reported by Bion (1994) in his seminars and later revisited as a key to thinking about what eludes the traditional analytic process – and which, not infrequently, manifests itself in the body as a last resort of expression. The case concerns a patient who was referred to him with a kind of "seal of approval"; he was, according to others, "highly suited" for analysis. And indeed, during the process everything seemed to be going well. The patient listened attentively to Bion's interpretations, agreed with them, and seemed receptive. Yet something troubled the analyst: behind that courteous acceptance, nothing was actually taking place. No transformation, no movement. It was as if the words, however precise or sensitive, failed to find a dwelling place.

Over time, Bion began to perceive something disturbing. The patient lived reclusively in his room, avoiding any contact with the outside world – as if human presence itself were a threat. He also found out that the man drank his own urine, an extreme gesture of self-sufficiency that rejected any form of exchange, any openness to the other. The outcome was tragic: the man took his own life.

This case became a turning point for Bion. He began to ask himself why certain individuals, even when they apparently understood what is being said in analysis, remain untouched, unaffected, as if the therapeutic process had never occurred. Some fall physically ill; others develop psychosomatic symptoms or descend into psychotic states. And there are those, like that man, whose pain finds only one outlet: the end of their own existence.

Such a deadlock revealed, to Bion, that something essential was escaping the grasp of contemporary psychoanalysis. There was a blind spot – a dimension of psychic suffering that was not being reached. It was at this point that he began to investigate the most remote origins of life, turning his attention to what precedes even birth itself.

Inspired by Freud (1926/1981) – who asserted that there is far greater continuity between intrauterine and postnatal life than the dramatic rupture of birth would lead us to believe – Bion began to consider the possibility that a similar line of deep continuity might exist within mental life. He imagined that, even in the womb, the foetus might endure unpleasant experiences, and that these experiences, however primitive, could be registered by a mind in formation. Faced with intolerable stimuli – for which no psychic structure yet existed to metabolise the pain – the foetus might perhaps defend itself by splitting off from the consciousness of such experiences, isolating parts of itself in order to survive.

These excluded psychic fragments would remain hidden, like silent zones of the self. The personality that develops later might appear functional, adapted to the demands of family and social life, yet would harbour, in its most intimate folds, this unprocessed core. At some point in life – particularly under the impact of intense emotional experiences, and even during the analytic process – these exiled parts might return, taking the form of psychotic symptoms, psychosomatic disturbances, or unexpected emotional collapses.

To Bion, the way Freud refers to birth – as a "caesura that would lead us to believe" in an absolute rupture – is revealing. He recognises that our way of thinking is conditioned by this cut, which insists on separating what may in fact be continuous. That means, we are trained to see body and mind as distinct domains while to Bion this is merely another *caesura* – that is, another conceptual obstacle preventing us from understanding the complex web that links the physical and the psychic from the very beginning of life.

This difficulty in communication between mind and body, or between split-off parts of the self, is one of the central themes in *A Memoir of the Future*, a work in which Bion explores – through poetic and symbolic language – the dialogues between internal agencies, such as the characters "Body" and "Mind", each seeking, in its own way, a possible path towards reconnection. Let us see:

Mind: You are borrowing [words] from me; do you get them through the diaphragm?

Body: They penetrate it. But the meaning does not get through. Where did you get your pains from?

Mind: Borrowed from the past. The meaning does not get through the barrier though. Funny – the meaning does not get through whether it is from you to me, or from me to you.

Body: It is the meaning of pain that I am sending to you; the words get through – which I have not sent – but the meaning is lost.

(Bion, 1991, pp. 433–434)

Bion used the term "soma-psychotic" to refer to an inverted perspective of what we typically call a true psychosomatic disorder. While the latter stems from a psycho-somatic unity that has been compromised by environmental failures and their repercussions in the body's pathological dramatisations, the former suggests the opposite trajectory: an eruption of the body that escapes the mind's domain, that has not been symbolised, not even thought, and remains as a psychotic core. These are markedly different ways of conceptualising psychosomatic issues in pathological contexts. To Winnicott the disturbance arises from the *lack* of psycho-somatic unity; in Bion's case, the issue is not the formation of this functional unity, but rather the inability to translate bodily dimensions into thought and symbolisation – dimensions that, in their raw state, persist as a psychotic nucleus.

In other words, to Winnicott the body is an intrinsic part of a functional unity that sustains existence; to Bion, it is a core of raw sensory formations to be thought, distilled, symbolised. In his own words, "[...] look at it from one side; there is a psycho-somatic complaint; turn it round; now it is soma-psychotic. It is the same... but what you see depends on which way you look at it" (Bion, 1976/1994, p. 244).

To Bion there is a deeper epistemological misunderstanding underlying all of this: the difficulty in imagining a primitive stage of psychic life in which neither the mental nor the physical stances have separated. He names this domain the *protomental system* – that is, an "archaic region", so to speak, prior to the split between thought and sensation, where emotional states are experienced in a raw form, without language, without mediation.

It is in this territory, still intrauterine, that the foetus, even in its immature stage of development, may undergo intolerable sensations – pain, threats, invasions – and, as a survival strategy, split off from them. There is not yet an "I" as such, but there is a body, and the body feels with an intensity that asks no permission to exist and to persist. The mind that comes later may never fully reconcile itself with these lost fragments. And so, from the very moment of birth the baby is already an incomplete being – yet one possessed of such precocious intelligence that this gap often goes unnoticed.

Bion wondered whether there might exist, within the body, a form of thinking that precedes conscious thought. A kind of bodily pre-thinking, perhaps inscribed within the autonomic nervous system – whether sympathetic or parasympathetic – or even within the glandular system. Adrenaline, for instance, secreted by the adrenal medulla, prepares the organism for fight or flight before we are even aware of what we are fleeing from. It is this state that leads the patient to say, "I feel afraid, but I don't know what I'm afraid of". In other words, for Bion, *the body knows before the mind can formulate.*

Yet how are we to access these archaic psychic zones, still unprocessed, where affection is experienced as raw pain, without a name? Bion refers to this as "thalamic pain" or "thalamic fear" – experiences that have not been modulated by the higher layers of the nervous system and which, as such, retain a degree of intensity that is nearly unimaginable. These are pains that cannot be represented, only inhabited.

In one of his lectures, entitled "Making the Best of a Bad Job" (1979/1994), Bion questions why we grant such prestige to the waking state at the expense of the dream state. We speak of the "work of the dream" – how dream organises itself from elements of waking life – yet we rarely consider the "work of waking", that which is devoted to disqualifying the dream as "just a dream". This hierarchy reveals our tendency to privilege the rational, even when it fails to transform that which truly moves us.

Bion's unease with the difficulty of accessing the most primitive layers of psychic reality is a constant theme. He believed that, at times, a crude word, an insult, a seemingly vulgar outburst, could contain an archaic vitality – that is, an abrupt contact with the raw real that civilisation seeks to tame. On the streets of London, he would say, it was enough for one man to point at another and say, "You cunt" for a fight to erupt. It was not merely an insult: it marked a point of fusion between language and flesh.

In his final years Bion became increasingly aware that analysis often failed to bring about real change. There were patients who seemed to have changed, who adopted analytic vocabulary, who mimicked the analyst's style – yet who remained unchanged within. They repeated words, but did not dream with them. They wielded concepts as shields rather than as tools of transformation. In such cases the alpha function was absent, and what emerged were evacuations of beta elements – raw residues of experience that had not been metabolised.

Bion probed the depths of foetal life in an attempt to understand why analysis sometimes fails. Why do certain cores of suffering remain untouched, even under sensitive listening? His effort to name the unnameable endures as the living legacy of a psychoanalysis that is not content with the mere appearance of healing, but seeks to touch the body of pain before it becomes symptom.

Some Notes on the Notion of "Somatic Reverie"

If, to Bion, the body senses before the mind can formulate, the pressing question becomes: who listens to what the body feels? Or, more precisely, what happens when pain that has not been thought breaks into the analytic setting – not through words, but through presence, silences, shivers, contractions, sighs?

It is at this point that the concept of *somatic reverie*, proposed by Giuseppe Civitarese (2021), becomes an essential tool to re-read Bion's legacy in light of the body. Unlike classical *reverie*, which involves the analyst's capacity to receive and metabolise the raw elements of the patient's experience through images, associations, or daydreams, *somatic reverie* is a form of listening that takes place in the body. A kind of bodily dreaming that, rather than representing, embodies.

Civitarese describes these experiences as sensory micro-events occurring in the countertransference: a sudden muscular tension, a tightening in the stomach, a change in the rhythm of breathing, and so forth. We are referring to subtle phenomena, yet laden with meaning, which point to something within the patient that has not been spoken – because it has not yet been thinkable – but which finds resonance in the analyst's body. As if the analyst, through their affective availability, were lending their flesh so that the other's suffering might find a passage.

In this field of silent reverberations, the analyst does not interpret immediately. They wait, hold, host. Like a body that dreams what the other is not yet able to say. Somatic reverie therefore requires a kind of floating attention that includes the analyst's own body as an instrument of listening, without yielding to the temptation to hastily translate what is still in the process of being formed. To quote the author:

> It is necessary to dream in the body (or rather, in the somatic field) what is happening, in order to come into contact with the crisis and to give it an initial representation – one that, in itself, offers virtual salvation. In the terms of Bion's model of the analytic field, sensory reveries (or rather, bodily reveries – that is, those without immediate representational content or evident perceptual quality) are a way of provoking initial transformations in the direction of thought. In particular, just as with "true" reveries and narrative derivations in the case of emotions, sensory reveries make it possible not only to grasp the vicissitudes of the most fundamental – or most subterranean – levels of identity that are at play, but also to construct a container, a structure, or a *semiotic chora* (Kristeva, 1974/1984), with the aim of giving meaning to the formless, the infinite, and the insensible.
>
> (Civitarese, 2021, p. 44)

That conception, then, broadens and deepens Bion's notion of the alpha function: it is not merely about transforming beta elements into thoughts, but about recognising that some experiences must first be felt in the body of another before they can become thinkable. In this sense, *somatic reverie* functions as a symbolic womb: it is in the analyst's body that raw experience may, at times, begin to be metabolised, slowly, until it can come to life as word, or as transformative silence.

In the film *The Lost Daughter* (2021), an adaptation of Elena Ferrante's novel of the same name, there is a scene in which time seems suspended. Leda, the protagonist, is alone on the beach, watching. The sun is scorching, the waves crash in the background, and a young mother struggles to contain the impulses of her small daughter. Nothing extraordinary seems to be happening. Yet there is something in the way Leda looks, as if that moment were not merely being observed, but lived from within, nerves exposed, skin bristling with unspoken memories.

She does not speak. There are no words. Only shallow breathing, a subtle touch to the chest, a gaze that hardens. The child cries, the mother becomes unsettled, and Leda leans in – not with her body, but with her soul. It is Leda's body that leans, that listens, being there. She feels a pain that is not hers, it reverberates within her as if it always had been there. She feels without knowing. Dreams without sleeping. Remembers without recalling.

At this moment the notion of *somatic reverie* becomes incarnate: Leda dreams, with her own body, the other woman's pain. The experience of another's woman's motherhood touches upon what remains unresolved in her own. We might think of it as a kind of "sensory return" – a murmur from the past that passes through the skin, the stomach, the chest. The other woman's pain pierces her silence as if it were her own. It seems to be a kind of "mutual possession", that is, a momentary fusion of stories inscribed in the flesh.

She does not translate. She does not interpret. She feels. And in that feeling, something – imperceptible, yet real – begins to shift. Experiences of her own motherhood, long dormant, stir beneath the surface.

As we have noted, *somatic reverie*, according to Civitarese (2021), requires neither image nor concept. It occurs in the somatic field, where the senses anticipate what the mind has not yet reached. On that beach, under the all-revealing sun, Leda is pierced. And what once appeared to be mere voyeurism reveals itself as the most delicate manifestation of analytic listening (or maternal listening): that which dreams in the body what the other has not yet been able to say.

We cite Civitarese:

> But what does the body think? In the totality of its being and at every moment, the body thinks or transforms the primary emotion that arises from contact with reality. What, then, would be the point of excluding action from analysis, relegating it to the category of enactment?
>
> (Civitarese, 2021, pp. 54–55)

Here the body ceases to be a mere passive receptor of unconscious content. It becomes an *agent of thought* – or rather, of *emotional transformation*.

Not by chance Civitarese (2021) challenges the traditional separation between action and symbolisation, proposing that certain gestures, silences, and sensory reactions in analysis are not simply enactments, but inaugural modes of thinking the unthought. Broadly speaking, what occurs between analyst and patient in such moments is not an enactment: it is the very *weaving of meaning* in its most rudimentary and original form.

Some Final Words

Finally, we may observe that while Winnicott approaches the matter of the body through the primitive constitution of the infant, linking psyche–soma integration to imaginative elaboration of body functioning – such as sucking, evacuating, and biting – Bion does not follow precisely this path. To Winnicott the body is experienced from the outset as a set of biological functions capable of psychic elaboration, and the psyche-soma is born sustained by an imaginative function that allows the psyche to emerge anchored in the body, making it its dwelling place. The body is not merely a support; it is the first territory of being.

In Bion's work, by contrast, the body emerges later and almost always as a response to a failure – a clinical sign that something has not been metabolised. Thalamic pain, nameless dread, the accumulation of beta elements that overwhelm the alpha function – all these point to an experience that has found no representation. When this occurs, it is the analyst's body that steps in as the final instrument of reception. Unlike Winnicott, Bion does not describe a process of psychic constitution rooted in bodily functions, but rather a clinic of the *unthinkable* – something of a mental order that, at times, can only be touched through the flesh.

If Winnicott offers a theory of *becoming* incarnate, Bion provides us with a form of listening for what never came to be. Two distinct gestures, yet they converge at the point where the analyst is faced with what does not speak, does not dream, does not present itself – only weighs. And there, among the undigested remnants of experience, the body may become language. Or, at the very least, a provisional container for the formless.

Concluding with this distinction is also stating that psychoanalysis is not made of concepts alone. It is made of presences. And, at times, of bodies that silently hold what cannot yet be spoken.

Notes

1 The text on "The Imaginative Elaboration of Body Functioning for Winnicott" was previously published as: Alfredo Naffah Neto (2011): The Imaginative Elaboration of Body Functioning and Maternal Holding: Winnicott and the Formation of the Psyche-Soma, *International Forum of Psychoanalysis*, DOI:10.1080/0803706X.2011.589408. However, for this book version, the text has been significantly expanded and revised.

2 Especially because, according to Winnicott, prior to the process by which the child's self takes ownership of instinctual impulses and erotic sensations – towards the establishment of a psychosomatic unity – strictly speaking, it is not yet possible to speak of infantile sexuality (a point that also applies to borderline-type patients). We shall develop this issue further later on.

3 Even when working with neurotic patients, whose dreams may indeed be understood as fulfilments of infantile sexual wishes, we still face a modality of imaginative elaboration of bodily functions – one that, in this case, is more directly linked to the sexual dimension of the body and its symbolisation within the field of desire.

4 For Winnicott, unconscious fantasy appears only later, after the so-called *use of an object stage* (cf. Winnicott, 1968/2017). In addition, he thought that the concept of death instinct or Thanatos, to give it its Greek name, was of no use, having developed a monistic conception of instincts (which considers the aggressive elements as part of the baby's primitive love impulse).

5 Winnicott was unable to consider the constitution of sexuality as something so automatic and immediate because of his contact with borderline patients who, as adults, had a completely false "sexuality" – one that operated mechanically or served some most basic functions of subsistence, such as, for instance, the fear of disintegration.

6 The uninterrupted nature of the flow of experience, sustained by maternal *holding*, is what allows that which Winnicott called the infant's *going on being*. When this experience is interrupted by a split false self, which isolates the true self from any contact and imitates surrounding human traits to adapt to environmental demands, the infant loses that continuity of *going on being*, thus simply subsisting in an "as if" way. It is the advent of psychoses.

7 *Incorporation* and *evacuation*, on the other hand, exist as processes from the very beginning.

8 The unconscious that existed until then has a purely descriptive statute – that is, it constitutes mechanisms and processes that function at a threshold incapable of reaching the conscience, which, in the initial stages, is not even entirely constituted as such.

9 In a different text, Winnicott describes a pathological form of the superego that seems to bear relations to this one: "in some cases there may have been *a false superego* development based in an abnormal way on the intrusion of a very powerful authoritarian influence derived from the environment of early years" (Winnicott, 1958/2017, p. 139, *emphasis added*). As, however, he does not elaborate further on the subject, it is difficult to be more precise regarding his thinking in this regard. We see this kind of false superego as an extremely active part in certain formations of the split false self, common to borderline patients, which functions as a formation of intensely oppressive psychic forces. However, it could also perfectly well describe the superego of certain melancholic or grave obsessive neurotic patients.

10 It is true that, for Winnicott, the mother performs an important mirror function, reflecting to the infant an image of itself. This, however, does not characterise a kind of *reverie*, as it does not imply a transformative digestion (of β elements into α ones, for example); the function of the maternal look is to *grant existence* to the infant at a period in which it lives dispersed rather than integrated.

References

Almeida, A. P. (2021). Empatia na psicanálise: um enfoque na teoria de Klein e Winnicott [Empathy in Psychoanalysis: An Approach Based on Klein and Winnicott's Theory]. *Psicanálise & Barroco em Revista*, 19(1): 162–183. https://doi.org/10.9789/1679-9887.2021.v19i1.162-183

Almeida, A. P., and Naffah Neto, A. (2022). O estágio da concernência e a elaboração do complexo de Édipo: revisitando Winnicott e o caso Piggle [The Stage of Concern and the Working-Through of the Oedipus Complex: Revisiting Winnicott and the Piggle Case]. *Psicologia Revista*, 31(1): 27–50. https://doi.org/10.23925/2594-3871.2022v31i1p27-50

Almeida, A. P. (2023). Transferência e introjeção: a metapsicologia ferencziana além da clínica [Transference and Introjection: Ferenczian Metapsychology Beyond the Clinic]. In A. P. Almeida, *Por uma ética do cuidado: Ferenczi para educadores e psicanalistas (vol. 1)* [*For an Ethics of Care: Ferenczi for Educators and Psychoanalysts (Vol. 1)*], pp. 139–172. São Paulo: Blucher.

Almeida, A. P., and Naffah Neto, A. (2024). Um estudo comparativo entre as teorias de Klein e Winnicott: analisando o conceito de fantasia [A Comparative Study of Klein and Winnicott's Theories: Analysing the Concept of Phantasy]. *Revista Latinoamericana de Psicopatologia Fundamental*, 27: 1–23. https://doi.org/10.1590/1415-4714.e230636

Bion, W. R. (1965). *Transformations*. London: Heinemann Medical Books.

Bion, W. R. (1991). *A Memoir of the Future*. London: Karnac Books.

Bion, W. R. (1994). *Clinical Seminars and Four Papers*. London: Karnac Books.

Bion, W. R. (1994). Evidence. In W. R. Bion, *Clinical Seminars and Four Papers*. London: Karnac Books. (Original work published in 1976)

Bion, W. R. (1994). Making the Best of a Bad Job. In W. R. Bion, *Clinical Seminars and Four Papers*. London: Karnac Books. (Original work published in 1979)

Chauí, M. (1981). *Da realidade sem mistérios ao mistério do mundo: Espinosa, Voltaire, Merleau-Ponty* [*From a Reality without Mysteries to the Mystery of the World: Spinoza, Voltaire, Merleau-Ponty*]. São Paulo: Brasiliense.

Civitarese, G. (2021). Campo incorporado e reverie somático [Embodied Field and Somatic Reverie]. *Revista Brasileira de Psicanálise*, 55(3): 43–57.

Dias, E. O. (2003). *A teoria de amadurecimento de D. W. Winnicott* [The Maturational Theory of D. W. Winnicott]. Rio de Janeiro: Imago.

Dias, E. O. (2007). Incorporação e introjeção em Winnicott [Incorporation and Introjection in Winnicott]. *Winnicott e-Prints*, 2(2): 1–30. http://pepsic.bvsalud.org/scielo.php?script=sci_arttext&pid=S1679-432X2007000200002&lng=pt&tlng=pt

Freud, S. (1981). Inhibition, Symptom and Anxiety. In S. Freud. *The Standard Edition of the Complete Psychological works of Sigmund Freud (Vol. 20)*, pp. 77–178. London: Hogarth Press. (Original work published in 1926)

Gyllenhaal, M. (director). (2021) *The Lost Daughter*. Endeavor Content.

Kaur, R. (2020). *Home Body*. Missouri: Andrews McMeel Publishing.

Laurentiis, V. R. F. (2016). *Corpo e psicossomática em Winnicott* [Body and Psychosomatics in Winnicott]. São Paulo: DWWeditorial.

Lejarraga, A. L. (2012). *O amor em Winnicott* [*Love in Winnicott*]. Rio de Janeiro: Garamond.

Lispector, C. (2018). *Todas as crônicas* [*All the Chronicles*]. Rio de Janeiro: Rocco.

Merleau-Ponty, M. (1964). *Le visible et l'invisible* [*The Visible and the Invisible*]. Paris: Gallimard.

Merleau-Ponty, M. (1994). *Fenomenologia da percepção* [*Phenomenology of Perception*]. São Paulo: Martins Fontes. (Original work published in 1945)

Naffah Neto, A. (2012). A construção do psiquismo: a singularidade da perspectiva winnicottiana diferindo de Freud, Klein e Bion [The Construction of the Psyche: The Uniqueness of the Winnicottian Perspective in Contrast to Freud, Klein and Bion]. In I. Sucar and H. Ramos (Orgs.), *Winnicott: ressonâncias* [*Winnicott: Resonances*], pp. 61–72. São Paulo: Sociedade Brasileira de Psicanálise de São Paulo/Primavera Editorial.

Naffah Neto, A. (2022). *Darkness Visible*: uma interpretação da patologia depressiva a partir de D. W. Winnicott [*Darkness Visible*: An Interpretation of Depressive

Pathology Based on D. W. Winnicott]. In A. P. Almeida & A. Naffah Neto (Orgs.), *Perto das trevas: a depressão em seis perspectivas psicanalíticas* [*Close to Darkness: Depression from Six Psychoanalytic Perspectives*], pp. 201–226. São Paulo: Blucher.

Winnicott, D. W. (2017). Primitive Emotional Development. In D. W. Winnicott, *The Collected Works of D. W. Winnicott (Vol. 2)*, pp. 357–368. Oxford: Oxford University Press. (Original work published in 1945)

Winnicott, D. W. (2017). Mind and Its Relation to the Psyche-Soma. In D. W. Winnicott, *The Collected Works of D. W. Winnicott (Vol. 3)*, pp. 245–258. Oxford: Oxford University Press. (Original work published in 1949)

Winnicott, D. W. (2017). Psycho-Analysis and the Sense of Guilt. In D. W. Winnicott, *The Collected Works of D. W. Winnicott (Vol. 5)*, pp. 135–148. Oxford: Oxford University Press. (Original work published in 1958)

Winnicott, D. W. (2017). Comments on Joseph Sandler's "On the Concept of the Superego". In D. W. Winnicott, *The Collected Works of D. W. Winnicott (Vol. 6)*, pp. 127–134. Oxford: Oxford University Press. (Original work published in 1960)

Winnicott, D. W. (2017). The Use of an Object and Relating Through Identifications. In D. W. Winnicott, *The Collected Works of D. W. Winnicott (Vol. 8)*, pp. 355–364. Oxford: Oxford University Press. (Original work published in 1968)

Winnicott, D. W. (2017). *Human Nature*. In D. W. Winnicott, *The Collected Works of D. W. Winnicott (vol. 11)*, pp. 25–186. Oxford: Oxford University Press. (Original work published in 1988)

Winnicott, D. W. (2017). What Do We Know About Babies Who Suck Cloths? In D. W. Winnicott, *The Collected Works of D. W. Winnicott (Vol. 5)*, pp. 115–118. Oxford: Oxford University Press. (Original work published in 1956)

10 The Origin of Psychosis According to Bion and Winnicott

*Alexandre Patricio de Almeida,
Filipe Pereira Vieira, and Alfredo Naffah Neto*

Bion's Early Studies on Psychosis

We open this chapter with a quotation from Clarice Lispector which, in our view, captures the most primal experience of the psychoses described by Bion and Winnicott: the radical difficulty of naming oneself:

> It is curious how I cannot say who I am. I mean, I know it well, but I cannot put it into words. Above all, I am afraid to speak, because the moment I try to, not only do I fail to express what I feel, but what I feel slowly turns into what I say.
>
> (Lispector, 2019, n.p.)

Driven by his observations from group work, Bion delved deeply into the analysis of schizophrenic patients using the classical technique of psychoanalysis. He himself remarked that he only worked with patients who could attend his consulting room, highlighting the delicate nature of this highly specific clinical task.

However, Bion's clinical work was not limited to cases of schizophrenia. He also treated severely neurotic patients and individuals struggling with substance dependence, publishing accounts of these experiences through clinical vignettes. These writings brought to light the phenomena of projective identification and the use of language and thought by schizophrenic patients.

These studies, carried out between 1950 and 1962, culminated in a landmark collection known in English as *Second Thoughts* (1963/2018). In his early writings the influence of Melanie Klein's theory is unmistakable – Bion himself continued to describe himself as a "Kleinian analyst" until the end of his career.

Bion conceived interpretation as a process linked to the function of thinking – the analyst's capacity to "transform" the patient's beta elements into alpha elements through the work of "alpha-function and reverie" (see Chapter 4 of this book). According to Bionian theory this process allows primitive emotional experiences to acquire meaning, becoming accessible

DOI: 10.4324/9781003642503-11

to symbolisation and psychic integration. His initial focus, therefore, lied on part-object relations, primary envy, and annihilation anxieties, as he explored the complexity of the defence mechanisms that arise in the face of such experiences.

Although Bion later reformulated his theoretical outlook – particularly from *Transformations* (1965/2020) onwards – his technique remained grounded in interpretation. From that point on, however, interpretation came to be understood differently, no longer merely as an instrument to analyse unconscious content, but as a process that should accompany – and even contain – the patient's capacity to think their own emotional experience.

That shift in the understanding of interpretation aligns with Bion's formulations on memory and desire – specifically the ideal of *without memory and without desire* – which underpin an analytic listening that refrains from imposing preconceived meaning. Rather than uncovering hidden unconscious content, interpretation becomes a means of fostering psychic growth, supporting the patient's effort to transform raw emotional experiences into something symbolisable and thinkable.

Thus, the analyst's role is not confined to *what* is interpreted, but extends itself to *how* and *when* – taking into account the patient's mental state as a crucial condition for metabolising the intervention. Interpretation, when offered prematurely or in a somewhat omniscient way, may "saturate" the psychic apparatus instead of helping its organisation.

The analyst is thus required to adopt a stance that embodies *negative capability* – a term coined by Keats and later taken up by Bion to describe the disposition to tolerate enigma, doubt, and uncertainty without rushing towards answers (Chuster, 2024). It is precisely this suspension of knowing that allows the analytic field to remain alive, fertile, and genuinely open to the emergence of the new.

As Hinshelwood highlights:

> The tradition of interpreting unconscious narratives in the session remains a key element derived from the idea of continuous unconscious phantasy in the deeper layers of the unconscious mind. The deepest of those phantasies can be discerned in the narratives accepted, enacted, and then discovered by introspection via the roles unconsciously required of the analyst. Bion's trajectory, though erratic in a theoretical sense as he found himself influenced by his reading (much of it outside of the psychoanalytic literature), tended to be in a consistent direction clinically. The lie is the careful manipulation of ideas, symbols, and memories. The truth of a session is the impact. That impact was something that Bion seemed to have remained true to even before he had started training as a psychoanalyst. The psychoanalytic session is less important in terms of the content of meaning and must be addressed in terms of process.
>
> (Hinshelwood, 2023, pp. 123–124)

It is also important to highlight that throughout his trajectory Bion demonstrated a consistent interest in the intersections between mass dynamics and the functioning of the psychotic mind. In his efforts to understand how individuals behave in group settings – and what implications this had on individual psychic life – he observed striking parallels between the mechanisms that govern collective behaviour and the internal processes of a psychotic mind. This articulation becomes particularly evident in a lecture delivered in São Paulo in 1978, in which he stated:

> So far we seem capable of having a mass psychosis in which we all agree to go about in disciplined and organised gangs of murderers, dedicated to the destruction of people who wear different clothes. Sometimes we don't even bother with the uniform if we can say, "I am black; he is white; therefore he is wrong."
>
> (Bion, 1977–1978/2018, p. 97)

Bion observed that, within a mass, individuality dissolves itself, and emotional elements – previously held in check by conscious control – emerge in an almost primitive state. In a similar fashion the psychotic mind may fragment under intense pressure, externalising destructive impulses and generating an internal (and external) environment of chaos. This externalisation of emotion may be experienced as an *attack on linking* (Bion, 1959/2018), when reality becomes distorted and the capacity for symbolisation is impaired – see Chapter 5 of this book.

We could also say that a central theme in his clinical work was the observation of the ongoing clash between life and death instincts – a conflict he frequently identified in his patients. *Instinctual curiosity* (epistemophilic drive),[1] which to Bion – following the Kleinian lineage – is closely linked to primary sadism, was often intensified by fantasies surrounding the oedipal scene. Bion placed considerable emphasis on the way a child begins to formulate questions even before acquiring verbal language, an aspect that recalls Freud's distinction between *thing-presentations* and *word-presentations* (see Freud, 1915/1981).[2]

Broadly speaking one could say that Bion proposed a theory in which schizophrenic language reflects a disconnection between thought and reality. To him, verbal thought is a fundamental component that allows the ego to establish links with both external and internal reality. However, he observed that contact with psychic reality becomes unbearable to the psychotic patient, resulting in a painful encounter with the depressive position.

Furthermore, as pointed out in previous chapters, Bion regarded schizophrenia as a raw (and brutal) expression of death instinct operating within the ego and disrupting the perception of internal reality. To the patient each broken link is not merely an isolated psychic disturbance; it represents the disintegration of an entire network of symbolic meaning, rendering the internal world unassimilable and chaotic.

In Bion's work the importance of the environment is expressed in the concept of *container*[3] – understood as the capacity to receive, hold, and transform emotional experiences. It refers to the ability to take in (contain) the infant's projections and return them in a *transformed* form, so that the infant may then assimilate them.

Without the capacity to think their own thoughts, these remain raw, as beta elements – impossible to comprehend within the infant's still-primitive psychic apparatus. The absence of a maternal container (alpha function) can thus be devastating for the development of the psyche, which becomes overwhelmed by indigestible and terrifying experiences (beta elements).

In order to develop those rather complex Bionian ideas we need to outline Bion's understanding of primitive psychic development and, subsequently, his conception of psychosis itself.

Reverie, Alpha Function and Containment: Primitive Development According to Bion

Bion takes the relationship between the infant and their breastfeeding mother to illustrate the development of thought. The Bionian baby is born with a preconception of the breast as a source of satisfaction, but the fulfilment of that expectation depends on their emotional experience with the object. When the real breast corresponds to the preconception, it leads to its transformation into a conception, thereby supporting the development of the capacity to think. But if the experience is marked by excessive frustration, the preconception may give way to states of confusion or psychic disorganisation.

In other words, when the mother meets the infant's needs a "positive realisation" occurs, confirming the presence of the desired object. However, when the baby is met with the absence of the breast, a "negative realisation" is experienced, being that absence perceived as a "bad" breast which generates suffering and anguish. Bion suggests that, at first, every necessary object is perceived as negative, since its absence causes pain.

In other words, if the infant is able to tolerate the frustration of absence, that experience is transformed into a proto-thought – that is, it becomes the foundation for the construction of a mental apparatus capable of thinking those sensations. That idea is compatible with Freud's (1911/1981), as he had emphasised the reality principle develops along with the capacity to think. However, when the infant is unable to tolerate such a frustration, the "non-breast" is internalised as a bad object, and the infant attempts to rid itself of the discomfort through projection and the omnipotent sense of control.

In this context the psyche may become structured in a "dysfunctional" way, leading to the mistaken belief that expelling a bad object is equivalent to obtaining a good one. This mechanism is frequently encountered in psychoanalytic practice, particularly when working with the "psychotic part of the personality" – a term we shall revisit and explore in more detail later.

Nevertheless, frustrating experiences, though difficult, are an essential part of human development. If the infant's ego can withstand the hatred generated by these frustrations, that results in the healthy formation of thought, made possible by the alpha function exercised by the caregiving figure.

On the other hand, when hatred is excessive and unbearable, the so-called "beta elements" emerge – raw proto-thoughts, unprocessed sensory experiences that cannot be mentally digested and must therefore be discharged through motor agitation, psychosomatic symptoms, or excessive projective identifications:

> Alpha-function operates on the sense impressions, whatever they are, and the emotions, whatever they are, of which the patient is aware. In so far as alpha-function is successful alpha elements are produced and these elements are suited to storage and the requirements of dream thoughts. If alpha-function is disturbed, and therefore inoperative, the sense impressions of which the patient is aware and the emotions which he is experiencing remain unchanged. I shall call them beta-elements. In contrast with the alpha-elements the beta-elements are not felt to be phenomena, but things in themselves. The emotions likewise are objects of sense. We are thus presented with a state of mind precisely contrasting with that of the scientist who knows he is concerned with phenomena but has not the same certitude that the phenomena have a counterpart of things in themselves.
>
> (Bion, 1962/2023, n.p.)

Beta elements can thus be understood as concrete and primitive experiences that have not been elevated to the level of abstraction – a fate reserved for alpha elements. Bion likens these representations to "psychological atoms", indicating that they do not exist as physical realities but rather as metaphors used to describe psychic processes.

Bion understands there needs to be a containing space to hold such intense projections and develops the idea of a "container" that receives and transforms projected anxieties. That points out the importance of the mother's capacity for reverie – a fundamental ability to receive and metabolise the infant's emotional experiences. As Levy states:

> Considering that the alpha function is not operative from the beginning of life, the infant depends on the mother's alpha function and her capacity for *reverie* to "alphabetise" (Ferro, 1995) their emotional experiences. The mother's *reverie* is understood by Bion (1962a/1988) as the "receptive organ for the harvest of sensations" (p. 106) that the baby has projected into her. It is *reverie* that fulfils the infant's need for love and understanding. If the feeding mother lacks the capacity for *reverie*, or if *reverie* occurs but without love for the baby or for its father (!!), this fact will be communicated to the infant, even if it is incomprehensible

to them. "*Reverie* is a factor of the mother's alpha function" (p. 59). In other words, from Bion's perspective, the mother comes to be seen as performing structuring functions of the infant's mind. Just as she nourishes the baby with milk, she nourishes them with "thoughts" by placing her alpha function at the baby's service. This goes far beyond merely presenting the object of the infant's need or desire.

(Levy, 2022, pp. 117–118, original emphasis)

In this sense, the infant's ability to deal with frustration depends not only on their own constitutional characteristics, but also – and above all – on the presence and responsiveness of the real mother, forming the model of "container-contained" (♀-♂). To Bion:

Container and contained are susceptible of conjunction and permeation by emotion. Thus conjoined or permeated or both they change in a manner usually described as growth. When disjoined or denuded of emotion they diminish in vitality, that is, approximate to inanimate objects. Both container and contained are models of abstract representations of psycho-analytic realizations. The next step in abstraction is dictated by the need for designation. I shall use the sign for the abstraction representing the container and for the contained.

(Bion, 1962/2023, n.p.)

In summary: for thought to be formed and made use of, it is crucial that these interactions unfold dynamically between the schizoid-paranoid and depressive positions (SP ↔ D).[4] According to Bion, such psychic movements are essential for the infant (and later, the adult) to develop the capacity to integrate experiences, tolerate frustration, and transform suffering into thought – thus enabling a mind capable of containing and processing its own emotions.

Bion argues that the way in which thoughts are used by the individual – whether to integrate and structure the ego, or to fragment and disorganise it – is closely linked to the movement from the schizoid-paranoid position (SP) to the depressive position (D). The formation of effective thoughts depends not only on the capacity to endure frustration, but also on the ability to engage with depressive states in a responsive and constructive manner. A successful passage through the depressive position is fundamental for thoughts to evolve and develop progressively. That elaboration is what enables the creation of symbols representing the inevitable losses inherent to development, allowing the individual to abstract, synthesise, and establish connections – thereby becoming more creative.

With his innovative perspective, Bion sought to simplify the complexity of theories concerning mental phenomena by introducing the concept of "function", borrowed from mathematical sciences. However, unlike its strictly mathematical usage, the alpha function in psychoanalysis refers to an unknown that must be filled with emotional experience in order to acquire meaning. That explains how different factors contribute to the way a personality operates; that is, a personality may function in a "psychotic" mode due to a combination of factors such as intense envy and exaggerated projective identifications. It is also worth mentioning that Bion proposed that distinct psychoanalytic theories, despite their differences, could be understood as factors in analytic practice.

The alpha function – considered the primary function of the psychic apparatus – is responsible for transforming raw sensory impressions and early emotional experiences into "alpha elements". If the alpha function succeeds those sensations and emotions become part of structured, processable thought. Otherwise, they remain in a raw state as beta elements which cannot be thought and must be expelled through projection or motor agitation.

Beta elements (β), although raw and unprocessed, may nonetheless exert a form of primitive communication. When projected into another person – particularly in an analytic setting – they tend to provoke a "counter-reaction" in the analyst, generating a kind of unconscious (and instinctive) dialogue. This constitutes a primitive mode of communication which, though chaotic, reveals something about the individual's mental state.

Alpha elements (α), in contrast, having been successfully processed by the alpha function, serve as the foundation for several vital mental functions; they support dream-thought, the production of dreams, unconscious thought during waking life, and memory, in addition to contributing to intellectual functioning.

Bion also uses the term "contact barrier"[5] – a structure composed of alpha elements which functions like a semi-permeable membrane. This barrier allows a regulated exchange between the conscious and unconscious, as well as between the internal and external worlds. It also prevents one of these spheres from invading the other, thereby maintaining the integrity of thought and psychic experience. The "contact barrier" performs a function analogous to that of dreaming: it protects sleep and supports our ability to distinguish between wakefulness and dream states, as well as between past, present and future. This psychic boundary is essential to preserve the mind's cohesion and to maintain balance between its different layers.

Beta elements (β), in turn, can accumulate in a disorganised manner, forming what Bion called the "beta screen (β)". Unlike the contact barrier, this structure does not allow any distinction between conscious and unconscious, or between fantasy and reality. Clinically this manifests in states of mental confusion in the patient who may not only experience chaotic thought but also induce a similar state in others, including the analyst.

In such cases language ceases to be a means of symbolisation and exchange of meaning and instead is used in a fragmented and disruptive way – evacuating anxiety and reinforcing psychic disarray instead of communicating.

Rather than integrating experience, discourse becomes an extension of the beta screen, perpetuating confusion and obstructing access to structured thought.

Language, when understood as a device for encounter, presupposes two subjectivities capable of mutual recognition. However, the patient who speaks from within a "survival language" (Machado Junior, 2023) – marked by trauma, absences, abandonment, and forged in a lifeless familial environment – may reveal traces of their pain without this constituting, on an emotional level, a true communicative experience:

> Since language capable of bridging the gap between two people with unique and separate minds reflects the developmental capacity for individuation, the patient lacking this capacity is unaware that he or she is speaking to a separate individual outside the self.
>
> (Reiner, 2012, p. 46)

It is no coincidence that Bion often asked himself what happened to words and metaphors when overused. As they pass hand to hand, sentence to sentence, they tend to lose their freshness, as though repetition empties them of meaning. They cease to resonate, becoming banal, almost lifeless. And yet, at times, something unexpected occurs: two words that had never met are placed side by side, and from this unlikely juxtaposition, a new vitality emerges. It is as if a collision of meanings restores to language its power to touch reality.

That kind of creation arises from "disconcertment" – particularly at the beginning of an analysis, when the patient's suffering has not yet found a viable form of expression, and the analyst is too at a loss for words. In that uncomfortable void, expressions that do not follow the rules of conventional speech come up, responding to an emergency.

They are words that did not exist before that moment, born of a specific encounter between two subjectivities that had never previously touched.

When that happens, we might speak of a kind of "birth". Yet alongside it, one must acknowledge that the encounter between two people is always "a little catastrophic". It disrupts predictability, what is already known. Suffering that finds expression in an unprecedented way, and the listening that dares to receive it – both unsettle the established order. From such a rupture, creativity may emerge: a way of giving form to chaos and, in doing so, beginning to inhabit it.

We feel particularly aligned with Bion's writings from the 1970s – a period in which his thought delves ever more deeply into the notion of "emotional experience" in its most refined dimension. At that point of his work, there is a shift towards a kind of phenomenology of living, in which the focus no longer lies in explanation, but in the lived experience of the enigma that constitutes us. By introducing the notion of "O", Bion proposes there is something of the order of the real that cannot be directly known, yet insists on making itself felt – as a process: something always in motion, a state of "becoming" that traverses and eludes us (Almeida, 2025).

It is not a truth that can be named, much less possessed. What Bion offers us, since the ideas published in *Transformations* (1965), is a path for thinking the unthinkable: a way of coming into contact with what has not yet gained "shape". Such contact is often accompanied by turbulence – disjointed fragments, abrupt images, bodily sensations that cannot yet be put into words. It is at that level of experience that analytic work typically begins: a territory where what is lived cannot yet be spoken.

That demands us to have long engaged with our own emotional life – and that we have, with other analysts, built a space where the unthinkable might begin to be thought. Personal analysis, supervision, exchanges with colleagues: such encounters constitute the shared ground from which a kind of listening may emerge, capable of receiving what has not yet been named.

Without such preparation we risk defending ourselves against experience precisely at the moment we ought to sustain its opacity. Working with unrepresented phenomena therefore calls for a kind of presence that can only be cultivated slowly – in the everyday companionship of doubt and not-knowing.

The Language of the Psychotic From a Bionian Perspective

According to Bion the formation of "beta screen" in psychotic patients prevails over the formation of contact barrier, just as the schizoid-paranoid position dominates the depressive one. This predominance hinders the development of the capacity for symbolisation, replacing it with "symbolic equations", as described by Segal (1957/1982) – a concept discussed at length in Chapter 5 of this book and in Almeida (2020). As a result, the thinking of a person with schizophrenia is unable to formulate concepts, synthesise, or abstract. Instead, thoughts become concrete, perceived as real objects that pose a threat and must be expelled, as if they were substances to be eliminated.

In other words: thought fails to reach a synthesis and thus remains in a primitive state of disorder (*synkrisis*), forming a heap of proto-thoughts. These raw elements – like physical objects – are merely accumulated, compressed, or discarded. Furthermore, the psychic apparatus responsible for processing projective identifications becomes hypertrophied, and thinking acquires a tone of omnipotence and magical quality, taking similar things as identical. As Symington and Symington aptly observe:

> Having mutilated his apparatus of awareness, which is intimately related to the development of verbal thought, the schizophrenic feels himself imprisoned by his state of mind because he cannot escape it by the use of verbal thought, that is, he cannot verbalize his feelings, or name a constant conjunction which would enable meaning to develop. He has destroyed the key to his escape. During analysis, he begins to develop this capacity for verbal thought and effects his escape from his imprisonment. But he is now more aware of his feelings of painful depression,

guilt and anxiety. He therefore splits off his newly acquired capacity for verbal thought and projects it into his analyst. Now, however, the lack of it makes him feel insane. Sometimes he believes that, Prometheus-like, he has been punished for daring to acquire it or else that the analyst has stolen it from him.

(Symington and Symington, 1996/2002, p. 145)

The last quotation from Symington and Symington (1996/2002) brings us to a central matter in the psychoanalytic understanding of schizophrenia: the relationship between the capacity for verbal thought and the psychic anguish that arises from that very function. When the schizophrenic patient resorts to the destruction of their own apparatus of perception and symbolisation – as an extreme defensive strategy in the face of unbearable suffering – they find themselves confined to a reality in which their experiences remain unnameable. Lacking symbolic resources to organise their internal chaos, everything they feel remains in a raw state, making any form of elaboration impossible.

As the analytic process goes on, however, that capacity slowly begins to be restored. And it is precisely at this point that previously diffuse or fragmented pains begin to emerge; guilt, anxiety, and depressive states now become more clearly defined. Facing this new emotional awareness the subject encounters a deadlock: instead of recognising the return of these functions as something of their own, the patient tends to project them onto the analyst. The temporary loss of that newfound capacity is thus not experienced as a natural oscillation of the process, but rather as a kind of dispossession – something felt as punishment, betrayal, or theft.

That dynamic may be illustrated by a clinical case in which, after months of fragmented and almost unintelligible speech, a patient began to construct more articulate sentences and to establish links between his experiences. Gradually, a new psychic organisation was taking shape. Yet as this transformation became more consolidated, he began to express increasing resentment towards the analyst. In one session, with a suspicious look, he said, "You understand everything. You took what was in my head and now I can't think without you."

His speech, both resentful and somewhat distrustful, revealed an ambivalent feeling: while he acknowledged the acquisition of a thinking function, he experienced it as though it had been taken from him. In the following session, he returned to a truncated language, full of neologisms and ruptures in meaning – as if he needed to regress in order to preserve something he now identified as "his own".

To individuals whose psychic organisation was structured from an early age around psychotic-type defences, emerging from the stagnation of nonthinking does not represent progress. Rather it poses a risk. The symbolic collapse, however devastating it may be, functions as a shield against primitive affections that have never found representation.

The "empty thought" often observed in psychotic patients is accompanied by what Bion called "nameless dread". The speech of such subjects – frequently described as a "word mix" – is entirely devoid of cohesion or structure.

In other words, in the psyche of the psychotic individual the capacity to think is replaced by fantasies of omnipotence; the experience of learning is exchanged for the illusion of omniscience; and the acceptance of dependence is suppressed by arrogance. Rather than seeking truth, the patient's mind becomes trapped in a "confusional state", in which a "supra-ego"[6] replaces the superego, establishing its own rules and expecting the external world to conform to them.

Indeed, expanding on Kleinian and Bionian ideas, Herbert Rosenfeld (1950) described "confusional states" as psychic experiences in which the subject loses the ability to differentiate between contradictory impulses – particularly love and hate – and confuses the boundaries between self and object. Present both in the earliest developmental phases and in severe psychotic conditions, these states are marked by a collapse in symbolisation functions and a chaotic emotional organisation. Instead of being able to work through affection the patient projects intolerable aspects onto others, which often leads to the perception of the other as a hostile and persecutory object. When reparative efforts do occur, they are typically incoherent, distorted by hatred. Frequently the projected object is reintrojected in a confused manner, becoming a cruel and self-destructive superego.

However, Rosenfeld emphasised that when these processes become visible within transference, the analyst can interpret them as enactment, enabling the patient to gradually regain psychic cohesion and reclaim the capacity to think.

Bion (1967) also proposed a third possibility, beyond the formation of alpha elements (linked to healthy thought development) and beta elements (which must be expelled): the "reversal of the alpha function". This concept refers to situations in which the alpha function begins to operate but, dealing with intense psychic pain, it retreats – producing beta elements that carry traces of the ego and the superego. These elements are referred to as "bizarre objects".

In cases of reversal of the alpha function, thought regresses from a normal level to a more concrete one (beta elements), and may then regress even further to a primitive language of bodily sensations, as observed in psychosomatic disorders. According to Meltzer (2022), this is one of the most compelling theories on psychosomatic functioning.

In summary, we can state that, clinically, the beta elements generated by such reversal may follow three main paths:

1 They may be discharged into the body, manifesting as somatisations and symptoms of hyperactivity.
2 They may be projected through the senses and return in the form of hallucinations.
3 Or they may be expressed through actions, such as acting-out or disjointed speech.

As we pointed in Chapter 4, Bion devoted himself tirelessly to exploring the relationship between the thinker and their thoughts through the "container-contained" model, which may take place in three distinct forms. The first is the parasitic form, in which thinker and thought weaken one another, feeding on falsehoods that serve as barriers to truth. The second, referred to as the commensal form, involves the thinker and the thought coexisting without major conflict – but also without producing significant development. The third form is symbiotic, in which both parties benefit, allowing the growth and integration of thought.

The mother's capacity of reverie – considered essential by Bion – plays a decisive role in this process. If the mother is able to receive and transform the infant's projected anxieties while also meeting their needs for affection and safety, she facilitates the process of "learning from experience". Otherwise, when the intense emotions projected do not find a suitable container they are reinternalised by the infant as "nameless dread", leading to an evasion of pain and inhibiting emotional growth.

> This aptitude for containing, which Bion called *reverie*, means *dreaming the undreamt dreams of the other* (the baby, the patient, etc.). In other words, it is the act of dreaming dreams that have not yet been given meaning (that have not yet been thought). Broadly speaking, *reverie* is part of the alpha-function. However, if the baby makes too many projective identifications into the environment, they tend to annihilate the caregiver's alpha-function.
>
> (Almeida, Naffah Neto and Vieira, 2024, p. 45)

Bion's theory encouraged psychoanalysts to pay closer attention to the levels of thought and language used by themselves and by their patients. From that point on, psychoanalysis began to place greater emphasis on the communicative exchange between primary and secondary mental processes. In more regressive cases, the analyst's role as a "container" – and as a facilitator of the capacity to think using alpha elements – becomes essential. The analyst helps the patient replace the need to "evacuate a bad breast" with a more integrated (and thoughtful) understanding.

Indeed, to Bion the act of thinking involves a "binocular vision" – that is, the joining of different perspectives, like the image formed by two eyes creating a single picture. In clinical practice, distinguishing kinds of thought allows the analyst to identify different levels of pathology: psychotic patients exhibit unintegrated thinking, while in obsessive neuroses or narcissistic personalities the thoughts are integrated but their use is problematic.

The primary task of the Bionian analyst, therefore, is to help the patient face and modify frustrations, rather than fleeing from them. Individuals who constantly avoid painful truths tend to approach analysis with attitudes of arrogance and omnipotence.

In Bion's theory of schizophrenia the destructiveness of death instinct – as described by Klein (1957) – is essential for understanding the attacks on the ego itself. According to Bion (1953) in schizophrenic patients these attacks occur with great intensity, *breaking the links that connect fantasies both to each other and to external reality*:

> Language is employed by the schizophrenic in three ways; as a mode of action, as a method of communication, and as a mode of thought. He will show a preference for *action* on occasions when other patients would realize that what was required was thought; thus, he will want to go over to a piano to take out the movement to understand why someone is playing the piano. Reciprocally, if he has a problem the solution of which depends on action, as when, being in one place, he should be in another, he will resort to thought – *omnipotent* thought – as his mode of transport.
>
> (Bion, 1953/2018, n.p., emphasis added)

The schizophrenic individual has an internal world composed of disconnected fragments, lacking cohesion or clarity between different parts of the self and the objects. That experience generates a state of terror and confusion, in which object fragments appear threatening and bizarre, recalling the "world catastrophe" described by Freud in the Schreber case (1911).

We may summarise the main causes and effects of schizophrenia as observed by Bion in his clinical analyses. According to Zimmerman (2004):

1 A fundamental cause lies in the infant's innate predisposition, whereby death instinct and envy lead to attacks on the bond with the maternal breast.
2 Another important factor is environmental response, especially that of the mother, dealing with such projections.
3 Bion emphasised the significance of early Oedipal fantasies which shape the infant's perception of their relationship with the parents (or caregiving figures).
4 The pursuit of knowledge, linked to the instinct of curiosity (epistemophilia), is often associated with sadism, resulting intellectual inhibition and lack of healthy curiosity.
5 Attacks on links prevent the transition from the schizoid-paranoid to the depressive position, thereby hindering psychic development.
6 Thought is replaced by fantasies of omnipotence, learning by the illusion of absolute knowledge, and the acceptance of helplessness by arrogance. As a result, verbal thought becomes impaired, and the mind remains in a confused state.
7 The inability to transform experiences into coherent thoughts leads to disorganised speech, often described as "word mix".

8 Unlike neurotic personalities, psychotic patients do not develop a "contact barrier" composed of alpha elements that help separate the conscious from the unconscious. Instead, there is a "beta screen" which fails to distinguish between these layers, generating confusion between fantasy and reality.

9 While neurotic individuals rely on repression, psychotic patients rely heavily on splitting, followed by massive projective identifications to evacuate what is intolerable. Bion distinguishes between "excessive projective identification", which damages the capacity to think by attacking mental links with hatred, from "realistic projective identification", which is healthy and supports psychic structuring. Realistic projective identification allows the child to internalise the mother's containing function and the alpha function, forming a "thinking breast" that supports thought. In clinical practice, distinguishing between these forms is essential, as they may either provoke pathological counter-identifications in the analyst or serve to foster empathy and understanding.

10 The fragments of objects and parts of the psychic apparatus – id, ego, superego – resulting from splitting are projected into the external environment in the form of "bizarre objects". These fragments return to the individual as threats and persecutions, creating a persistent sense of harassment and fear.

11 The projection of such anxieties – particularly fears of destruction and death – must be received and processed by an environment capable of containing and transforming them. The mother's function, in this context, is fundamental: she must take in and return these contents in a "detoxified" form, with meanings and names the child can integrate. When this containment fails, the child ends up reabsorbing the projected anxieties, often mixed with the mother's own distress, creating a state of "nameless dread".

12 The difficulty in reaching the depressive position leads to a limited capacity to create and use symbols. That inability results in the substitution of symbols with symbolic equations, in which imaginary ideas are perceived as concrete realities. A schizophrenic patient takes fantasies as reality.

13 Bion associated the primitive and pre-verbal thoughts of schizophrenics with ideograms, such as those found in Chinese writing, where vision prevails over hearing and word-based perception. Any attacks on links compromise the connections between these ideograms, undermining the function of thinking and preventing the formation of dreams and the capacity for fantasy. Bion often remarked that schizophrenic patients do not dream in the traditional sense; the dreams they report are usually composed of fragmented daytime content, lacking symbolic elaboration – more a discharge of proto-thoughts than genuine dreams.

14 Due to attacks on links and the lack of symbolisation, schizophrenics struggle to articulate and integrate thoughts, resulting in accumulation and confusion. Words lose their symbolic function and are experienced as the very things they were meant to represent, further complicating communication.

15 Schizophrenic language may be used in four distinct ways:

a As a form of acting out: just as with the desperate cries of an infant, language replaces thought with action, serving as a discharge of various anxieties (oral, anal, sadistic, narcissistic, etc.).

b As a form of primitive communication: this kind of language may be understood through the analyst's countertransference which captures the patient's raw emotional states.

c As a form of thought: the absence of symbols and the presence of "word mix" reflect the chaotic state of the patient's thinking, revealing the difficulty in organising and structuring ideas.

d As a means of producing effects on the other: language may be used to impact the analyst's mind, provoking dissociation in associative links and interfering with the therapist's capacity to understanding and respond.

In the clinical work with psychotic patients Bion draws attention to the challenges involved in countertransference. The analyst must contend with envious attacks that often manifest as negative therapeutic reactions, as well as confront intense projective identifications and potentially dangerous behaviours. These attacks on the analytic bond can lead the patient into mental states marked by emotional blindness, distorted curiosity, arrogant attitudes, and self-destructive tendencies. As a consequence, the analyst may feel bored, paralysed, or impotent – signs that they are being affected by a profoundly disturbed relational field.

To Bion, what sustains this situation is not, primarily, the strength of aggressive impulses, but rather the intensity of mechanisms that deny the possibility of knowing. This movement of repudiating knowledge, which he designates as "–K", becomes central to psychotic conditions. When pushed to an extreme, functioning in –K disrupts the capacity to symbolise, to think, and, in the most severe cases, the very relation with reality itself.

Bion introduced the symbols K, H, and L in his work to represent different types of links or mental functions operating within the psychic dynamic. These concepts were developed in his book *Learning from Experience* (1962/2023), as well as in later writings in which he sought to explore how thinking and learning processes unfold both in the mind and in the analytic interaction.

K (Knowledge) refers to the link with knowledge and the capacity to learn from experience. In clinical practice, K is used to describe the patient's pursuit of understanding, assimilating both internal and external experiences.

The absence or denial of K (termed –K) indicates a resistance or rejection of knowledge, typical of psychotic states, in which there is a refusal to recognise painful truths and a tendency to disconnect from reality.

H (Hate) represents the link with hatred. In practice H reflects how hatred may interfere with the capacity to form bonds and maintain coherence in thought. Any attack on linking associated with H is a defensive mechanism whereby the patient fragments psychic experience to avoid suffering or anxiety.

L (Love) symbolises the link with love. Clinically L is essential to create positive bonds and integrate experiences and emotions. The presence of L enables the patient's movement towards the depressive position, where repair and the integration of "good" and "bad" aspects become possible.

Considering the phenomenology of the clinical encounter, Bion used those symbols to comprehend and interpret transference and countertransference interactions, as well as the processes of resistance or acceptance that emerge throughout analysis. For example, a patient with strong –K may show a systematic refusal to learn from experience, thus hindering therapeutic progress. Excessive H, in turn, may manifest in attacks on mental links themselves, or in attempts to put the relationship with the analyst to an end.

Psychotic and Non-psychotic Personalities

Another particularly interesting aspect of Bion's writings is his reference to "psychotic and non-psychotic personalities" (1957). He did not make it entirely clear whether the psychotic characteristics he described are confined to severely regressed patients or whether they may also be present, in latent form, in all of us. In the book *Bion in New York and São Paulo* (1977–78/2018), he discusses the importance of considering, even among markedly psychotic patients, a distinction between "sane psychotics" and "insane psychotics", emphasising that in the former there are always "vestiges of rational, conscious behaviour" (p. 125) which can be developed in analysis – an aspect that, in the latter case, proves impossible.

Likewise, a person may be mentally sane and yet display modes of thought that are both psychotic and non-psychotic in nature. Along these lines, Chuster (1999) states:

> [...] in every individual there exists a psychotic part [...] and a non-psychotic part. [Bion] does not use the term neurosis and makes psychosis the fundamental clinical reference in human beings. In psychotic patients, the psychotic part dominates the personality, destroying and paralysing the non-psychotic parts. In non-psychotic individuals, psychotic movements also occur, varying in duration, and may or may not go unnoticed.
>
> (p. 70)

For many scholars of Bion, the term "psychotic personality" is synonymous with the "psychotic part of the personality", which means that it does not refer to a specific psychiatric diagnosis, but rather to a mode of mental functioning that coexists alongside other modes. In this sense, Symington and Symington state:

> When writing about psychotic patients, Bion refers not only to the overtly schizophrenic patient, with manifest thought disorder, but also to the psychotic part of the personality in borderline and neurotic patients. Thus, the mechanisms described in psychotic patients do not comprise some esoteric theory but are applicable to all patients, including oneself. The dominance of the psychotic part over the non-psychotic part in any personality interferes with mental functioning.
>
> (1996/2002, p. 144)

In our point of view the expression "psychotic personality" may be reserved for regressive situations with clinically psychotic manifestations, whereas the "psychotic part of the personality" refers to the primitive nuclei of the psyche present in all of us, without necessarily implying a psychiatric diagnosis. This premise leads us to conclude that, just as a psychotic patient possesses a neurotic part, every neurotic patient harbours a latent psychotic part. An analysis that fails to address this "psychotic part" may therefore be superficial and incomplete – herein lies one of Bion's most fundamental contributions to contemporary clinical practice.

It is also worth remarking that the difference between the psychotic part submerged within the personality and full-blown schizophrenia may be "quantitative"; however, the nature of the psychic dynamic remains analogous. Beyond this quantitative variation – which defines the degree of sanity – Bion also identifies a qualitative distinction that plays a relevant role in the configuration of psychosis. One of our author's insights was the recognition that the psychotic's use of excessive projective identifications serves not only to evacuate intolerable contents, but also to establish a primitive form of non-verbal communication. Through such projections the patient communicates sensations and anxieties that cannot yet be expressed in words. Those projections generate effects that allow the analyst to grasp the emotional experience before it acquires name or meaning.

It is through that process that the analyst experiences the effects of the patient's projected anxieties, through countertransference.

Regarding the features that characterise the psychotic personality, Grinberg, Sor, and De Bianchedi (1974) consider that:

> The intolerance of frustration, and the predominance of destructive impulses are among the most outstanding characteristics of the psychotic personality. These become apparent as a violent hatred of reality, either internal or external – a hatred which extends to the senses, to those

parts of the personality and psychic elements which may be used to recognize and make contact with this reality, to consciousness, and to all the functions associated with it. Owing to the intensity of the destructive impulses, love becomes sadism, and no solution to the conflict between life and death instincts is ever reached. The psychotic personality is further characterized by the fear of imminent annihilation, and it is this which gives form to the specific type of object relations which it tends to establish (among these, the analytic transference); these object relations, hasty and premature, are established in a tenacious manner, while being, on the other hand, extremely precarious and fragile.

(Grinberg, Sor, and De Bianchedi, 1974, p. 159)

Bion is particularly emphatic in stating, in the article *The Differentiation of the Psychotic from the Non-Psychotic Personality* (1957/2018), the importance of the innate factor in the constitution of schizophrenia:

To return now to the characteristics I listed as intrinsic to the schizophrenic personality. These constitute an *endowment* that makes it certain that the possessor of it will progress through the paranoid-schizoid and depressive positions in a manner markedly different from that of one not so endowed.

(Bion, 1957/1984, n.p., emphasis added)

In a beautiful essay, Judith S. T. C. Andreucci translates into clinical terms what Bion sought to express theoretically about these parts of the psyche:

A. had been hospitalised several times for extended periods in psychiatric institutions before the analysis began. The treatment commenced at the end of her last hospitalisation, with the patient attending sessions accompanied by a nurse from the sanatorium. It was clear she was in no condition to decide anything. She came like an automaton, as she would to any other hospital activity, sent by the psychiatrist. With a vacant stare, disjointed speech, and a static face devoid of any trace of life, she would enter the consulting room and throw herself onto the couch like a dead body or an object placed somewhere. Gradually, something from that strange, unknown world seemed to take shape and became possible to perceive and verbalise for the patient, as a fragile form of communication began to emerge between us. The patient became less absent and disjointed. She began attending analysis sessions on her own and refused to lie down. She would look at me and lament: "They sent me here, they want this." She always spoke in the plural, never identifying herself in the first person singular. Upon entering, she would invariably ask: "How are we?", looking at me with a piercing gaze that I felt entered me, enveloped me, and overflowed. It was as though it pierced through me and was lost in the distance, as if she could not distinguish between us or locate herself. I reflected this back to her. She seemed to quickly reintroject something of herself that she had projected, making a slight movement that suggested concentration, then greeting me again: "How are you?" As I observed the patient, I was struck by the idea that, in her fragmentation and projection – "They sent me here, they want this" – there were parts of her that wanted to come to me, that longed for the encounter, while in other areas of the mind this meeting was experienced as disastrous and fiercely resisted, a conflict made evident in the anguished, plaintive tone of her voice. It seemed to me that the patient's mind contained what I will attempt to describe using the expression *the two worlds*, and our entire work was dominated by an oscillation between one and the other – that is, between the world that cooperated and the one that hated and destroyed any form of connection.

(Andreucci, 2016, pp. 120–121, original emphasis)

As we can see, Bion (1957) highlights four central characteristics of the psychotic personality:

1 A predominance of destructive impulses.
2 An aversion to reality.
3 A constant fear of annihilation.
4 The rapid and premature formation of object relations.

These characteristics become more comprehensible when viewed from the perspective of an infant's earliest experiences. Events that cause pain or frustration are perceived as real threats to survival – which may correspond to reality, as a hungry baby who is not fed is indeed at risk of death. It is hardly surprising, then, that such primitive experiences evoke intense, urgent emotions, characteristic of life-and-death situations. As previously mentioned, in order to withstand this overload, the infant resorts to projective identification: it expels raw perceptions and affections (beta elements), seeking another mind capable of transforming them through the alpha function, making them more digestible and ready to be reintegrated.

We must also emphasise that the mind's psychotic part may present itself throughout life, especially when faced with intense frustrations, taking over mental functioning and provoking a reversal of the alpha function. When it occurs, it leads to the collapse of the internal container-contained pairs, reducing the "valency" of internal objects. "Valency", a term borrowed from chemistry, refers to the capacity of an atom to combine with others to form new substances through the exchange or sharing of electrons.

To Bion (1962/2018) mental growth involves expanding the ability to observe and understand both the external world and the self. Such psychic maturation, however, presupposes the capacity to internally sustain the emotions stirred by one's own perceptions – without rejecting them or prematurely displacing them into defences. It is an affective crossing that includes the possibility of recognising oneself as lovable, hateful, and, above all, knowable. As we welcome what we feel – even when uncomfortable or contradictory – we move closer to an intimate truth that is continuously unfolding, converting emotional experience into meaning, and rooting the subject in their own psychic reality.

An emblematic example of that dynamic takes place in the film *Joker* (2019), directed by Todd Phillips. The character Arthur Fleck (played by Joaquin Phoenix) has a mother who is unable to exercise a proper function of reverie – she cannot receive and transform her son's anxieties into something comprehensible and tolerable. Although Fleck openly displays psychotic symptoms and violent behaviour after repeated frustrations and traumas, his non-psychotic part had remained for a long time latent, silent, and repressed.

At the beginning of the story Fleck attends regular appointments with a social worker responsible for his psychotherapeutic support and medication management. In those sessions he seeks some form of human contact and attempts, although precariously, to process his anguish, while the social worker acts (or is supposed to act) as an emotional container – receiving his projections, offering reverie, and helping him to understand his emotions and frustrations better.

But due to an abrupt government budget cut Fleck has his psychological treatment and access to medication denied. In a crucial scene the social worker tells him his sessions will no longer take place.

That abrupt interruption – quite impactful to the viewer, it must be said – perfectly symbolises the failure of the container-contained relationship described by Bion. The sudden termination of therapeutic care and the loss of active listening by the social worker represent the collapse of the alpha function and the emotional transformation capacity needed to metabolise Fleck's projected anxieties. On his own he finds himself emotionally abandoned, completely unable to process his intense and destructive emotions all by himself.

That is when his psychotic functioning intensifies, and Fleck's non-psychotic part – which had been tenuously sustained through therapeutic support – disappears. Later re-emerging in an explosive, intense, and deeply disturbing form as Joker.

The film's tragic narrative illustrates, in our view, key aspects of Bion's theory: when the containing capacity of the mother/environment fails and the infant has innate difficulties in tolerating frustration, healthy mental development is compromised, resulting in an individual unable to attribute meaning to their own emotions and to external reality.

We will now turn to Winnicott's conception of psychosis, highlighting its development from the theory of emotional maturation.

Psychosis in Winnicott: Initial Considerations

To Winnicott psychosis is, at its core, intimately linked to an emotional privation occurring at such an early stage of development that the infant is not yet
capable of perceiving absence itself:

> The basis for mental health is being laid down by the mother from con-
> ception onwards through the ordinary care that she gives her infant
> because of her special orientation to that task. Mental ill-health of psy-
> chotic quality arises out of delays and distortions, regressions and mud-
> dles, in the early stages of growth of the environment-individual set-up.
> (Winnicott, 1952/2017, p. 43)

That is a form of privation that occurs prior to any possibility of awareness
regarding the presence or absence of emotional provision. In that context,
failure is not limited to the concrete environment but concerns the complete absence of something the infant might perceive as sufficiently good.
We are not speaking here of loss in the classical sense – in which something
that once existed is later taken away. What is at stake is something more
"primitive" and, paradoxically, more imperceptible: there is no cessation of
a positive experience because there was never anything that could be felt
as such. What is disrupted is the very *coming-into-being* of the subject – an
original discontinuity, faceless and nameless because it occurs at a moment when the infant has not yet differentiated itself from the environment
to which it remains fused: "The second type of experience, with failure of
good-enough active environmental adaptation, produces a psychotic distortion of the environment-individual set-up. Relationships produce *loss of the
sense of self*, and the latter is only regained by return to isolation" (Winnicott, 1953/2017, p. 38).

It is worth highlighting the distinction Winnicott proposes between what is
"primitive" and what is "deep". Although this differentiation may appear subtle, it carries significant implications for understanding emotional maturation
and for clinical listening.

What Winnicott refers to as "deep" belongs to the subject's internal psychic reality – that is, it presupposes the existence of an already constituted
"inner world", populated by unconscious fantasies, repressed contents, imagination, and conflict. "Primitive", on the other hand, refers to the very early
stages of development, when there is not yet a sufficiently structured psychic
apparatus capable of generating depth.

In the first months of life the infant does not yet possess an internal past
or an organised psychic memory. At this stage there is neither repression nor
fantasy. Experience is immediate, bodily, and therefore not symbolisable. That
is why Winnicott states, "an infant needs a degree of maturity before becoming gradually able to be deep" (Winnicott, 1958/2017, p. 251). Prior to that
the child is immersed in a state of total dependence, in a "mother-infant fu-
sional unit".

According to Winnicott himself that insight was decisive in his development as an analyst, as it allowed him to draw close to Klein's theory without becoming bound to it. He realised that, in certain clinical cases, "what is early is not deep", and he came to understand that certain clinical phenomena point to a more archaic level of functioning – one that cannot be approached using the same conceptual tools employed in the treatment of neuroses.

Some psychic mechanisms – such as those observed in schizoid formations, for instance – belong to the register of the primitive, whereas others, such as depression, pertain to the domain of the deep. Confusing those dimensions is, therefore, a theoretical and technical error that compromises clinical treatment.

It is important to emphasise that "primitive" is not simply an earlier version of "deep". It operates according to a different logic: there is not yet a personal psychic reality, nor symbolic representation or language. Experiences are preverbal and, when healthy, are later forgotten – not repressed – forming what Winnicott calls the "primary unconscious" (or "general unconscious"), distinct from the "repressive unconscious" that structures neuroses.

When it comes to clinical work that distinction demands those primitive disturbances – such as those found in certain psychotic or borderline states – be approached with a different stance from the analyst. It is not a matter of interpreting internal conflicts, but of sustaining the regressed state, offering a kind of care that closely resembles the facilitating environment of the absolute dependence phase. In such cases the management of the setting and the concrete conditions of the patient's life become essential components of the therapeutic process.

That is why the distinction between psychosis and neurosis – which parallels the difference between primitive and deep – is fundamental. Those are not matters of differing degrees of severity, but rather of distinct modes of *self-organisation*. Each requires its own theoretical models and specific clinical approaches that are attuned to the developmental stage in which the patient finds themselves.

When such privation of care occurs during the phase of absolute dependence, we may consider that the psyche becomes "trapped" in a state of indeterminacy, in which the origin of the failure is so primitive and undefined that it does not result in a loss that can be located or felt, but rather in an absolute incapacity to relate to objects. As a consequence, the relationship with the external world is impaired, and psychic development is marked by a structural failure that pervades the entire process of self-construction.

As we can see, Winnicott offers a markedly different aetiological conception of the origins of psychosis. He is not merely reorganising familiar concepts in new language. His perspective places central importance on the *misattunement* of the environment, and only secondarily considers the child's reaction to that failure. This premise stands in sharp contrast to the Kleinian tradition, which places unconscious fantasy at the heart of psychic organisation, thereby minimising the importance of the external object in the constitution of subjectivity – even though Klein constantly refers to the "introjected good object" (on this, see Chapter 2 of this book).

However, Winnicott also reminds us that the primitive experiences at play in psychoses are not exclusive to such states. What defines psychosis, according to him, are "primitive defences" that emerge as a result of environmental failures occurring during the earliest stages of development:

> It is my intention to show here that what we see clinically is always a defence organization, even in the autism of childhood schizophrenia. The underlying agony is unthinkable. It is wrong to think of psychotic illness as a breakdown, it is a defence organization relative to a primitive agony, and it is usually successful (except when the facilitating environment has been not deficient but tantalizing, perhaps the worst thing that can happen to a human baby).
>
> (Winnicott, 1963/2017, p. 526)

As the environment provides the necessary provision during the phase of absolute dependence, these defences do not become organised as they do in psychotic states. Thus, the lack of a facilitating environment compromises the evolution of the personality and the self, leading to what Winnicott refers to as schizophrenia:

> Rather am I trying to make a statement of the way in which emotional development in its primitive or earliest stages concerns exactly the same phenomena that appear in the study of adult schizophrenia, and of the schizoid states in general and of the *organized defences* against confusion and un-integration.
>
> (Winnicott, 1952/2017, p. 38, emphasis added)

At some point during the early stages of development the infant was forced to respond to an experience that exceeded their capacity for psychic integration. In response a "defensive system" was established as the only possible means of preventing the repetition of such a devastating experience. Behind every defensive mechanism lies the persistent threat of psychic disintegration – a confusion that undermines the sense of "continuity of being".

The only way the infant can attempt to protect themselves from what Winnicott calls "unthinkable agony" is by deploying defences that stave off imminent collapse. Even though this manoeuvre may preserve the infant's apparent intactness, it comes at a cost: a disconnection from their most fundamental needs. By becoming invulnerable, the individual avoids trauma, but also sacrifices the possibility of genuine communication, reliable relationships, and contact with their internal reality. They become, in this sense, impermeable to help.

In the clinical context what often appears as symptom or psychopathological structure is not the manifestation of a future collapse, but the defensive organisation constructed to prevent the return of a collapse already suffered – even if not representable. Life choices, relationships, and even symptoms are guided by that defensive logic to avoid anything that might lead back to the psychic danger zone. Nothing is lived spontaneously; everything revolves around precaution.

That is why Winnicott warns us that psychosis does not represent the moment of collapse, but the indication that the maturation process was interrupted prematurely. The collapse that may eventually emerge is not the beginning of illness, but the breakdown of the defences that had up to then held the psychic structure together.

The central defence, in this context, consists in the interruption of emotional maturation through splitting. This mechanism operates by isolating what remains of the self in order to protect it from further injury. Instead of continuing the integrative movement of bringing together the various aspects of being – through contact with reality and lived experience – a rupture occurs: one part of the self becomes inaccessible, while the other assumes the task of maintaining the defence at all costs, attempting to ward off the return of the original pain.

In his text "Fear of Breakdown and the Unlived Life" (2014), Ogden establishes a fruitful dialogue with Winnicott's essay "Fear of Breakdown" (1963), emphasising that the persistence of parts of life that remain unlived is inherent to the human condition. These parts call for integration so that the individual may become whole – fully becoming who they are. As reinterpreting Winnicott's concept of breakdown, Ogden suggests that the rupture of the bond between mother and infant throws the latter into an extreme state of helplessness, threatening their very existence. However, he states that this condition should not be confused with a psychotic episode, for psychosis constitutes a defence against that original experience of rupture, against what Winnicott described as "unthinkable agonies".[7]

When separated from the mother the infant resorts to the psychotic defence of disintegration as a paradoxical means of escaping the agony of being unable to organise itself – a state that may lead to psychic self-annihilation. Since the individual, in early childhood, does not yet possess a sufficiently consolidated psychic structure to withstand the breakdown of the bond with the mother, they grow up with a fear of collapse – a collapse that has, in fact, already occurred, but was never consciously experienced.

Ogden (2014) expands Winnicott's thought by proposing that what moves the patient to confront the source of this fear is the felt absence of essential parts of the self – parts that must be recovered in order for the individual to feel whole. What remains of their life is, in a sense, an unlived life.

It is worth briefly clarifying how Winnicott conceptualises splitting. He reserves the term *splitting* for the most archaic defensive mechanisms, frequently observed in schizophrenic or borderline personalities, or in cases of latent schizophrenia. The notion of *dissociation*, by contrast, is used in situations in which it is possible to engage with a central self in relation to dissociated parts of the personality.

To Winnicott, splitting does not arise from instinctual conflict, nor is it pathological by definition – as he did not work with Freud's concept of the "death instinct". According to Winnicott, splitting is present in all individuals and constitutes an essential feature of human structure. It becomes problematic when environmental failures, instead of promoting integration, exacerbate this early separation in the infant.

Under favourable conditions of care, as psychic maturation progresses, this divided state tends to be absorbed and integrated. Splitting, then, ceases to have a disorganising impact and may be understood as dissociation – a feature which, though present, does not compromise the subject's functioning. Being healthy implies a progressive capacity to gather the fragmented parts of the personality and to restore the continuity of being.

According to Winnicott:

> A description of the extreme degree of the splitting leads the way to a description of the lesser degrees of splitting and indeed of the way in which some degree of what is being described is present in all children and is inherent in life itself. In the extreme degree the child has no reason for living at all but in the commoner lesser degrees there is some degree of a sense of futility in regard to the false living, and a constant search for the life that feels real, even if it leads to death, as by starvation. In the lesser degrees there are objects in the secret inner relatedness of the true self and these objects have been derived from some degree of success at the stage of the theoretical first feed. In other words, in the lesser degrees of this illness it is not so much the primary state of splitting which is to be found as a secondary organisation of splitting which implies regression from difficulties encountered at a later stage of emotional development.
>
> (Winnicott, 1988/2017, pp. 125–126)

In psychosis, however, the collapse in the process of self-constitution is so primitive that it renders even the possibility of perceiving that something unviable is missing. It is an emptiness prior to absence – a state in which even the notion of lack cannot be represented. That is, emotional development encounters such a radical deadlock that the psyche retreats, forming an extreme defence against unthinkable anxiety, resulting in a state of "psychic non-existence" (a true *non-being*).

The fundamental issue in psychotic states, according to Winnicott, is not directly related to the loss of reality testing, but to the failure in the constitution of a cohesive self and the capacity to establish contact with the external world. In the earliest stages of development, such contact does not yet exist – and indeed cannot exist – given the infant's extreme level of immaturity. This is why Winnicott devotes much of his work to describing how this bond with reality can only be formed gradually, supported by a sufficiently good environment.

What emerges, then, is a surprising proposition: external reality, as we know it, cannot be taken for granted. It is a construction that only acquires meaning through the illusion sustained by the maternal figure in the earliest phases of life. For the infant, objects and external events have no intrinsic meaning. They belong to another world – a world that only becomes accessible as the child can create, through illusion, bridges between the subjective universe and what lies outside.

It is this capacity to "create the world" that makes the world real for the child. And such creation is only possible when the mother, through her active adaptation, allows the baby to believe that everything he encounters has, in some way, been produced by him. Without this inaugural experience of creation, reality remains devoid of value and meaning. In Winnicott's words, "it is only from the state of *not being* that *being* can begin" (quoted in Almeida and Naffah Neto, 2021).

We are thus left with two fundamental poles: on one side, the original emptiness, *the essential solitude of being*. On the other, the innate tendency towards integration, which drives the subject into a living relationship with the world. This split between the subjective and the objective is not something that can be eliminated. It forms part of the very nature of the human condition. However, in situations of healthy development, this division tends to be gradually absorbed over the course of maturation.

When this occurs, the individual can function as a "whole person", even having gone through states of non-integration. Primordial splitting continues to exist, but it loses its pathological status. In psychotic states, however, the process has failed: the splitting has intensified and become rigidly embedded within the defensive system. This rigidity becomes the only possible way of maintaining psychic stability. Any movement is perceived as a threat to the fragile organisation achieved.

One of Winnicott's patients, for example, recounted a symbolic dream during analysis: she was at a train station, but the train never departed – as if any attempt to move could be the risk of catastrophe. And indeed, to those living in such a state, psychic life becomes organised around the prevention of anything new from happening.

Winnicott is unequivocal: this state cannot be mistaken for health. To some individuals – those whose early lives were marked by sufficiently good care – there was never a traumatic rupture in basic trust. These subjects developed an implicit sense that the world is a reliable place, and that it is worth investing affectively in relationships. This deep-seated sense of security allows them to live without ever realising how fortunate they were. As a result, they often fail to understand the struggles of those who carry throughout their lives an invisible wound – an experience of absolute helplessness that compromises their relationship both with reality and with themselves.

It is precisely through his clinical work with these patients that Winnicott locates the origin of the most severe forms of psychic suffering – not the classical neuroses, but schizophrenic and borderline conditions. In this trajectory, he develops the notion of "regression", **emphasising its therapeutic benefits – an aspect that would radically shape his understanding of these pathologies.** According to him: "The advantage of a regression is that it carries with it the opportunity for correction of inadequate adaptation- to-need in the past history of the patient, that is to say, in the patient's infancy management" (Winnicott, 1955/2017, p. 289).

In this context, the author distinguishes between two types of regression. In some cases, what occurs is a collapse of the defensive system in the face of unbearable external demands. The subject finds no way out and regresses in a disorganised fashion, with no sense of their own needs. This is a chaotic return, one that interrupts the maturation process.

However, there is another kind of regression entirely different in nature – although it may appear similar at first glance. In this case, the individual senses, even unconsciously, the present environment is safe enough to hold their fragility. They allow themselves to return to a state of dependence, thereby creating the possibility of repairing what was once interrupted. In such cases, regression may hold therapeutic value, as it reactivates early experiences of care, and supports a renewed path of emotional integration.

Alongside those dynamics, Winnicott also identified a third pathway – subtler and more usual than one might assume: the so-called "flight into health". We might think of those individuals who have succeeded in masking their original pain through an apparently healthy mode of functioning. These are people who maintain successful careers, stable relationships, and a socially functional image. Yet that adaptation has been achieved at the cost of a disconnection from the true self.

To remain functional, they created a *false self* – a kind of defensive persona that acts as a protective barrier. In many cases intelligence was instrumentalised at an early stage, and thinking began to operate split off from emotional experiences – what Winnicott termed *split-off intellect*.

These strategies are often effective until an external factor – such as a loss, a crisis, or an unbearable demand – triggers the original trauma. When this occurs, the collapse does not refer to something new, but rather to the return – in a new guise – of a very old pain, surprising those around them, who often say that "everything seemed fine so far", revealing how deeply that pain had been hidden beneath a façade of apparent normality.

Winnicott also speaks of another type of psychosis that does not arise strictly during the stage of absolute dependence, but at later stages of maturation (relative dependence), particularly during the elaboration of the Oedipus complex – a time when the child is required to internally sustain their ambivalent feelings (Almeida and Naffah Neto, 2022). Thus, if the child's personality has been developed in an extremely fragile manner – through the early stages only

in a rudimentary way, without acquiring the capacity to bear ambivalence –
a deep fear of collapse may emerge, giving rise to psychotic defences:

> The term psychosis is used to imply either that as an infant the indi-
> vidual was not able to reach to the degree of personal health which
> makes sense of the concept of the Oedipus complex, or alternatively
> that the organization of the personality had weaknesses which became
> revealed when the maximal strain of the Oedipus complex had to be
> borne. It will be seen that there is a very thin line between this second
> type of psychosis and psycho-neurosis. In the extreme of the first type
> of psychosis there is but little resemblance to psycho-neurosis, since no
> significant Oedipus stage has ever been reached, and castration anxiety
> was never a major threat to an intact personality.
>
> (Winnicott, 1959/2017, p. 451)

In other words, he considers this second type of psychosis to be closer to
neurosis, prompting us to reflect on borderline structures which always stand
somewhere between psychosis and neurosis. We shall return to this issue
later.

Some Notes on the Notions of False and True in Winnicott's Work

So far, we have seen that, to Winnicott, an individual is considered psychotic
when they chronically rely on *psychotic defences* over a significant period.
This concept encompasses not only schizophrenic, melancholic, and manic-
depressive patients, but also those classified as borderline, since all make use
of psychotic defences – differing only in the intensity and manifestation of
symptoms.

Among these defences, the first is a certain form of *invulnerability*, frequently observed in autistic withdrawal, in which the individual shields themselves from the external world to avoid any contact that might be experienced
as invasive. The second is the splitting between intellectual functions and the
psychosoma – a mechanism whereby the intellect becomes hypertrophied to
anticipate potential environmental failures and protect against them. When
this defence becomes rigid, thinking begins to operate as a kind of *bodyguard*
for the self, imposing constant vigilance and an unrelenting state of alertness,
which prevents the subject from relaxing.

Another central defence is the splitting between the *true* and *false self*.
In this case the false self assumes the role of a shield, protecting the true
self both from external intrusions and from the intensity of internal impulses.
However, as this structure is built through mimicry of the environment, it
proves to be quite fragile; when it collapses, it exposes the true self to forces
it cannot withstand, potentially triggering a psychotic breakdown.

Finally, there is *active disintegration*, a defence in which the self deliber-
ately fragments as a means of protection. Rather than bearing the anxiety of

environmental intrusions or the pressure of instinctual forces, the individual dissolves into multiple parts, becoming unable to integrate their experiences. This extreme fragmentation, however, intensifies psychic disorganisation, reinforcing the state of internal collapse.[8]

When working with patients who live on the *edges* of psychic experience, we must set aside the established criteria used to assess neurotic patients. As Winnicott (1954/2017) points out, neurotics are individuals whose psychic structure is relatively integrated, allowing a distinction between the internal and external worlds. These are the:

> [...] patients who operate as *whole persons* and whose difficulties are in the realm of interpersonal relationships. The technique for the treatment of these patients belongs to psycho-analysis as it developed in the hands of Freud at the beginning of the century.
> (Winnicott, 1954/2017, p. 202, emphasis added)

That differentiation enables them to experience conflict, repress it, and even render it unconscious.

However, when dealing with patients whose psychic structure is not yet sufficiently consolidated, analytic listening must be guided by different frameworks. In such cases the classical techniques of psychoanalysis – those built upon the analysis of intrapsychic conflict and repression – are not sufficient to address the complexity of their suffering. Compared to this, the condition of neurotic patients is almost a luxury, given that borderline individuals are still struggling to *come into being* – that is, to feel real.[9]

We need an approach that considers the more primitive states of emotional development, in which the very constitution of the self is still in the process of formation, *in order to face those cases.*

Unfortunately, many psychoanalysts still fail to realise that, in Winnicott's vocabulary, the terms *true* and *false* have an eminently clinical meaning (Naffah Neto, 2023). This distinction is far from expressing a moral judgement; rather, it concerns the *quality of the experience of being*. Feeling true is being connected to one's inner world, living with presence and authenticity. The false self, by contrast, translates into a disconnection from that subjective core: the person starts acting according to external expectations, driven by automatisms that do not express their emotional truth. In more severe cases, this condition leads to an intense existential void, as if life were being guided by a force that is alien to one's own will and experience of self.

In such contexts, one may speak of *faulty adaptation*, in which the environment imposes itself intrusively upon the child, turning the individual into a mere reactor to that invasion. "The sense of self is lost in this situation and is only regained by a return to isolation" (Winnicott, 1953/2017, p. 38).

At the extreme opposite of this excessive adaptation, some withdrawal emerges as an attempt to preserve what remains of the true self. When the environment fails to offer emotional support and invades the child's psychic space the subject may respond by drastically retreating from all forms of relatedness. Isolation is not merely social withdrawal, but a psychic strategy of self-protection against intrusion. This is the context in which many patients with schizoid traits are found: individuals who inhabit a threshold where contact with reality becomes tenuous, and the experience of self loses consistency. Withdrawing into silence, solitude or fantasy is not a free choice; it represents a mode of subjective survival in the face of the impossibility of existing authentically in a world felt to be threatening.

"True" and "false" are thus not metaphysical or epistemological notions, but clinical concepts, descriptive of the experiences of two types of patients: those who experience *life as something true*, and those who feel and evaluate it as something false, inconsistent (Naffah Neto, 2023).

Winnicott also mentions the existence of true and false selves in individuals considered healthy, referring to complementary aspects of the same psychic structure: true self corresponding to the isolated and incommunicable core of identity, and false self relating to the subject's social dimension – the inevitable compromises we all must make to exist in society.

However, as we move closer to the field of psychoses, false self may take on a pathological character, becoming a formation entirely split off from the rest of the personality and wholly submitted to the demands of the environment. In this condition, the adjective *false* acquires an even greater weight, as Winnicott (1960) observes. In the schizoid patient, for example, withdrawal functions as a defence against subjugation to an environment perceived as persecutory. Yet, in adopting this defence, part of the experience of being is also relinquished:

> Being isolated, however, becomes less and less pure the further the child is from the beginning, involving more and more defensive organization in *repudiation of environmental impingement*. Therapy in respect of such a disorder must provide active adaptation to the child and must gradually build up a respect for processes.
>
> (Winnicott, 1953/2017, p. 38, emphasis added)

However, even before Winnicott, Nietzsche had already said:

> The concept of the "real, truly existing" is derived, first and foremost, from that which "concerns us"; the more our interests are affected, the more we believe in the "reality" of a thing or a being. "This exists" means I feel myself existing in contact with it.
>
> (Nietzsche, 1886–1887/1978, p. 193)

The sentence is exemplary in highlighting the value of analysis in the treatment of psychotic patients or those with borderline personalities. An analysis may be considered successful when it manages to reach the individual's most primitive needs, gradually supporting the construction of a sense of personal existence – that is, tending to what was missing in the original process of becoming. Thus, the patient may one day be able to say, "I feel like I exist in contact with you", or "At least I feel real when I'm with you"; and from that point, begin to extend this sense of existence and reality to the rest of life (Naffah Neto, 2023).

An Important Addendum on the Origins of Psychosis in Winnicott's Theory

When studying psychoses within the Winnicottian framework it is essential to attend to the distinction between psychoses of a *schizophrenic nature* and those within in the *field of depressions*. That differentiation only makes sense within a theoretical perspective that conceives emotional maturation as a continuous process, marked by progressive stages that shape the constitution of the self.

In *schizophrenic psychoses* the environment fails at a very early stage, causing a traumatic rupture during the initial phases of emotional life – from the very first moments up to the point when the infant begins to recognise the independent existence of the other and achieves the basic experience of "I AM". The severity of this disorder is proportional to the precocity of the interruption, determining how much of the early integrative capacity was preserved after the trauma. That explains the spectrum ranging from severe cases of developed schizophrenia to infantile autism, borderline personality organisation and schizoid types – although the latter may also be associated with the second kind of psychosis described below.

In all such manifestations the central issue concerns the formation of an integrated self and the ability to establish a functional relationship with external reality – a task that, even in psychologically healthy individuals, is never entirely complete. It is, therefore, in that first encounter with the external world, marked by the experience of what Winnicott termed the "first theoretical feed", that this struggle begins. He affirms that nearly all suffering in these patients can be traced back to the failure in establishing contact with what is real. However, it is important to stress once again that the difficulties in accessing reality vary according to the specific developmental moment at which the interruption occurred.

In contrast, *depressive psychoses* emerge from failures taking place at later stages of development when the individual is already capable of perceiving themselves as someone separate and distinct from environment (Vieira, 2024). This stage is characterised by anxieties related to responsibility, guilt, and loss – typical of the concern phase. The individual must learn to manage destructive/aggressive impulses and feelings connected to separation and care for the other. Psychotic depression, manic-depressive illness, and hypochondria fall within this category.

Curiously Winnicott's clinical work places greater emphasis on the field of schizophrenic psychoses: autism, borderline states, and schizoid conditions.

According to him it is precisely in these extreme cases, marked by the most primitive failures, that we can most clearly grasp the fundamental questions of what it means to be human. To Winnicott, the true advancement of psycho-analysis lies in the investigation of such complex cases and thus constructing a robust theory of psychotic illness.

We recall a patient who, over the course of treatment, revealed a defensive pattern oscillating between total withdrawal and outbursts of persecutory anxiety. In moments of great emotional tension, he described the feeling of "falling apart", with intense episodes of depersonalisation and derealisation. In one session, while speaking about his relationship with his father, he recalled a moment in childhood when he felt that he could not exist in his father's presence. "He would walk into the room and I just knew I had to disappear", he said. This psychic disappearance – which, in his childhood, had functioned as a survival mechanism – reappeared in adulthood whenever he was confronted with emotionally charged situations, leading to a subjective collapse that interrupted his continuity of being.

The constant fluctuation between the wish to be seen and the fear of invasion made each analytic encounter a highly delicate exercise in proximity. In some sessions his speech would become discursive and impersonal, as if he were shielding a part of himself from exposure. In others silence would dominate, accompanied by a distant gaze – as if he were trying to avoid a contact that threatened him at the deepest level.

This clinical case points us to a specific form of psychic suffering which, although structured around extremely primitive experiences, only becomes evident at later stages of emotional development – often during the "Oedipal period". It refers to a type of psychosis that does not present itself with the classical signs of a break from reality, such as delusions or hallucinations but, instead, operates silently and exerts a deeply structuring influence on the subject's internal world.

Those patients frequently display a psychological functioning that, at first glance, might be mistaken for a well-compensated neurosis: they speak clearly, articulate conflicts logically, and appear to demonstrate a high degree of social adaptation. Yet, beneath this coherent surface, lies a core of profound fragility, sustained by psychotic defences – such as depersonalisation, extreme withdrawal, and the intensive use of false self. On this issue, Winnicott warns us:

> *Only the true self can be analysed.* Psycho-analysis of the false self; analysis that is directed at what amounts to no more than an internalized environment, can only lead to disappointment. There may be an apparent early success. It is being recognized in the last few years that in order to communicate with the true self where a false self has been given pathological importance it is necessary for the analyst first of all to provide conditions which will allow the patient to hand over to the analyst the burden of the internalized environment, and so to become a

highly dependent but a real, immature, infant; then, and then only, the analyst may analyse the true self.

(Winnicott, 1959/2017, pp. 453–454, original emphasis)

In the case described, for instance, the patient oscillated between an apparently controlled speech and moments of psychic dissolution, in which he described the sensation of "falling to pieces". This experience was not merely metaphorical; it referred to a *real sense* of disintegration, reactivated whenever he faced emotionally intense situations – particularly those evoking figures of authority or intimacy, such as his father during childhood.

The "disappearance" reported in session – "he walked into the room and I knew I had to disappear" – reveals how this defensive mechanism was established as a gesture of survival. That is, it was a necessary psychic adaptation in the face of an environment experienced as intrusive and annihilating. In adulthood, this same mechanism re-emerged as episodes of subjective collapse: withdrawal, a vacant gaze, and silence as desperate attempts to protect against what threatened to dissolve their self.

Unlike more overt psychotic conditions where splitting and a rupture with reality are clearly visible, in such cases the suffering is concealed beneath a kind of apparent normality. Analysis may proceed for months – sometimes years – before the analyst realises that what seemed to be a neurotic defence was, in fact, a more primitive strategy for preserving a self that never fully came into being. The subjective "emptiness" experienced by these patients is not a mere lack of meaning, but rather the expression of a structural hole – a gap where the experience of continuity of being failed to take root (Vieira, 2024).

Faced with this kind of functioning, therapeutic management requires a mode of listening that goes beyond interpretation, one capable of holding the patient's fragility without offering premature constructions or answers. The analyst's role, in those situations, aligns closely with Winnicott's idea of "survival" (Almeida, 2023): it is essential to endure the patient's withdrawal without intrusion, to receive their discontinuity without demanding immediate coherence and, above all, recognise that the analytic relationship, already represents both a threat and a promise – a threat of repetition of past failures, and the promise that this time, perhaps, it may be possible to exist without having to "break apart" (Almeida, 2024).

Notes

1 *Epistemophilia* is a term that refers to an intense desire for knowledge. It derives from the Greek *episteme* (knowledge) + *philia* (love, affinity). In psychoanalysis – particularly in Melanie Klein's theory – epistemophilia is linked to the infantile desire to know and understand the world. For Klein, that impulse may stem from an innate curiosity, and also from primitive anxieties, such as the fear of losing the object of love or attempts to repair destructive fantasies. This longing for knowledge may carry a healthy dimension, related to creativity and inquiry, but it may

also serve as a defensive function – becoming a means of control or a protection against anxiety. "We frequently find that, when the epistemophilic instinct is early associated with sexual interests, the result is inhibition or obsessional neurosis and brooding mania" (Klein, 1923/2011, n.p.).

2 "Thing-presentation" and "word-presentation" are concepts proposed by Freud (1915/1981) to explain different levels of psychic symbolisation. The *thing-presentation* refers to the mental image of an object that arises from direct sensory and perceptual experiences, forming the most primitive basis of thought. The word-presentation, in turn, is the association of this image with a specific word, which enables more elaborate thought and access to conscious discourse. Together these representations form the foundation of symbolic functioning and the capacity to formulate more complex ideas.

3 According to *The Language of Bion: A Dictionary of Concepts*, by Paulo C. Sandler:

> [...] his experiences in war also provided him with an experiential background that gave sense to Klein's observations; more specifically, the idea of a warring army containing the enemies. As late as 1970 he would use the metaphor in the clinical depiction of the container and containment: *"[...] a man speaking of an emotional experience in which he was closely involved began to stammer badly as the memory became increasingly vivid to him. The aspects of the model that are significant are these: the man was trying to contain his experience in a form of words; he was trying to contain himself, as one sometimes says of someone about to lose control of himself; he was trying to 'contain' his emotions within a form of words, as one might speak of a general attempting to 'contain' enemy forces within a given zone* (AI, 94)".
>
> (Sandler, 2005, pp. 161–162, emphasis original)

4 This idea, however, began to be developed by Melanie Klein herself towards the end of her work, particularly in the paper *"A Note on Depression in the Schizophrenic"* (1960). In that essay, Klein suggests that guilt, stemming from the destruction of the "good breast", already emerges in the schizoid-paranoid position. However, if the maternal figure does not enable the repair of this destruction the infant finds no alternative but to split the ego, remaining fixed in the paranoid-schizoid position. In other words, the child experiences guilt but does not process it as expected in the depressive position. In this context of ongoing suffering the schizophrenic defence becomes a psychic resource for the subject.

> It is only in the analysis of deep layers of the mind that we come across the schizophrenic's feelings of despair about being confused and in bits. Further work enables us in some cases to get access to the feeling of guilt and depression about being dominated by destructive impulses and about having destroyed oneself and one's good object by splitting processes. As a defence against such pain we might find that fragmentation occurs again; it is only by repeated experiences of such pain and the analysis of it that progress can be made.
>
> (Klein, 1960/2011, n.p.)

5 It is worth noting that in *Project for a Scientific Psychology* (1895/1981), Freud introduced the idea of a "contact barrier" when discussing the functioning of the psychic apparatus. That barrier relates to the way the mother helps regulate the infant's excessive stimuli, acting as a kind of protective filter in response to instinctual demands. Although Freud did not further develop this concept in his later works Bion revisited and expanded it – retaining the same term, but approaching it with a more refined and conceptually developed perspective.

6 That idea of an extremely stiff and tyrannical superego is presented by Bion through his idea of "primitive conscience" – a very controversial matter. Primitive conscience is mentioned by Bion during supervisions in Brazil in 1978 and remains in his later elaborations about the mind. By primitive conscience he refers to an archaic psychic stance, previous to superego, that reacts instinctively to emotional experiences, without any mediation of internalised moral values. Mattos and Braga (2009, p.141), mention an excerpt not fully published where Bion says, "[..] there seems to exist a form of innate morality, in the way, for example, the Roman Catholic Church refers to Original Sin. [..] We are born with a sense of guilt, we are born with what will one day become a form of moral conscience" (Bion, São Paulo, 1978, supervision S12).

7 The "unthinkable agonies" are described by Winnicott (1963/2017) as intensely primitive emotional states that threaten the very existence of the self. These include feelings of disintegration, endless falling, loss of bodily orientation, collapse of psychic reality, and annihilation. Winnicott explains that such states of anguish arise when the environment fails to provide the necessary support during the infant's early development, resulting in a direct threat to the integrity of the self. These experiences are deemed "unthinkable" precisely because they lack spatiotemporal articulation. In other words, they are lived experiences devoid of clear boundaries of time and space, as the infant has not yet developed the internal structures necessary to integrate these dimensions.

8 Winnicott describes schizoid functioning as a psychotic defence mechanism in which the individual withdraws into their subjective world in response to a chaotic and unpredictable environment. Facing an environment that failed to offer them a sufficiently safe space, the schizoid person avoids external contact whenever possible. This retreat, however, prevents the psyche from maturing – it remains in a primitive and unintegrated state, making it impossible to construct a cohesive identity due to the lack of lived experience and elaboration. Nonetheless, such a withdrawal proves insufficient when environmental demands become unavoidable, and the false self can no longer sustain the necessary adaptation. Faced with this threat, the schizoid individual resorts to a final defensive resource: active disintegration. This process involves the multiplication and reorganisation of primitive splittings, fragmenting the self even further to create a sense of invulnerability and avoid confrontation with objective reality. Rather than exposing themselves to the impact of the external world, the individual dissolves themselves into smaller parts, making it impossible to face directly that which threatens their fragile psychic organisation (Naffah Neto, 2018).

9 However, some analysts from the Kleinian tradition often argue that the treatment of schizophrenic patients should follow the same classical approach used with neurotic individuals. A striking example is Hanna Segal who, during a scientific meeting of the British Society, defended the view that there is no difference between the clinical management needs of a neurotic and those of a psychotic patient. Her statement, however, did not go unnoticed. On 22 January 1953, Winnicott wrote her a letter in which he challenged this perspective, "If you really believe, as many of us do, that the psychotic patient is in an infantile state in the transference situation, then what you are really saying is that there is no essential difference between the management needs of an infant and those of a grownup. Yet in conversation I am sure that you would admit that whereas a mature person can take part in his own management a child can only take part to some extent and an infant at the beginning is absolutely dependent on an environment which can either choose to adapt to the infants needs or to fail to adapt and to ignore those needs. I would say that the management problems are essentially different according to the level of development. If this is so, then management problems must be different in the analysis of psychotics and neurotics" (Winnicott, 1987/2017, p. 71).

References

Almeida, A. P. (2020). Melanie Klein e o processo de formação dos símbolos: revisitando o caso Dick [Melanie Klein and the Process of Symbol Formation: Revisiting the Case of Dick]. *Estilos da Clínica*, 25(3), 552–567. https://dx.doi.org/10.11606/issn.1981-1624.v25i3p552-567

Almeida, A. P., and Naffah Neto, A. (2022). O estágio da concernência e a elaboração do complexo de Édipo: revisitando Winnicott e o caso Piggle [The Stage of Concern and the Elaboration of the Oedipus Complex: Revisiting Winnicott and the Piggle Case]. *Psicologia Revista*, 31(1): 27–50. https://doi.org/10.23925/2594-3871.2022v31i1p27-50

Almeida, A. P. (2023). Novas compreensões para a agressividade infantil: uma visão winnicottiana [New Understandings of Childhood Aggression: A Winnicottian Perspective]. In A. P. Almeida, *Por uma ética do cuidado: Winnicott para educadores e psicanalistas (vol. 2)* [*For an Ethics of Care: Winnicott for Educators and Psychoanalysts (Vol. 2)*], pp. 233–274. São Paulo: Blucher.

Almeida, A. P. (2024). O voo silencioso: o lugar da interpretação psicanalítica em Winnicott [The Silent Flight: The Place of Psychoanalytic Interpretation in Winnicott]. *Berggasse 19*, 14(2): 22–36.

Almeida, A. P. (2025). O obsceno e a homossexualidade: considerações a partir da psicanálise ontológica [The Obscene and Homosexuality: Considerations from an Ontological Psychoanalytic Perspective]. *Ide*, 47(79): 57–70. https://doi.org/10.5935/0101-3106.v47n79.07

Almeida, A. P., Naffah Neto, A., and Vieira, F. P. (2024). A construção do pensar: Um estudo comparativo entre Bion e Winnicott [The construction of thinking: A comparative study between Bion and Winnicott]. *Natureza Humana*, 26(1): 40–59. https://doi.org/10.59539/2175-2834-v26n1-692

Andreucci, J. S. T. C. (2016). Considerações sobre a análise de uma personalidade psicótica [Considerations on the analysis of a psychotic personality]. *Revista Brasileira de Psicanálise*, 50(1): 119–132.

Bion, W. R. (2018). Notes on the Theory of Schizophrenia. In W. R. Bion, *Second Thoughts: Select Papers on Psychoanalysis*. London: Routledge. E-book. (Original work published in 1953)

Bion, W. R. (2018). Differentiation of the Psychotic from the Non-Psychotic Personalities. In W. R. Bion, *Second Thoughts: Select Papers on Psychoanalysis*. London: Routledge. E-book. (Original work published in 1957)

Bion, W. R. (2018). On Hallucination. In W. R. Bion, *Second Thoughts: Select Papers on Psychoanalysis*. London: Routledge. E-book. (Original work published in 1958)

Bion, W. R. (2018). A Theory of Thinking. In W. R. Bion, *Second Thoughts: Select Papers on Psychoanalysis*. London: Routledge. E-book. (Original work published in 1962)

Bion, W. R. (2018). Attacks on Linking. In W. R. Bion, *Second Thoughts: Select Papers on Psychoanalysis*. London: Routledge. E-book. (Original work published in 1959)

Bion, W. R. (2018). Commentaries. In W. R. Bion, *Second Thoughts: Select Papers on Psychoanalysis*. London: Routledge. E-book. (Original work published in 1967)

Bion, W. R. (2018). *Attention and Interpretation*. London: Routledge. E-book. (Original work published in 1970)

Bion, W. R. (2023). *Learning From Experience*. London: Routledge. E-book. (Original work published 1962)

Bion, W. R. (2018). *Bion in New York and São Paulo and Three Tavistock Seminars*. London: The Harris Meltzer Trust. (Original work presented in 1977–1978)

Chuster, A. (1999). *W. R. Bion: novas leituras. A psicanálise: dos modelos científicos aos princípios ético-estéticos* [*New Readings of W. R. Bion: Psychoanalysis from Scientific Models to Ethical-Aesthetic Principles*]. São Paulo: Companhia de Freud.

Chuster, A. (2024). *Linguagem de alcance psicanalítico: a diferença transcendental em W. R. Bion* [*Psychoanalytically Oriented Language: The Transcendental Difference in W. R. Bion*]. São Paulo: Blucher.

Freud, S. (1981). Project for a Scientific Psychology. In S. Freud, *The Standard Edition of the Complete Psychological Works of Sigmund Freud (Vol. 1)*, pp. 283–387. London: Hogarth Press. (Original work published in 1895)

Freud, S. (1981). Formulations on the two principles of mental functioning. In, S. Freud, *The Standard Edition of the Complete Psychological Works of Sigmund Freud (Vol. 12)*, pp. 213–226. London: Hogarth Press. (Original work published in 1911)

Freud, S. (1981). Psycho-analytic Notes on an Autobiographical Account of a Case of Paranoia (*Dementia Paranoides*). In S. Freud, *The Standard Edition of the Complete Psychological Works of Sigmund Freud (Vol. 12)*, pp. 9–82. London: Hogarth Press. (Original work published in 1911)

Freud, S. (1981). The Unconscious. In S. Freud, *The Standard Edition of the Complete Psychological Works of Sigmund Freud (Vol. 14)*, pp. 159–216. London: Hogarth Press. (Original work published in 1915)

Grinberg, L., Sor, D., and De Bianchedi, E. T. (1974). Bion's concepts of psychosis. *Contemporary Psychoanalysis*, 10(2): 157–171.

Hinshelwood, R. D. (2023). Content and Process. In Abram, J. and Hinshelwood, R. D., *The Clinical Paradigms of Donald Winnicott and Wilfred Bion: Comparisons and Dialogues*. London: Routledge.

Klein, M. (2011). Early Analysis. In M. Klein, *Love, Guilt and Reparation and Other Works (1921–1945)*. London: Vintage Books. E-book (Original work published in 1923)

Klein, M. (2011). A Note on Depression in the Schizophrenic. In M. Klein, *Envy and Gratitude and Other Works (1946–1963)*. London: Vintage Books. E-book. (Original work published in 1960)

Levy, R. (2022). *A simbolização na psicanálise: os processos de subjetivação e a dimensão estética da psicanálise* [*Symbolisation in Psychoanalysis: The Processes of Subjectivation and the Aesthetic Dimension of Psychoanalysis*]. São Paulo: Blucher.

Lispector, C. (2019). *Perto do coração selvagem* [*Near to the Wild Heart*]. E-book. Rio de Janeiro: Rocco.

Lispector, C. (2020). *Uma aprendizagem ou o livro dos prazeres* [*An Apprenticeship or The Book of Pleasures*]. E-book. Rio de Janeiro: Rocco.

Machado Junior, P. P. (2023). *A linguagem perdida das gruas e outros ensaios de rasuras e revelações* [*The Lost Language of Cranes and Other Essays of Erasures and Revelations*]. São Paulo: Blucher.

Mattos, J. A. J., and Braga, J. C. (2009). Consciência moral primitiva: um vislumbre da mente primordial [Primitive Moral Conscience: A Glimpse of the Primordial Mind]. *Revista Brasileira de Psicanálise*, 43(3): 141–158.

Meltzer, D. (2022). *Vida onírica: uma revisão da teoria e a técnica psicanalítica* [*Dream-Life: A Revision of Psychoanalytic Theory and Technique*]. São Paulo: Blucher.

Naffah Neto, A. (2018). Apontamentos sobre a análise de uma paciente esquizoide, de uma perspectiva winnicottiana [Notes on the Analysis of a Schizoid Patient from a Winnicottian Perspective]. *Jornal de Psicanálise*, 51(95): 59–72.

Naffah Neto, A. (2023). Falso self e patologia borderline no pensamento de Winnicott: antecedentes históricos e desenvolvimentos subsequentes [False self and borderline pathology in Winnicott's thought: historical antecedents and subsequent developments]. In A. Naffah Neto, *Veredas psicanalíticas: à sombra de Winnicott*. São Paulo: Blucher.

Nietzsche, F. (1978). *Fragmento póstumo 5[19], verão de 1886–outono de 1887* [*Posthumous Fragment 5[19], Summer 1886–Autumn 1887*]. *Oeuvres philosophiques complètes* [*Complete Philosophical Works*]. Paris: Gallimard, 8, Vol. XII, pp. 193–194.

Ogden, T. (2014). Fear of breakdown and the unlived life. *International Journal of Psychoanalysis*, *95*: 205–223.

Pessoa, F. (2014). *Cancioneiro* [Songbook]. São Paulo: Textos para a Reflexão. E-book. (Original work published 1935)

Phillips, T. (director). (2019). *Joker*. Warner Bros. Pictures.

Reiner, A. (2012). *Bion and Being*. London: Karnac Books.

Rosenfeld, H. (1950). Note on the Psychopathology of Confusional States in Chronic Schizophrenias. *International Journal of Psychoanalysis*, *31*: 132–137.

Sandler, P. C. (2005). *The Language of Bion: A Dictionary of Concepts*. London: Karnac Books.

Segal, H. (1982). Notas a respeito da formação de símbolos [Notes on Symbol Formation]. In H. Segal, *A obra de Hanna Segal: uma abordagem kleiniana à prática clínica* [*The Work of Hanna Segal: A Kleinian Approach to Clinical Practice*], pp. 77–98. Rio de Janeiro: Imago. (Original work published in 1957)

Symington, J., and Symington, N. (2002). *The Clinical Thinking of Wilfred Bion*. New York: Taylor and Francis/Routledge. (Original work published in 1996)

Vieira, F. P. (2024). A depressão em adolescentes na atualidade: um estudo comparativo a partir da psicanálise de Freud e Winnicott [Depression in Contemporary Adolescents: A Comparative Study Based on the Psychoanalysis of Freud and Winnicott]. *Revista Da Faculdade Paulo Picanço*, *4*(3): 1–17. https://doi.org/10.59483/rfpp.v4n3121

Winnicott, D. W. (2017). Psychoses and Child Care. In D. W. Winnicott, *The Collected Works of D. W. Winnicott (Vol. 4)*, pp. 35–44. Oxford: Oxford University Press. (Original work published in 1953)

Winnicott, D. W. (2017). Metapsychological and Clinical Aspects of Regression Within the Psycho-Analytical Set-Up. In D. W. Winnicott, *The Collected Works of D. W. Winnicott (Vol. 4)*, pp. 201–218. Oxford: Oxford University Press. (Original work published 1954)

Winnicott, D. W. (2017). Withdrawal and Regression. In D. W. Winnicott, *The Collected Works of D. W. Winnicott (Vol. 4)*, pp. 283–289. Oxford: Oxford University Press. (Original work published 1955)

Winnicott, D. W. (2017). On the Contribution of Direct Child Observation to Psycho-Analysis. In D. W. Winnicott, *The Collected Works of D. W. Winnicott (Vol. 5)*, pp. 249–254. Oxford: Oxford University Press. (Original work published 1958)

Winnicott, D. W. (2017). Classification: Is There a Psycho-Analytic Contribution to Psychiatric Classification? In D. W. Winnicott, *The Collected Works of D. W. Winnicott (Vol. 5)*, pp. 445–460. Oxford: Oxford University Press. (Original work published 1959)

Winnicott, D. W. (2017). Ego Distortion in Terms of True and False Self. In D. W. Winnicott, *The Collected Works of D. W. Winnicott (Vol. 6)*, pp. 159–174. Oxford: Oxford University Press. (Original work published 1960)

Winnicott, D. W. (2017). Fear of Breakdown. In D. W. Winnicott, *The Collected Works of D. W. Winnicott (Vol. 6)*, pp. 523–532. Oxford: Oxford University Press. (Original work published 1963)

Winnicott, D. W. (2017). Letter to Hanna Segal. In D. W. Winnicott, *The Collected Works of D. W. Winnicott (Vol. 4)*, pp. 71–72. Oxford: Oxford University Press. (Original work published in 1987)

Winnicott, D. W. (2017). Human Nature. In D. W. Winnicott, *The Collected Works of D. W. Winnicott (Vol. 11)*, pp. 25–186. Oxford: Oxford University Press. (Original work published in 1988)

Zimerman, D. E. (2004). *Bion: Da teoria à prática – uma leitura didática* [*Bion: From Theory to Practice – a Didactic Reading*]. Porto Alegre: Artmed.

Index

220   *Index*

107, 108, 111, 114, 118, 119, 121,
122, 126, 127, 128, 129, 132, 134,
141, 144, 147, 148, 153, 154, 155,
156, 162, 163, 164, 165, 166, 167,
174, 176, 182, 183, 184, 190, 191,
192, 198, 199, 202, 204, 212
mothers, 18, 43, 57, 60, 94, 100, 125
mourning, 48, 52, 54, 122

narcissism, 21, 131, 141, 168
neurosis, 2, 14, 19, 23, 24, 30, 76,
101, 108, 114, 154, 194, 200, 206,
210, 212
normal, 30, 34, 46, 101, 102, 108, 162,
163, 164, 165, 166, 189
not-me, 39, 126, 130

object, 10, 11, 16, 18, 19, 21, 22, 28,
29, 30, 36, 37, 39, 40, 42, 47, 49,
50, 51, 52, 53, 54, 56, 57, 58, 59,
60, 64, 65, 66, 67, 68, 69, 70, 71,
72, 73, 75, 76, 83, 85, 86, 87, 88,
89, 91, 93, 94, 101, 108, 113, 114,
117, 118, 119, 120, 121, 122, 123,
128, 132, 133, 134, 135, 137, 141,
143, 144, 146, 147, 148, 151, 156,
161, 162, 163, 164, 176, 180, 182,
184, 189, 191, 196, 197, 200, 201,
211, 212
objectivity, 72
object-relating, 36, 37, 73
Oedipus complex, 2, 29, 43, 53, 55,
59, 76, 108, 114, 125, 142, 143,
145, 149, 152, 153, 155, 156, 164,
165, 206
omnipotence, 16, 33, 34, 37, 53, 54,
71, 83, 108, 120, 127, 129, 135,
144, 151, 161, 163, 164, 187, 189,
190, 191

paradox, 52, 156
paranoid-schizoid position, 21, 29, 30,
51, 52, 117, 118, 120, 123, 124,
133, 134
parents, 41, 49, 83, 141, 142, 143, 144,
150, 153, 155, 165, 166, 191
patient, 3, 14, 5, 8, 9, 10, 12, 13, 14,
15, 18, 19, 20, 21, 22, 38, 49, 55,
66, 67, 75, 76, 77, 78, 86, 87, 90,
91, 92, 93, 94, 95, 96, 103, 104,
105, 106, 107, 109, 110, 111, 113,
114, 117, 123, 130, 131, 133, 134,
135, 136, 137, 138, 150, 151, 154,
155, 159, 168, 169, 170, 172, 173,

175, 179, 180, 181, 183, 185, 186,
188, 189, 190, 192, 193, 194, 195,
196, 197, 200, 202, 205, 208, 209,
210, 211, 213
patients, 3, 7, 11, 4, 5, 6, 8, 12,13, 14,
17, 19, 22, 23, 24, 27, 40, 55, 68,
86, 87, 92, 93, 94, 95, 99, 103, 105,
106, 110, 113, 114, 125, 132, 138,
154, 167, 172, 176, 179, 181, 187,
189, 190, 191, 192, 193, 194, 195,
204, 205, 206, 207, 208, 209, 210,
211, 213
perception, 29, 32, 36, 42, 47, 50, 51,
54, 65, 69, 87, 102, 117, 122, 123,
126, 127, 129, 156, 158, 181, 188,
189, 191, 192
persecution, 12, 146, 147
persecutory, 5, 12, 22, 29, 38, 51, 58,
67, 83, 85, 86, 87, 119, 120, 121,
123, 124, 132, 134, 143, 144, 145,
146, 147, 163, 189, 208, 210
perversion, 150
phantasy, 4, 11, 24, 27, 30, 31, 40, 41,
42, 43, 55, 120, 123, 180
play, 4, 12, 13, 14, 15, 31, 38, 52, 56,
58, 70, 72, 73, 82, 84, 86, 144, 159,
173, 201
playing, 15, 38, 73, 84, 86, 131, 132,
153, 191
pleasure, 3, 51, 71, 78, 107, 159, 161, 162
positions, 1, 4, 5, 21, 46, 49, 117, 184
potential space, 15, 16, 39, 72, 166
primary, 2, 13, 14, 21, 30, 36, 41, 42,
43, 55, 56, 59, 69, 70, 71, 72, 85,
112, 113, 118, 120, 126, 129, 131,
135, 141, 144, 145, 146, 147, 151,
154, 160, 161, 163, 166, 167, 174,
180, 181, 185, 190, 200, 203
projection, 22, 28, 38, 42, 52, 54, 74,
75, 77, 85, 102, 114, 120, 132, 133,
137, 144, 145, 146, 156, 163, 182,
185, 192, 197
projective identification, 14, 51, 65, 66,
67, 68, 69, 74, 75, 77, 95, 100, 101,
103, 111, 114, 115, 137, 146, 156,
167, 183, 185, 187, 192, 193, 195
psyche-soma, 5, 42, 60, 70, 71, 108,
114, 127, 133, 151, 156, 159,
168, 175
psychoanalysis, 1, 2, 3, 11, 12, 13, 15, 2,
4, 9, 23, 27, 30, 39, 40, 42, 43, 48, 49,
78, 83, 91, 95, 103, 107, 120, 125,
130, 136, 137, 144, 149, 159, 160,
170, 172, 175, 184, 190, 207, 211

222   *Index*

For Product Safety Concerns and Information please contact our EU
representative GPSR@taylorandfrancis.com
Taylor & Francis Verlag GmbH, Kaufingerstraße 24, 80331 München, Germany

www.ingramcontent.com/pod-product-compliance
Lightning Source LLC
Chambersburg PA
CBHW050352270326
41926CB00016B/3710